HARRAP'S VERBES ANGLAIS

par

LEXUS

avec

Jane Goldie

HARRAP

Edition publiée en France 1989
par Chambers Harrap Publishers Ltd
7 Hopetoun Crescent, Edinburgh EH7 4AY
Grande-Bretagne

Edition d'un format plus grand,
publiée en 1998

© Chambers Harrap Publishers Ltd 1998

ISBN 0 245 50363 3

Réimprimé 1999

Dépôt légal : janvier 1998

Imprimé en France

Introduction

Cet ouvrage se compose en majeure partie d'un dictionnaire de verbes composés, éléments dynamiques et essentiels de la langue anglaise ; plus de 1 000 verbes ont été analysés et mis en contexte. Mais cet ouvrage est bien plus que cela, il se concentre sur l'étude de la structure du verbe anglais : les auxiliaires, la forme des temps, les modaux et les gérondifs. Tous ces termes grammaticaux sont expliqués de façon claire et précise tout au long de l'ouvrage ainsi que dans un glossaire que vous trouverez de la page 7 à la page 11. L'objectif principal de ce volume est donc de montrer par l'emploi de nombreux exemples les divers aspects des verbes et des constructions verbales de l'anglais d'aujourd'hui.

Table des Matières

1 Glossaire des Termes Grammaticaux — 7

2 Les Formes Verbales : les Concepts de Base — 12

3 Les Auxiliaires — 14

4 Les Temps — 16

5 Les Verbes Modèles — 18

6 Le Passif — 22

7 Liste des Verbes Irréguliers — 25

8 Les Contractions — 34

9 Les Questions — 36

10 La Forme Négative — 39

11 L'Impératif — 41

12 Exprimer la Condition — 43

13 Le Gérondif, l'Infinitif — 47

14 Le Subjonctif — 49

15 Les Auxiliaires Modaux — 51

    CAN-COULD — 51

    MAY-MIGHT — 55

    MUST-HAD TO — 58

OUGHT TO 60

SHALL-SHOULD 61

WILL-WOULD 63

USED TO 65

DARE, NEED 66

HAVE, GET 67

16 Exprimer le Présent **68**

17 Exprimer le Passé **71**

18 Exprimer le Futur **76**

WILL et SHALL 76

BE GOING TO 78

BE TO 80

BE ABOUT TO 81

19 Les Particules des Verbes Composés **83**

20 Les Types de Verbes Composés **111**

Dictionnaire des Verbes Composés 115

Index **240**

1 Glossaire des Termes Grammaticaux

AUXILIAIRE

Les auxiliaires sont employés pour former les temps composés d'autres verbes, par exemple : *il est venu* (l'auxiliaire est le verbe "être").

COMPLEMENT

Il existe deux sortes de complément : **direct** et **indirect**. La phrase *j'ai écrit une lettre à mon frère* a deux compléments. *Une lettre* est le complément d'objet direct (ce que j'ai écrit); *mon frère* est le complément d'objet indirect (à qui je l'ai écrite). Dans la phrase, *j'ai vu mon frère samedi,* cependant, *mon frère* est le complément d'objet direct.

CONDITIONNEL

Mode verbal employé pour exprimer ce que quelqu'un ferait ou ce qu'il arriverait si une condition était remplie, par exemple : *il **viendrait** s'il le pouvait*; *la chaise **se serait cassée** s'il s'était assis dessus.*

CONJUGAISON

La conjugaison d'un verbe est l'ensemble des formes d'un verbe à des temps et à des modes différents.

FAMILIER

Le langage familier est le langage courant d'aujourd'hui employé dans la langue parlée mais pas à l'écrit, comme dans les lettres officielles, les contrats, etc.

FORME PROGRESSIVE

La forme progressive d'un verbe se forme avec *to be* + **participe présent**, comme dans *I am thinking, he has been writing all day, will she be staying with us?*

GERONDIF

Le gérondif est aussi appelé le "verbe substantivé". En anglais, il a la même forme que le **participe présent** d'un verbe, c.-à-d. radical + **ing**. Par exemple : **skiing is fun** *le ski, c'est amusant,* **I'm fed up with waiting** *j'en ai assez d'attendre.*

IMPERATIF

On emploie ce mode pour exprimer l'ordre (par exemple : *va-t'en, tais-toi !*) ou pour faire des suggestions (*allons-y*).

INDICATIF

C'est le mode le plus courant, celui qui décrit l'action ou l'état, comme dans *j'aime, il est venu, nous essayons.* Il s'oppose au subjonctif, au conditionnel et à l'impératif.

INFINITIF

L'infinitif en anglais est la forme de base, comme on la trouve dans les dictionnaires précédée ou non de *to* : *to eat* ou *eat.* On appelle cette forme sans *to* le radical.

INTERROGATIF

Les mots interrogatifs sont employés pour poser des questions, par exemple : *qui ?, pourquoi ?* La forme interrogative d'une phrase est la question, par exemple *le connaît-il ?, dois-je le faire ?, peuvent-ils attendre un peu ?*

MODE

Le mode représente l'attitude du sujet parlant vis-à-vis de l'action dont il est question dans la phrase. Voir INDICATIF, SUBJONCTIF, CONDITIONNEL, IMPERATIF.

PARTICIPE PASSE

En français, c'est la forme *mangé, vendu*, etc. Le participe passé anglais est la forme verbale employée après *have*, comme dans *I have **eaten***, *I have **said***, *you have **tried***, *it has **rained***.

PARTICIPE PRESENT

Le participe présent en anglais est la forme verbale qui se termine en *-ing*.

PERSONNE

Pour chaque temps, il y a trois personnes du singulier (1ère : *je*, 2ème : *tu*, 3ème : *il/elle/on*) et trois personnes du pluriel (1ère : *nous*, 2ème : *vous*, 3ème : *ils/elles*).

PRONOM

Un pronom est un mot qui remplace un nom. Il en existe différentes sortes. Les pronoms personnels sont *je*, *me*, *moi*, *tu*, *te*, *toi*, *il*, *se*, *soi*, *etc*. Les pronoms démonstratifs sont *ce*, *ça*, *celui-ci*, *celui-là*, *etc*.

PROPOSITION

Une proposition est un groupe de mots qui contient au moins un sujet et un verbe : *il chante* est une proposition. Une phrase peut être composée de plusieurs propositions : *il chante/quand il prend sa douche/et qu'il est content*.

PROPOSITION SUBORDONNEE

Une proposition subordonnée est une proposition qui dépend d'une autre. Par exemple dans : *il a dit qu'il viendrait*, *qu'il viendrait* est la proposition subordonnée.

RADICAL

voir INFINITIF.

SUBJONCTIF

Par exemple : *il faut que je **sois** prêt*, ***vive** le Roi*. Le subjonctif est un mode qui n'est pas très souvent employé en anglais.

SUJET

Le sujet d'un verbe est le nom ou le pronom qui accomplit l'action. Dans les phrases *je mange du chocolat* et *Pierre a deux chats*, *je* et *Pierre* sont des sujets.

TEMPS

Le temps d'un verbe indique quand l'action a lieu, c'est-à-dire le présent, le passé, le futur.

TEMPS COMPOSES

Les temps composés sont composés de plus d'un élément. Ils sont formés par l'**auxiliaire** et le participe **présent** ou **passé** du verbe conjugué en anglais. Par exemple : **I am reading** *je lis*, **I have gone** *je suis allé*.

VERBE

Le verbe est le mot de la phrase qui décrit une action (*chanter*, *marcher*). Il peut aussi décrire un état (*être*, *paraître*, *espérer*).

VERBE COMPOSE

Un verbe composé (en anglais) est un verbe comme *ask for* ou *run up*. Leur sens est généralement différent de la somme des sens des deux parties qui les composent, par exemple : **he goes in for skiing in a big way** *il adore faire du ski* (différent de : **he goes in for a medical next week** *il va se faire examiner la semaine prochaine*), **he ran up an enormous bill** *ça lui a fait une note énorme* (différent de : **he ran up the road** *il a monté la rue en courant*).

VERBE MODAL

Les verbes modaux en anglais sont *can/could*, *may/might*, *must/had to*, *shall/should*, *will/would*, de même que *ought to*, *used to*, *dare* et *need*. Une de leurs caractéristiques est qu'aux formes interrogative et négative, ils se construisent sans *do*.

VERBE REFLECHI

Les verbes réfléchis renvoient l'action sur leur propre sujet (*je me suis coiffée*).

VOIX

Il existe deux voix pour les verbes : la voix active et la voix passive.

VOIX ACTIVE   La voix active est la forme de base du verbe, comme dans *je le surveille.* Elle s'oppose à la forme passive (*il est surveillé par moi*). On l'appelle aussi l'actif.

VOIX PASSIVE   Un verbe est à la voix passive lorsque le sujet ne fait pas l'action mais la subit : *les tickets sont vendus à l'entrée*. En anglais, la voix passive est formée avec le verbe *to be* et le participe passé du verbe, par exemple : **he was rewarded** *il fut récompensé*. On l'appelle aussi le passif.

2 Les Formes Verbales : les Concepts de Base

Les concepts de base sont :

l'infinitif ou le radical
le participe présent
le participe passé

i) L'**infinitif** ou **radical** est la forme du verbe donnée dans le dictionnaire des verbes composés de ce livre ou dans l'index. Cette forme peut être employée avec ou sans **to**. **Watch** est à l'infinitif dans :

do you want to watch?
veux-tu regarder ?

I can't watch
je ne peux pas regarder

ii) Le **participe présent** est la forme du verbe qui se termine en **-ing** :

is anyone watching?
est-ce que quelqu'un regarde ?

they were watching us
ils/elles nous regardaient

Remarquez que, comme dans le dernier exemple, le participe présent est aussi employé pour former d'autres temps que le présent.

Pour les détails concernant la formation du participe présent, voir section 5.

iii) Il existe deux formes de base pour le **participe passé** d'un verbe. Pour les verbes réguliers, le participe passé a la même forme que le prétérit simple, c'est-à-dire : radical + **-(e)d** :

watch – watched

dance – danced

Pour les détails concernant le changement d'orthographe du participe passé, voir section 5.

Les participes passés des verbes irréguliers sont donnés dans la liste page 25. En voici des exemples :

go – gone
teach – taught
stand – stood

3 Les Auxiliaires

Les verbes **be**, **do** et **have** sont appelés des auxiliaires ordinaires.

Ils fonctionnent aussi comme verbes à part entière et dans ce cas ils signifient : **être** (be), **faire** (do), **avoir** (have).

Les auxiliaires sont employés pour former certains temps :

what ARE you doing?
qu'est-ce que tu fais (maintenant) ?

what DO you do?
qu'est-ce que tu fais (en général, d'habitude) ?

what HAVE you done?
qu'est-ce que tu as fait ?

Les formes de ces auxiliaires au présent et au passé sont :

BE
Présent

	singulier	*pluriel*
1ère	**I am**	**we are**
2ème	**you are**	**you are**
3ème	**he/she/it is**	**they are**

Prétérit

	singulier	*pluriel*
1ère	**I was**	**we were**
2ème	**you were**	**you were**
3ème	**he/she/it was**	**they were**

DO
Présent

	singulier	*pluriel*
1ère	**I do**	**we do**
2ème	**you do**	**you do**
3ème	**he/she/it does**	**they do**

Prétérit

	singulier	*pluriel*
1ère	**I did**	**we did**
2ème	**you did**	**you did**
3ème	**he/she/it did**	**they did**

HAVE
Présent

	singulier	*pluriel*
1ère	**I have**	**we have**
2ème	**you have**	**you have**
2ème	**he/she/it has**	**they have**

Prétérit

	singulier	*pluriel*
1ère	**I had**	**we had**
2ème	**you had**	**you had**
2ème	**he/she/it had**	**they had**

4 Les Temps

En anglais, la plupart des verbes prennent la même terminaison à toutes les personnes d'un même temps. On a, par exemple :

I/you/he/she/it/we/they went

L'exception majeure concerne la troisième personne du singulier du présent. Elle prend **-s** ou **-es** (voir les verbes modèles à la section 5). On a, par exemple :

	singulier	*pluriel*
1ère	**I watch**	**we watch**
2ème	**you watch**	**you watch**
2ème	**he/she/it watches**	**they watch**

Les temps des verbes se forment de la manière suivante (pour l'emploi des temps, voir sections 16-18, pour Le Passif voir section 6) :

infinitif	**(to) watch**
infinitif progressif	**(to) be watching** (**be** + participe présent)
infinitif passé	**(to) have watched** (**have** + participe passé)
infinitif passé progressif	**(to) have been watching**
présent simple	**(I/you/he,** etc.**) watch(es)**
présent progressif	" **am/are/is watching**
*futur simple**	" **will watch**
*futur progressif**	" **will be watching**
prétérit simple	" **watched**
prétérit progressif	" **was/were watching**
present perfect	" **have/has watched**
present perfect progressif	" **have/has been watching**
plus-que-parfait	" **had watched**
plus-que-parfait progressif	" **had been watching**

futur antérieur	" **will have watched**
futur antérieur progressif	" **will have been watching**
conditionnel présent	" **would watch**
conditionnel présent progressif	" **would be watching**
conditionnel passé	" **would have watched**
conditionnel passé progressif	" **would have been watching**

*Selon les théories modernes, le "futur" n'est pas considéré comme un temps à part entière en anglais mais comme un mode.

5 Les Verbes Modèles

On propose dans cette section une classification des verbes en différents modèles selon les variations orthographiques qu'ils subissent. Les verbes qui figurent dans l'index de ce livre sont codés et renvoient à un verbe modèle.

Pl

	ajouter
"he/she/it" au présent	**-s**
participe présent	**-ing**
participe passé	**-ed**

Par exemple :

look : looks – looking – looked

P2

	ajouter
"he/she/it" au présent	**-es**
participe présent	**-ing**
participe passé	**-ed**

Par exemple :

watch : watches – watching – watched

REMARQUE : **-es** est ajouté aux verbes qui se terminent en **-s, -z, -ch** et **-sh**.

P3

	ajouter
"he/she/it" au présent	**-s**
participe présent	**-ing**
participe passé	**-d**

Par exemple :

agree : agrees – agreeing – agreed

P4

	enlever	*ajouter*
"he/she/it" au présent		**-s**
participe présent	**-e** final	**-ing**
participe passé		**-d**

Par exemple :

hate : hates – hating – hated

P5

	changer	*ajouter*
"he/she/it" au présent		**-s**
participe présent	doubler consonne finale	**-ing**
participe passé	doubler consonne finale	**-ed**

Par exemple :

grab : grabs – grabbing – grabbed
occur : occurs – occurring – occurred

REMARQUE : ce doublement de la consonne a lieu après une voyelle courte accentuée, comme dans les exemples donnés ci-dessus. Mais il ne se produit pas dans le cas suivant :

keep : keeps – keeping

où la voyelle est longue. Ni dans :

vomit : vomits – vomiting – vomited

où la voyelle n'est pas accentuée.

En anglais BRITANNIQUE, ce doublement de consonne se produit dans quelques cas même après une voyelle finale non accentuée comme dans :

travel : travels – travelling – travelled
kidnap : kidnaps – kidnapping – kidnapped

Mais en anglais AMERICAIN, on n'écrit ces formes verbales qu'avec une seule consonne :

kidnap – kidnaping – kidnaped
travel – traveling – traveled

(*Am*) dans l'index indique les verbes qui se construisent sur le modèle américain.

P6

	changer	*ajouter*
"he/she/it" au présent	le **y** final en **ies**	
participe présent		**-ing**
participe passé	le **y** en **ied**	

Par exemple :

accompany : accompanies – accompanying – accompanied
cry : cries – crying – cried

P7

	changer	*ajouter*
"he/she/it" au présent		**-s**
participe présent	le **ie** final en **y**	**-ing**
participe passé		**-d**

Par exemple :

die : dies – dying – died

P8

	changer	*ajouter*
"he/she/it" au présent		**-s**
participe présent	le **c** final en **ck**	**-ing**
participe passé	le **c** final en **ck**	**-ed**

Par exemple :

picnic : picnics – picknicking – picknicked

P9

Ce code est employé pour marquer des verbes dont le participe passé est irrégulier (voir page 25) :

choose : chooses – choosing – chosen

Ces verbes portent deux codes. Dans le cas de **choose**, on trouvera les codes suivants : P4P9. Le P9 signifie que le verbe est irrégulier et que les formes irrégulières, étant fixes, ne subissent pas de changement orthographique. Pour les autres formes le verbe suit le modèle P4.

P10

ajouter

"he/she/it" au présent	**-ses**
participe présent	**-sing**
participe passé	**-sed**

Une forme rare :

nonplus : nonplusses – nonplussing – nonplussed

6 Le Passif

Dans la phrase :

I follow
je suis

le verbe **follow** a un sens actif et le sujet **I** accomplit l'action de suivre. Mais dans la phrase :

I am followed
je suis suivi

le verbe **am followed** a un sens passif et le sujet **I** subit l'action d'être suivi.

i) Le passif se forme avec le verbe **be** + participe passé. Par exemple, pour le verbe **hide**, on a :

infinitif	**(to) be hidden**
infinitif passé	**(to) have been hidden**
infinitif progressif	**(to) be being hidden**
présent simple	**am/are/is hidden**
présent progressif	**am/are/is being hidden**
futur simple	**will be hidden**
futur progressif	**will be being hidden**
prétérit simple	**was/were hidden**
prétérit progressif	**was/were being hidden**
present perfect	**have/has been hidden**
present perfect progressif	**have/has been being hidden**
plus-que-parfait	**had been hidden**
plus-que-parfait progressif	**had been being hidden**
futur antérieur	**will have been hidden**

conditionnel présent	**would be hidden**
conditionnel présent progressif	**would be being hidden**
conditionnel passé	**would have been hidden**
conditionnel passé progressif	**would have been being hidden**

Exemples :

it was hidden under some old papers
il était caché sous de vieux papiers

it had deliberately been hidden by his assistant
il avait été caché délibérément par son assistant

it was thought to have been hidden by the Romans
on pensait qu'il avait été caché par les Romains

he objected to this information being hidden away at the bottom of the form
il protesta que le renseignement était caché à la fin du formulaire

if he were a suspect, he would be being asked a lot of questions by now
s'il était un suspect, on lui poserait des questions à l'heure qu'il est

if he had made any comment it would almost certainly have been ignored
s'il avait fait des critiques, elles auraient certainement été ignorées

ii) Remarquez que la phrase active :

they sent him the wrong letter
ils lui ont envoyé la mauvaise lettre

peut être exprimée au passif de deux façons différentes :

the wrong letter was sent to him
he was sent the wrong letter
la mauvaise lettre lui a été envoyée

iii) Les verbes intransitifs peuvent souvent être employés avec un sens passif :

it opens at the front
ça s'ouvre devant

the sentence reads better like this
cette phrase est plus correcte comme ceci

this material won't wash very well
ce tissu ne se lave pas très bien

7 Liste des Verbes Irréguliers

Les américanismes sont indiqués par *. Les formes peu courantes, archaïques ou littéraires sont données entre parenthèses. Les traductions ci-dessous ne sont pas restrictives et ne donnent qu'un des sens de base.

Infinitif		Prétérit	Participe Passé
abide	*(supporter)*	**(abode)** [1]	**abided**
arise	*(surgir)*	**arose**	**arisen**
awake	*(s'éveiller)*	**awoke, awaked**	**awoken, (awaked)**
bear	*(porter)*	**bore**	**borne** [2]
beat	*(battre)*	**beat**	**beaten** [3]
become	*(devenir)*	**became**	**become**
befall	*(arriver)*	**befell**	**befallen**
beget	*(engendrer)*	**begot**	**begotten**
begin	*(commencer)*	**began**	**begun**
behold	*(apercevoir)*	**beheld**	**beheld**
bend	*(courber)*	**bent**	**bent** [4]
bereave	*(priver)*	**bereaved**	**bereft** [5]
beseech	*(implorer)*	**besought**	**besought**
bestride	*(chevaucher)*	**bestrode**	**bestridden**
bet	*(parier)*	**bet, betted**	**bet, betted**
bid	*(offrir)*	**bid**	**bid**
bid	*(commander)*	**bade**	**bidden**
bind	*(attacher)*	**bound**	**bound**
bite	*(mordre)*	**bit**	**bitten**
bleed	*(saigner)*	**bled**	**bled**
blow	*(souffler)*	**blew**	**blown**
break	*(casser)*	**broke**	**broken** [6]
breed	*(élever)*	**bred**	**bred**
bring	*(apporter)*	**brought**	**brought**
broadcast	*(diffuser)*	**broadcast**	**broadcast**
build	*(construire)*	**built**	**built**
burn	*(brûler)*	**burnt, burned**	**burnt, burned**
burst	*(éclater)*	**burst**	**burst**
buy	*(acheter)*	**bought**	**bought**

Infinitif		Prétérit	Participe Passé
cast	(*jeter*)	cast	cast
catch	(*attraper*)	caught	caught
chide	(*gronder*)	chid, chided	chid, (chidden), chided
choose	(*choisir*)	chose	chosen
cleave	(*fendre*)	clove, cleft,	cloven, cleft [7]
cleave	(*adhérer*)	cleaved, (clave)	cleaved
cling	(*s'accrocher à*)	clung	clung
clothe	(*habiller*)	clothed, (clad)	clothed, (clad)
come	(*venir*)	came	come
cost	(*coûter*)	cost	cost
creep	(*ramper*)	crept	crept
crow	(*chanter*)	crowed, (crew)	crowed
cut	(*couper*)	cut	cut
dare	(*oser*)	dared, (durst)	dared, (durst)
deal	(*traiter*)	dealt	dealt
dig	(*fouiller*)	dug	dug
dive	(*plonger*)	dived, dove*	dived
draw	(*dessiner, tirer*)	drew	drawn
dream	(*rêver*)	dreamt, dreamed	dreamt, dreamed
drink	(*boire*)	drank	drunk [8]
drive	(*conduire*)	drove	driven
dwell	(*demeurer*)	dwelt, dwelled	dwelt, dwelled
eat	(*manger*)	ate	eaten
fall	(*tomber*)	fell	fallen
feed	(*nourrir*)	fed	fed
feel	(*sentir*)	felt	felt
fight	(*battre*)	fought	fought
find	(*trouver*)	found	found
fit	(*aller à*)	fit*, fitted	fit*, fitted
flee	(*s'envoler*)	fled	fled
fling	(*lancer*)	flung	flung
fly	(*voler*)	flew	flown
forbear	(*s'abstenir*)	forbore	forborne
forbid	(*interdire*)	forbad(e)	forbidden
forget	(*oublier*)	forgot	forgotten
forgive	(*pardonner*)	forgave	forgiven
forsake	(*abandonner*)	forsook	forsaken
freeze	(*geler*)	froze	frozen

Infinitif		Prétérit	Participe Passé
get	(*obtenir*)	**got**	**got, gotten*** [9]
gild	(*dorer*)	**gilt, gilded**	**gilt, gilded** [10]
gird	(*ceindre*)	**girt, girded**	**girt, girded** [10]
give	(*donner*)	**gave**	**given**
go	(*aller*)	**went**	**gone**
grind	(*grincer*)	**ground**	**ground**
grow	(*pousser*)	**grew**	**grown**
hang	(*pendre*)	**hung, hanged** [11]	**hung, hanged** [11]
hear	(*entendre*)	**heard**	**heard**
heave	(*lever*)	**hove, heaved** [12]	**hove, heaved** [12]
hew	(*tailler*)	**hewed**	**hewn, hewed**
hide	(*cacher*)	**hid**	**hidden**
hit	(*frapper*)	**hit**	**hit**
hold	(*tenir*)	**held**	**held**
hurt	(*blesser*)	**hurt**	**hurt**
keep	(*garder*)	**kept**	**kept**
kneel	(*s'agenouiller*)	**knelt, kneeled**	**knelt, kneeled**
knit	(*tricoter*)	**knit, knitted** [13]	**knit, knitted** [13]
know	(*savoir, connaître*)	**knew**	**known**
lay	(*coucher*)	**laid**	**laid**
lead	(*mener*)	**led**	**led**
lean	(*s'appuyer*)	**leant, leaned**	**leant, leaned**
leap	(*sauter*)	**leapt, leaped**	**leapt, leaped**
learn	(*apprendre*)	**learnt, learned**	**learnt, learned**
leave	(*laisser*)	**left**	**left**
lend	(*prêter*)	**lent**	**lent**
let	(*laisser*)	**let**	**let**
lie	(*coucher*)	**lay**	**lain**
light	(*allumer*)	**lit, lighted**	**lit, lighted** [14]
lose	(*perdre*)	**lost**	**lost**
make	(*faire*)	**made**	**made**
mean	(*signifier*)	**meant**	**meant**
meet	(*rencontrer*)	**met**	**met**
melt	(*fondre*)	**melted**	**melted, molten** [15]
mow	(*faucher*)	**mowed**	**mown, mowed**
pay	(*payer*)	**paid**	**paid**
plead	(*plaider*)	**pled***, **pleaded**	**pled***, **pleaded** [16]
put	(*poser*)	**put**	**put**

Infinitif		Prétérit	Participe Passé
quit	*(quitter)*	**quit, (quitted)**	**quit (quitted)** [17]
read	*(lire)*	**read**	**read**
rend	*(déchirer)*	**rent**	**rent**
rid	*(débarrasser)*	**rid, (ridded)**	**rid**
ride	*(monter à)*	**rode**	**ridden**
ring	*(sonner)*	**rang**	**rung**
rise	*(se lever)*	**rose**	**risen**
run	*(courir)*	**ran**	**run**
saw	*(scier)*	**sawed**	**sawn, sawed**
say	*(dire)*	**said**	**said**
see	*(voir)*	**saw**	**seen**
seek	*(chercher)*	**sought**	**sought**
sell	*(vendre)*	**sold**	**sold**
send	*(envoyer)*	**sent**	**sent**
set	*(mettre)*	**set**	**set**
sew	*(coudre)*	**sewed**	**sewn, sewed**
shake	*(secouer)*	**shook**	**shaken**
shear	*(tondre)*	**sheared**	**shorn, sheared** [18]
shed	*(perdre)*	**shed**	**shed**
shine	*(briller)*	**shone** [19]	**shone** [19]
shoe	*(chausser)*	**shod, shoed**	**shod, shoed** [20]
shoot	*(abattre, tirer)*	**shot**	**shot**
show	*(montrer)*	**showed**	**shown, showed**
shrink	*(rétrécir)*	**shrank, shrunk**	**shrunk, shrunken** [21]
shut	*(fermer)*	**shut**	**shut**
sing	*(chanter)*	**sang**	**sung**
sink	*(couler)*	**sank**	**sunk, sunken** [22]
sit	*(s'asseoir)*	**sat**	**sat**
slay	*(tuer)*	**slew**	**slain**
sleep	*(dormir)*	**slept**	**slept**
slide	*(glisser)*	**slid**	**slid**
sling	*(lancer)*	**slung**	**slung**
slink	*(s'en aller furtivement)*	**slunk**	**slunk**
slit	*(fendre)*	**slit**	**slit**
smell	*(sentir)*	**smelt, smelled**	**smelt, smelled**
smite	*(frapper)*	**smote**	**smitten** [23]
sneak	*(entrer, etc. à la dérobée)*	**snuck*, sneaked**	**snuck*, sneaked**
sow	*(semer)*	**sowed**	**sown, sowed**

Infinitif		Prétérit	Participe Passé
speak	(*parler*)	**spoke**	**spoken**
speed	(*aller vite*)	**sped, speeded**	**sped, speeded**
spell	(*écrire*)	**spelt, spelled**	**spelt, spelled**
spend	(*dépenser*)	**spent**	**spent**
spill	(*renverser*)	**spilt, spilled**	**spilt, spilled**
spin	(*filer*)	**spun**	**spun**
spit	(*cracher*)	**spat, spit***	**spat, spit***
split	(*se briser*)	**split**	**split**
spoil	(*abîmer*)	**spoilt, spoiled**	**spoilt, spoiled**
spread	(*étendre*)	**spread**	**spread**
spring	(*bondir*)	**sprang**	**sprung**
stand	(*se tenir*)	**stood**	**stood**
steal	(*voler*)	**stole**	**stolen**
stick	(*enfoncer, coller*)	**stuck**	**stuck**
sting	(*piquer*)	**stung**	**stung**
stink	(*puer*)	**stank**	**stunk**
strew	(*répandre*)	**strewed**	**strewn, strewed**
stride	(*avancer à grands pas*)	**strode**	**stridden**
strike	(*frapper*)	**struck**	**struck, stricken** [24]
string	(*enfiler*)	**strung**	**strung**
strive	(*s'efforcer*)	**strove**	**striven**
swear	(*jurer*)	**swore**	**sworn**
sweat	(*suer*)	**sweat*, sweated**	**sweat*, sweated**
sweep	(*balayer*)	**swept**	**swept**
swell	(*gonfler*)	**swelled**	**swollen, swelled** [25]
swim	(*nager*)	**swam**	**swum**
swing	(*se balancer*)	**swung**	**swung**
take	(*prendre*)	**took**	**taken**
teach	(*enseigner*)	**taught**	**taught**
tear	(*déchirer*)	**tore**	**torn**
tell	(*dire*)	**told**	**told**
think	(*penser*)	**thought**	**thought**
thrive	(*fleurir*)	**thrived, (throve)**	**thrived, (thriven)**
throw	(*jeter*)	**threw**	**thrown**
thrust	(*pousser*)	**thrust**	**thrust**
tread	(*marcher*)	**trod**	**trodden**

Infinitif		Prétérit	Participe Passé
understand	(*comprendre*)	**understood**	**understood**
undertake	(*s'engager*)	**undertook**	**undertaken**
wake	(*se réveiller*)	**woke, waked**	**woken, waked**
wear	(*porter*)	**wore**	**worn**
weave	(*tisser*)	**wove** [26]	**woven** [26]
weep	(*pleurer*)	**wept**	**wept**
wet	(*mouiller*)	**wet*, wetted** [27]	**wet*, wetted** [27]
win	(*gagner*)	**won**	**won**
wind	(*remonter*)	**wound**	**wound**
wring	(*tordre*)	**wrung**	**wrung**
write	(*écrire*)	**wrote**	**written**

(1) Régulier dans la construction **abide by** "se conformer à, suivre" : **they abided by the rules**.

(2) Mais **born** au passif = "né" ou comme un adjectif : **he was born in France/a born gentleman**.

(3) Remarquez la forme familière **this has me beat/you have me beat there** *cela me dépasse/tu m'as posé une colle* et **beat** dans le sens de "très fatigué, épuisé" : **I'm (dead) beat**.

(4) Remarquez la phrase **on one's bended knees** *à genoux*.

(5) Mais **bereaved** dans le sens de "endeuillé" comme dans **the bereaved received no compensation** *la famille du disparu ne reçut aucune compensation*. Comparez : **he was bereft of speech** *il en perdit la parole*.

(6) Mais **broke** quand il s'agit d'un adjectif = "fauché" : **I'm broke**.

(7) **cleft** n'est employé qu'avec le sens de "coupé en deux". Remarquez **cleft palate** *palais fendu* et **(to be caught) in a cleft stick** *(être) dans une impasse*, mais **cloven foot/hoof** *sabot fendu*.

(8) Quand c'est un adjectif placé avant le nom, **drunken** "ivre, ivrogne' est parfois employé (**a lot of drunk(en) people** *beaucoup de gens ivres*) et il **doit** toujours être employé devant les noms représentant des objets inanimés (**one of his usual drunken parties** *une de ses soirées habituelles où l'on boit*).

(9) Mais **have got to** se dit aussi en américain avec le sens de "devoir, être obligé de" : **a man has got to do what a man has got to do** *un homme doit faire ce qu'il doit faire.* Comparez avec : **she has gotten into a terrible mess** *elle s'est fourrée dans une sale situation.*

(10) Les formes du participe passé **gilt** et **girt** sont très couramment employées comme adjectif placé avant le nom : **gilt mirrors** *des miroirs dorés*, **a flower-girt grave** *une tombe entourée de fleurs* (mais toujours **gilded youth** *la jeunesse dorée*, dans lequel **gilded** signifie 'riche et bienheureux').

(11) Régulier quand il a le sens de "mettre à mort par pendaison".

(12) **Hove** est employé dans le domaine nautique comme dans la phrase **heave into sight** : **just then Mary hove into sight** *et Mary pointa à l'horizon/apparut.*

(13) Irrégulier quand il a le sens de "unir" (**a close-knit family** *une famille unie*), mais régulier lorsqu'il a le sens de 'fabriquer en laine' et quand il fait référence aux os = 'se souder'.

(14) Lorsque le participe passé est employé comme un adjectif devant un nom, **lighted** est souvent préféré à **lit** : **a lighted match** *une allumette allumée* (mais : **the match is lit, she has lit a match** *l'allumette est allumée, elle a allumé une allumette*). Dans les noms composés, on emploie généralement **lit** : **well-lit streets** *des rues bien éclairées*. Au sens figuré (avec **up**), **lit** uniquement est employé au prétérit et au participe passé : **her face lit up when she saw me** *son visage s'illumina lorsqu'elle me vit.*

(15) On emploie **molten** uniquement comme un adjectif devant les noms, et seulement lorsqu'il signifie 'fondu à une très haute température', par exemple : **molten lead** *du plomb fondu* (mais **melted butter** *du beurre fondu*).

(16) En anglais d'Ecosse et en américain, on emploie **pled** au passé et au participe passé.

(17) En américain, les formes régulières ne sont pas employées, et elles sont de plus en plus rares en anglais britannique.

(18) Le participe passé est normalement **shorn** devant un nom
(**newly-shorn lambs** *des agneaux tout juste tondus*) et toujours
dans la phrase **(to be) shorn of** *(être) privé de* : **shorn of his
riches he was nothing** *privé de ses richesses, il n'était plus
rien*.

(19) Mais régulier quand il a le sens de 'cirer, astiquer' en
américain.

(20) Quand c'est un adjectif, on n'emploie que **shod** : **a well-shod
foot** *un pied bien chaussé*.

(21) **Shrunken** n'est employé que lorsqu'il est adjectif : **shrunken
limbs/her face was shrunken** *des membres rabougris/son
visage était ratatiné*.

(22) **Sunken** n'est employé que comme un adjectif : **sunken eyes**
des yeux creux.

(23) Verbe archaïque dont le participe passé **smitten** s'emploie
encore comme adjectif : **he's completely smitten with her** *il
est complètement fou d'elle*.

(24) **Stricken** n'est utilisé que dans le sens figuré (**a stricken
family/stricken with poverty** *une famille accablée/accablée par
la pauvreté*). Il est très courant dans les noms composés (accablé
par) : **poverty-stricken**, **fever-stricken**, **horror-stricken** (aussi
horror-struck), **terror-stricken** (aussi **terror-struck**), mais on
dit toujours **thunderstruck** *frappé par la surprise, abasourdi de
surprise*.

C'est aussi un emploi américain **the remark was stricken from
the record** *la remarque a été rayée du procès-verbal*.

(25) **Swollen** est plus courant que **swelled** comme verbe (**her face
has swollen** *son visage a gonflé*) et comme adjectif (**her face
is swollen/a swollen face**). **A swollen head** *une grosse tête*,
pour quelqu'un qui a une haute opinion de soi-même, devient **a
swelled head** en américain.

(26) Mais il est régulier lorsqu'il a le sens de 'se faufiler' : **the
motorbike weaved elegantly through the traffic** *la moto se
faufila avec élégance dans la circulation*.

(27) Mais irrégulier aussi en anglais britannique lorsqu'il a le sens de "mouiller par de l'urine" : **he wet his bed again last night** *il a encore mouillé son lit la nuit dernière.*

8 Les Contractions

Les formes contractées sont très courantes dans l'anglais parlé d'aujourd'hui et dans l'anglais écrit non-officiel :

BE

I am	I'm
you are	you're
he/she/it is	he's/she's/it's
we/they are	we're/they're

I am not	I'm not
you are not	you're not, you aren't
he/she/it is not	he's/she's/it's not, he/she/it isn't
we/they are not	we/they aren't

am I not?	aren't I?
are you not?	aren't you?
is he/she/it not?	isn't he/she/it?
are we/they not?	aren't we/they?

DO

I/you/we/they do not	I/you/we/they don't
he/she/it does not	he/she/it doesn't

do I/you/we/they not?	don't I/you/we/they?
does he/she/it not?	doesn't he/she/it?

HAVE

I have	I've
you/we/they have	you've/we've/they've
he/she/it has	he's/she's/it's (plus courant avec le present perfect comme dans : I've seen etc.)

I/you/we/they have not	I/you/we/they haven't
he/she/it/has not	he/she/it hasn't

have I/you/we/they not?	haven't I/you/we/they?
has he/she/it not?	hasn't he/she/it?

I/he/she/it was not **you/we/they were not**	**I/he/she/it wasn't** **you/we/they weren't**
I, etc. **did not**	**I**, etc. **didn't**
I/you, etc. **will**	**I'll/you'll**, etc.
I/he, etc. **will not**	**I/he**, etc. **won't**
I shall	**I'll**
I shall not	**I shan't**
I/you, etc. **would***	**I'd/you'd**, etc.
I/you, etc. **would not***	**I/you**, etc. **wouldn't**
I/he, etc. **would have***	**I'd've/ he'd've**, etc.
I/he, etc. **would not have***	**I/he**, etc. **wouldn't have**

*aussi **should** à la première personne

Les contractions ne sont pas seulement utilisées avec les pronoms personnels :

that'll he the day!
Mummy's just gone out

Voir aussi Les Auxiliaires Modaux, page 51.

9 Les Questions

i) Lorsqu'aucun autre auxiliaire n'est utilisé (**be**, **have** ou **will**) on forme les questions avec l'auxiliaire **do** :

do you like whisky?
aimez-vous le whisky ?

how do you spell it?
comment ça s'écrit ?

doesn't she expect you home?
est-ce qu'elle ne vous attend pas à la maison ?

did you talk to him?
lui avez-vous parlé ?

didn't I tell you so!
est-ce que je ne vous l'avais pas dit ?!

ii) Si un autre auxiliaire est utilisé, alors on inverse l'ordre du sujet et du verbe :

he is Welsh
il est Gallois

is he Welsh?
est-il Gallois ?

they're going home tomorrow
ils/elles rentrent à la maison demain

are they going home tomorrow?
est-ce qu'ils/elles rentrent à la maison demain ?

Daphne will be there too
Daphné sera là aussi

will Daphne be there too?
est-ce que Daphné sera là aussi ?

I can't understand
je ne peux pas comprendre

why can't I understand?
pourquoi ne puis-je pas comprendre ?

iii) Si le sujet est un pronom interrogatif, **do** n'est pas utilisé :

who made that noise?
qui a fait ce bruit ?

what happened?
qu'est-ce qui s'est passé ?

iv) Les question-tags (n'est-ce pas ?) :

a) Une affirmation est suivie par un question-tag négatif,
et vice-versa :

you can see it, can't you?
tu peux le voir, n'est-ce pas ?

you can't see it, can you?
tu ne peux pas voir ça, si ?

Si le question-tag ne s'emploie pas pour poser une question
mais sert à renforcer le sens de la phrase principale, alors un
question-tag positif suit une phrase affirmative :

so you've seen a ghost, have you?
alors vous avez vu un fantôme, n'est-ce pas ?
(incrédulité, sarcasme)

he's got married again, has he?
alors il s'est encore marié, hein ? (surprise, intérêt)

Remarquez que le question-tag reprend le temps de la phrase
principale :

you want to meet him, don't you?
tu veux le rencontrer, n'est-ce pas ?

you wanted to meet him, didn't you?
tu voulais le rencontrer, n'est-ce pas ?

you'll want to meet him, won't you?
tu voudras le rencontrer, n'est-ce pas ?

b) Si la proposition précédente est régie par un auxiliaire, on
répète cet auxiliaire dans le question-tag :

he has been here before, hasn't he?
il est déjà venu ici, n'est-ce pas ?

they aren't stopping, are they?
ils ne s'arrêtent pas, si ?

you will sign it, won't you?
tu le signeras, n'est-ce pas ?

c) S'il n'y a pas d'auxiliaire dans la proposition précédente, on utilise **do** dans le question-tag :

he lives in France, doesn't he?
it vit en France, n'est-ce pas ?

she left yesterday, didn't she?
elle est partie hier, n'est-ce pas ?

d) Si le question-tag suit un impératif, l'auxiliaire (et surtout **will/would**) est utilisé. Ces question-tags permettent d'adoucir la phrase, d'éviter un ton abrupt :

leave the cat alone, will you?
laisse donc ce chat tranquille

take this to Mrs Brown, would you?
tu veux bien apporter ça à Madame Brown ?

Dans les cas suivants, la forme négative **won't** représente une invitation :

help yourselves to drinks, won't you?
servez-vous à boire, je vous en prie

10 La Forme Négative

i) Quand il n'y a pas d'autre auxiliaire (**be**, **will**, etc.) on emploie **not** après **do** (voir aussi Les Contractions, page 34) :

I like it
ça me plaît

I do not (don't) like it
ça ne me plaît pas

she agrees with them
elle est d'accord avec eux

she does not (doesn't) agree with them
elle n'est pas d'accord avec eux

I expected him to say that
je m'attendais à ce qu'il dise cela

I didn't expect him to say that
je ne m'attendais pas à ce qu'il dise cela

ii) Si un autre auxiliaire est employé, alors on emploie seulement **not** :

I will (I'll) take them with me
je les prendrai avec moi

I will not (won't) take them with me
je ne les prendrai pas avec moi

they are just what I'm looking for
c'est exactement ce que je cherche

they are not really what I'm looking for
(contraction = they aren't/they're not)
ce n'est pas vraiment ce que je cherche

iii) **Not** est employé avec les infinitifs et les gérondifs :

to be or not to be
être ou ne pas être

please try not to be so stupid
s'il te plaît évite d'être si stupide

it would have been better not to have mentioned it at all
il aurait mieux valu ne pas en parler du tout

he's worried about not having enough money
il a peur de ne pas avoir assez d'argent

Voir aussi L'Impératif, page 41.

11 L'Impératif

i) Pour exprimer l'impératif, on emploie le verbe à l'infinitif (sans **to**) :

stop that!
arrête ça !

well, just look at him!
eh bien, regarde-le, celui-là !

somebody do something!
que quelqu'un fasse quelque chose !

have another
prenez-en un autre

try one of mine
essayez l'un des miens

ii) Pour faire une suggestion ou une proposition à la première personne du pluriel, on emploie **let's** + infinitif sans **to** :

let's leave it at that for today
restons-en là pour aujourd'hui

let's just agree to differ
acceptons seulement de ne pas être du même avis

iii) L'interdiction ou la commande négative :

Pour exprimer l'interdiction ou la commande négative, on emploie **do not** ou **don't** placés devant l'infinitif. En anglais courant et parlé **don't** est de beaucoup la forme la plus fréquente, à moins qu'on veuille donner plus d'emphase à la phrase :

don't listen to what he says
n'écoute pas ce qu'il dit

please don't feel you have to accept
ne te sens pas obligé d'accepter, je t'en prie

look, I've told you before, do not put your hands on the hotplate!
écoute, je te l'ai déjà dit, ne mets pas tes mains sur la plaque chauffante !

Avec la forme **let's**, on place **not** entre **let's** et le verbe. On peut aussi employer la forme **don't let's** :

let's not go just yet
don't let's go just yet
ne partons pas encore

iv) **Do not** est très couramment employé sur les panneaux d'indication :

do not feed the animals
ne pas nourrir les animaux

v) Pour renforcer un impératif, l'auxiliaire **do** peut être employé :

oh, do be quiet!
oh, reste tranquille !

12 Exprimer la Condition

La phrase :

if you don't hurry, you'll miss your train
si tu ne te dépêches pas, tu vas manquer ton train

est une phrase conditionnelle. La condition est exprimée dans la proposition subordonnée (commençant par **if**) qui peut être placée avant ou après la proposition principale (**you'll miss your train**).

La forme des verbes varie selon la **référence temporelle** et le degré de **probabilité de réalisation** de la condition.

i) Référence temporelle au présent/futur :

a) forte "probabilité de réalisation" :

Les verbes dans la proposition commençant par **if** sont au présent ou au present perfect : le verbe de la proposition principale est **will** + infinitif : (parfois **shall** + infinitif, à la première personne) :

if I see her, I'll tell her
si je la vois, je le lui dirai

if you have finished that one, I'll give you another
si tu as fini celui-ci, je t'en donnerai un autre

Il y a trois exceptions majeures :

★ Si le verbe de la proposition principale est aussi au présent, on s'attend à une conséquence logique, par automatisme ou habitude. Dans ce cas, **if** a le sens de **when(ever)** (chaque fois, quand) :

if the sun shines, people look happier
quand le soleil brille, les gens ont l'air plus heureux

if you're happy, then I'm happy
si ça te va, ça me va

★ Quand **will** est employé dans la proposition qui commence par **if**, le locuteur fait allusion à la volonté ou à l'intention de quelqu'un de faire quelque chose :

if you will kindly look this way, I'll try to explain the painter's approach
si vous voulez bien regarder par ici, je vous expliquerai l'approche du peintre

well if you will mix your drinks, what can you expect!
si tu tiens absolument à faire des mélanges d'alcool, que veux-tu qu'il arrive ?!

Quand on emploie cette forme pour faire une demande, on peut rendre la phrase plus polie en employant **would** :

if you would be kind enough to look this way . . .
si vous voulez bien regardez par ici . . .

★ Lorsque **should** est employé dans la proposition commençant par **if** (à n'importe quelle personne), la condition semble avoir moins de chance de se réaliser. Ces propositions avec **should** sont souvent suivies de l'impératif, comme dans le premier exemple :

if you should see him, please ask him to ring me
si vous deviez le rencontrer, pourriez-vous lui demander de me téléphoner ?

if they should not be there, you will have to manage by yourself
si par hasard ils/elles ne sont pas là, il faudra bien que vous vous débrouilliez par vous-même

Dans un style plus soutenu, **if** peut être omis et la phrase peut commencer avec une proposition subordonnée employant **should** :

should the matter arise again, telephone me at once
si le problème se pose encore, téléphonez-moi immédiatement

b) "probabilité de réalisation" moins forte :

Si la condition n'est pas supposée se réaliser ou si elle présente un caractère de doute ou si elle est contredite par des faits connus, le verbe de la proposition commençant par **if** est au passé : le verbe de la proposition principale est

would (ou aussi **should** à la première personne) + infinitif :

if I saw her, I would (I'd) tell her
si je la voyais, je le lui dirais

if I had known that, I would have done something about it
si j'avais su cela, je m'en serais occupé

Remarquez que ce type de phrase n'indique pas toujours une différence dans le degré de probabilité de réalisation de la condition. Il y a souvent très peu de différence entre ce type de phrase et celui décrit en i) a) :

if you tried harder, you would pass the exam (= if you try harder, you will pass the exam)
si tu travaillais davantage, tu réussirais tes examens

L'emploi du passé rend la phrase plus amicale ou plus polie.

ii) Référence au passé :

a) La condition ne s'est pas réalisée. Le verbe de la proposition subordonnée est au plus-que-parfait ; on trouve **would** (ou aussi **should** à la première personne) + infinitif passé dans la proposition principale :

if I had seen her, I would have told her
si je l'avais vue, je le lui aurais dit

if you had finished that one, I would have given you another one
si tu avais fini celui-ci, je t'en aurais donné un autre

Dans un style légèrement plus soutenu, **if** peut être omis et la proposition subordonnée peut commencer avec **had** :

had I seen her, I would/should have told her
si je l'avais vue, je le lui aurais dit

b) Exceptions :

★ Si la proposition principale exprime un état **présent** de non-réalisation d'une condition passée, on peut aussi employer **would** + infinitif (présent) :

if I had studied harder, I would be an engineer today
(= if I had studied harder, I would have been an engineer today)
si j'avais plus travaillé je serais ingénieur aujourd'hui

★ Le passé est employé dans les deux propositions si, comme nous l'avons vu en a) i), une conséquence d'automatisme ou d'habitude est sous-entendue (**if** = when(ever) "chaque fois, quand") :

if people had influenza in those days, they died
si les gens attrapaient la grippe à cette époque-là, ils en mourraient

★ Si la condition est supposée avoir eu lieu, les restrictions sur les formes verbales ne sont plus valables. En effet dans ce cas, **if** signifie souvent "comme" ou "puisque" :

if he was rude to you, why did you not walk out?
puisqu'il était impoli avec toi, pourquoi n'es-tu pas sorti ?

if he was rude to you, why have you still kept in touch?
puisqu'il était impoli avec toi, pourquoi es-tu resté en contact avec lui ?

if he was rude to you, why do you still keep in touch?
puisqu'il était impoli avec toi, pourquoi restes-tu en contact avec lui ?

13 Le Gérondif, l'Infinitif

Le gérondif, que l'on appelle aussi verbe substantivé, a la forme du participe présent (terminaison en **-ing**) mais un différent champ d'application. Il peut être employé :

i) Comme un nom :

driving is fun
conduire, c'est sympa

smoking is not good for you
fumer n'est pas bon pour la santé

I love reading
j'adore lire

ii) Avec les caractéristiques d'un verbe (prenant un complément, un sujet ou un attribut) :

writing this letter took me ages
la rédaction de cette lettre m'a pris longtemps

being left-handed has never been a problem
être gaucher n'a jamais été un problème

the thought of Douglas doing that is absurd
penser que Douglas fasse cela est absurde

iii) Avec un adverbe qui le modifie :

it's a question of precisely defining our needs
il s'agit de définir précisément quels sont nos besoins

iv) Avec un possessif :

L'emploi d'un adjectif possessif (**my**, **his**, etc.) placé devant un gérondif est plus courant dans le style écrit (soutenu) qu'oral :

we were suprised about you/your not being chosen
nous avons été surpris que vous ne soyez pas sélectionnés

v) Comparaison du gérondif et de l'infinitif :

On peut parfois employer l'un ou l'autre après un verbe :

I can't stand seeing him upset
I can't stand to see him upset
je ne supporte pas de le voir inquiet

Mais il y a parfois une différence importante :

we stopped having our rest at 3 o'clock (= ended it)
nous avons arrêté notre sieste à 3 heures

we stopped to have our rest at 3 o'clock (= started it)
nous avons arrêté pour faire la sieste à 3 heures

Voici des verbes fréquemment employés qui ne sont suivis que de l'infinitif :

demand	exiger
expect	s'attendre à
hope	espérer
want	vouloir
wish	souhaiter

Verbes fréquemment employés qui ne sont suivis que du gérondif :

avoid	éviter
consider	considérer
dislike	ne pas aimer
enjoy	apprécier
finish	finir
keep	garder
practise	pratiquer, faire
risk	risquer

vi) La césure de l'infinitif

On dit que l'infinitif "se coupe" lorsqu'un adverbe est placé entre **to** et le radical :

they then decided to definitely leave
ils/elles ont alors décidé de partir pour de bon

Cette forme est souvent considérée de mauvais style, et on lui préfère la forme :

they then decided definitely to leave

14 Le Subjonctif

On reconnaît le subjonctif à l'omission du **-s** à la troisième
personne du singulier, à l'emploi de **be** au lieu de **is** et à l'emploi
de **were** au lieu de **was**. Ce mode n'est pas aussi courant en anglais
qu'en français. Emplois principaux :

i) Dans des locutions fixes qui expriment le souhait :

   long live the King!
   vive le Roi !

   God rest his soul
   Dieu ait son âme

   Heaven be praised
   Dieu soit loué

ii) Dans l'expression **if need be** (si besoin est) :

   well, if need be, you could always hire a car
   eh bien, si besoin est, vous pourriez toujours louer une voiture

iii) Dans des propositions comme :

   it is vital that he understand this
   il est très important qu'il comprenne cela

   they recommended she sell the house
   ils lui ont conseillé de vendre la maison

   we propose that this new ruling be adopted
   nous proposons que cette nouvelle loi soit adoptée

On trouve cet emploi du subjonctif dans un style plus soutenu.
Dans la langue parlée, il est plus fréquent en anglais américain
qu'en anglais britannique.

iv) **if I was/were** :

Comparez :

(a) **if I was in the wrong, it wasn't intentional**
si j'avais tort, ce n'était pas voulu

(b) **if I were in the wrong, I would admit it**
si j'avais tort, je le reconnaîtrais

Dans l'exemple (a) le locuteur n'émet aucun doute sur le fait qu'il/elle avait tort, mais précise l'absence d'intention malveillante. Dans l'exemple (b), par contre, le locuteur n'accepte pas qu'il/elle a ou avait tort ; pour le locuteur, un doute persiste concernant ce point. D'où l'emploi du subjonctif **were**.

Dans la phrase (b), on pourrait aussi employer **was** tout en conservant le même sens. **Was** serait d'un style plus familier que **were**.

15 Les Auxiliaires Modaux

i) CAN-COULD

Les formes contractées négatives sont **can't-couldn't**. La forme négative non contractée du présent est **cannot**.

a) Pour exprimer la capacité, le fait de pouvoir faire qch (= **be able to**) :

can machines "think"?
est-ce que les machines peuvent "penser" ?

I can explain that
je peux l'expliquer

when I was a student I could explain that sort of thing easily
quand j'étais étudiant, je pouvais expliquer facilement ce genre de choses

Pour ce dernier exemple (facultativement), et pour les autres temps, on emploie les formes de **be able to** :

I used to be able to explain that sort of thing easily
je pouvais expliquer ce genre de choses facilement

I'll be able to tell you the answer tomorrow
je pourrai te donner la réponse demain

I've never been able to understand her
je n'ai jamais pu la comprendre

Remarquez que dans une proposition conditionnelle, **could** + infinitif fait référence au présent ou au futur (Comparez avec **would** dans la section Exprimer la Condition, page 43) :

you could do a lot better if you'd only try
vous pourriez faire bien mieux si seulement vous essayiez

b) Pour exprimer la permission :

can/could I have a look at your photos?
puis/pourrais-je voir vos photos ?

Remarquez que **could** fait autant référence au présent et au futur que **can**. La seule différence réside dans le fait que **could** est un peu plus poli ou moins affirmatif. Par exemple, un enfant ne dira pas :

could I go out and play?
pourrais-je aller jouer ?

Could peut parfois être employé pour exprimer une permission dans le passé, lorsque il est évident que le contexte est dans le passé :

for some reason we couldn't smoke in the lounge yesterday; but today we can
pour d'obscures raisons, nous ne pouvions pas fumer dans le salon hier ; mais aujourd'hui nous le pouvons

Pour ce dernier exemple (facultativement), et pour les autres temps, on emploie les formes de **be allowed to** :

we weren't allowed to see him, he was so ill
nous ne pouvions pas le voir, il était trop souffrant

will they be allowed to change the rules?
est-ce qu'on leur permettra de changer les règles ?

c) Pour exprimer la possibilité :

that can't be right
cela ne peut être possible

what shall I do? – you can always talk to a lawyer/you could talk to a lawyer
que vais-je faire ? – vous pouvez toujours vous adresser à un avocat/vous pourriez vous adresser à un avocat

Remarquez que **could** ne fait pas référence au passé, mais au présent ou au futur. Si l'on souhaite faire référence au passé, **could** doit être suivi par l'infinitif passé :

you could have talked to a lawyer
vous auriez pu vous adresser à un avocat

I know I could have, but I didn't want to
je sais que j'aurais pu, mais je ne le voulais pas

★ **Could** et **may** sont parfois interchangeables lorsqu'ils expriment la possibilité, l'éventualité :

you could/may be right
vous avez peut-être raison

Mais il existe parfois une différence importante entre **can** et **may** dans leur rapport à la possibilité, à l'éventualité :

(a) **your comments can be overheard**
   on peut entendre vos remarques

(b) **your comments may be overheard**
   il est possible qu'on entende vos remarques

(a) signifie qu'il est possible que l'on entende les commentaires (parce qu'ils sont dits à voix haute, par exemple) sans spécifier si quelqu'un le fera effectivement ou non. (b) signifie qu'il existe une probabilité, une chance que les commentaires soient réellement entendus.

La différence existe aussi avec la forme négative :

don't worry, he can't have heard us
ne t'inquiète pas, il ne peut pas nous avoir entendus (il est impossible qu'il nous ait entendus)

because of all the noise, he may not have heard us
avec ce bruit il se peut qu'il ne nous ait pas entendus

d) Pour exprimer la suggestion : (**could** uniquement)

you could have talked to a lawyer
vous auriez pu vous adresser à un avocat

they could always sell their second house if they need money
ils pourraient toujours vendre leur deuxième maison s'ils ont besoin d'argent

e) Pour exprimer le reproche, l'ennui, l'agacement :
(**could** uniquement)

you could have told me I had paint on my face!
tu aurais pu me dire que j'avais de la peinture sur la figure !

ii) **MAY-MIGHT**

La forme contractée négative **mayn't** n'est pas courante dans le sens de "permission" de **may**. On emploie à la place **may not** ou **must not/mustn't**. La forme négative contractée de **might** est **mightn't**.

a) Pour exprimer la permission :

may I open a window? – no, you may not!
puis-je ouvrir la fenêtre ? – non, pas question !

L'emploi de **may** donne une forme légèrement plus polie que **can**. Un locuteur qui emploie **might** pour demander une permission se montrerait extrêmement poli :

I wonder if I might have another of those cakes
je me demande si je pourrais avoir un autre de ces gâteaux

might I suggest we stop there for today?
pourrais-je suggérer que nous nous arrêtions ici pour aujourd'hui ?

Remarquez que **might** se réfère au présent ou au futur. Il se réfère très rarement au passé quand il est employé dans une proposition principale. Comparez :

he then asked if he might smoke (**might** dans la proposition subordonnée)
alors il a demandé s'il pouvait fumer

he then asked if he was allowed to smoke
alors il a demandé s'il pouvait fumer

et

he wasn't allowed to smoke
il ne pouvait pas fumer, il n'avait pas le droit de fumer

On ne peut pas employer **might** dans le dernier exemple ; on a recours aux formes de **be allowed to** à la place.

b) Pour exprimer la possibilité :

it may/might be still be possible
c'est peut-être encore possible

they may/might change their minds
ils/elles vont peut-être changer d'avis

it mayn't/mightn't be necessary after all
ça ne sera peut-être pas nécessaire après tout

she may/might have left a note upstairs
elle a peut-être laissé un mot en haut

c) Pour exprimer la surprise, l'agacement : (**might** habituellement)

and who may/might you be?
pour qui est-ce que tu te prends ?

and what might that be supposed to mean?
et qu'est-ce que c'est supposé vouloir dire ?

d) Pour exprimer la suggestion : (**might** uniquement)

they might at least apologize
ils pourraient au moins s'excuser

you might like to try one of these cigars
vous serez peut-être curieux d'essayer un de ces cigares

Remarquez que dans cet usage, on a presque un ordre :

you might take this down the road to your Gran
apporte donc cela à ta grand-mère

you might like to read the next chapter for Monday
vous voudrez bien lire le chapitre suivant pour lundi

e) Pour exprimer le reproche, l'agacement : (**might** uniquement)

you might have told me he was deaf!
tu aurais pu me dire qu'il était sourd !

they might have written back to us at least!
ils auraient pu au moins nous répondre !

f) Pour exprimer le souhait :

may you have a very happy retirement
je vous souhaite d'avoir une très heureuse retraite

may all your dreams come true!
je souhaite que vos rêves se réalisent !

may/might you be forgiven for telling such lies!
que le Bon Dieu te pardonne de dire de tels mensonges !

Cet usage est normalement limité aux locutions fixes ou à un
style rhétorique ou littéraire.

iii) **MUST-HAD TO**

La forme contractée négative est **mustn't** (pour **have**, voir page 34).

a) Pour exprimer l'obligation :

we have no choice, we must do what he wants
nous n'avons pas le choix, nous devons faire ce qu'il veut

must you go already?
tu dois déjà partir ?

On peut aussi employer **have to**, ou dans un style plus familier, **have got to** :

we have no choice, we have (got) to do what he says
nous n'avons pas le choix, nous devons faire ce qu'il dit

do you have to go already/have you got to go already?
faut-il que tu partes déjà/dois-tu déjà partir ?

Le sens est souvent le même. Mais dans certains cas quand une obligation externe est sous-entendue (c.-à-d. quelqu'un vous a dit de faire quelque chose) **have to** est plus souvent employé :

I have to be there for my interview at 10 o'clock
je dois être là pour mon entretien à 10 heures

Pour le passé et le futur, on emploie **have to** :

we had to do what he wanted
nous devions faire ce qu'il voulait

I'll have to finish it tomorrow
il faudra que je le finisse demain

b) La forme négative :

i) **Must not** est employé pour exprimer l'interdiction :

you mustn't drink and drive
il ne faut pas boire et conduire

ii) **Don't have to** ou **haven't got to** sont employés pour signifier une absence d'obligation :

we don't have to drive all night, we could always stop off at a hotel
nous n'avons pas besoin de conduire toute la nuit, nous pourrions nous arrêter dans un hôtel

Pour i) au passé, on emploie **be allowed to** :

when we were children we weren't allowed to . . .
quand nous étions enfants, on ne nous autorisait pas à . . .

La forme passée de ii) suit la conjugaison de **have** :

you didn't have to buy one, you could have used mine
tu n'avais pas besoin d'en acheter un, tu aurais pu prendre le mien

c) Pour exprimer la probabilité :

hello, you must be Susan
bonjour, vous devez être Susan

that must be my mistake
ça doit être une erreur de ma part

she must have been surprised to see you
elle a dû être surprise de te voir

Have to est souvent employé dans ce sens aussi :

you have to be kidding!
vous voulez rire !

de même que **have got to**, surtout en anglais britannique :

well if she said so, it's got to be true (it's = it has)
si elle le dit, ça doit être vrai

iv) **OUGHT TO**

La forme contractée négative est **oughtn't to**. L'infinitif après **ought** prend **to**, à la différence des autres auxiliaires modaux.

a) Pour exprimer l'obligation :

Ought to a le même sens que **should** quand il exprime l'obligation :

you oughtn't even to think things like that
tu ne devrais même pas penser à des choses pareilles

and he ought to know!
et il est bien placé pour le savoir !

Mais **ought to** est moins fort que **must** dans ces sens. Comparez :

I must/have to avoid fatty foods (obligation ferme ou nécessité)
je dois éviter les aliments gras

I ought to avoid fatty foods (obligation moins stricte)
je devrais éviter les aliments gras

Must ou **have (got) to** remplacent normalement **ought to** dans les questions :

must you/do you have to/have you got to visit your mother every Sunday?
faut-il que vous rendiez visite à votre mère tous les dimanches ?

b) Pour exprimer la probabilité :

she ought to be halfway to Rome by now
elle doit être maintenant à mi-chemin de Rome

£50? – that ought to be enough
50 livres ? – cela devrait suffire

v) **SHALL-SHOULD**

Les formes contractées négatives sont **shan't-shouldn't**.
Pour le conditionnel, voir page 43. Pour exprimer le futur,
voir page 76.

a) Pour exprimer l'obligation (souvent morale) : (**should**
seulement)

you should take more exercise
tu devrais faire plus d'exercice

you shouldn't talk to her like that
tu ne devrais pas lui parler comme ça

what do you think I should do?
qu'est-ce que tu crois que je devrais faire ?

something was obviously not quite as it should be
quelque chose n'allait pas aussi bien que ça aurait dû

with a new fuse fitted it should work
avec un nouveau fusible, ça devrait marcher

b) Pour exprimer la probabilité : (**should** seulement)

it's after ten, they should be in Paris by now
il est plus de dix heures, ils/elles doivent être à Paris
maintenant

**if doing one took you two hours, then three shouldn't
take longer than six hours, should it?**
si tu en fais un en deux heures, tu dois pouvoir en faire
trois en six heures, non ?

**is it there? – well, it should be because that's where I
left it**
il est là ? – eh bien il devrait, parce que c'est là que je
l'ai laissé

c) Pour exprimer **would** d'une façon légèrement plus polie :
(**should** seulement)

I should just like to say that . . .
je voudrais juste dire que . . .

I should hardly call him a great innovative mind but . . .
je ne l'appellerais pas vraiment un grand esprit
innovateur, mais . . .

d) Pour exprimer la surprise, l'agacement, l'ennui :

there was a knock at the door, and who should it be but . . .
il y a eu un coup à la porte, et qui est entré . . . ?

where's the money gone? – how should I know?
où est l'argent ? – comment le saurais-je ?

e) **shall** est employé dans le langage légal ou officiel :

these sums shall be payable monthly
ces sommes seront payables mensuellement

as shall be stipulated by the contract
comme il sera stipulé dans le contrat

the bearings shall have a diameter of no less than . . .
le diamètre minimum des paliers sera de . . .

vi) **WILL-WOULD**

Les formes négatives contractées sont **won't-wouldn't**. Pour les phrases au conditionnel, voir page 43. Pour exprimer le futur, voir page 76.

a) **Will** est employé pour décrire des capacités ou des talents naturels, des goûts, ou des comportements caractéristiques :

concrete will not normally float
normalement le béton ne flotte pas

the paint will normally last for two to three years
la peinture doit durer deux ou trois ans

the tank will hold about 50 litres
ce réservoir a une contenance d'environ 50 litres

leave him alone and he'll play for hours
laisse-le seul, et il s'amusera pendant des heures

they will keep getting the address wrong!
ils persistent à mettre une adresse incorrecte !
(agacement)

the car won't start on damp mornings
la voiture ne démarre pas le matin quand il fait humide

On emploie **would** pour faire référence au passé :

let him alone and he would play for hours
on le laissait seul, et il jouait pendant des heures

they would insist on calling me "Jacko"
ils/elles tenaient absolument à m'appeler "Jacquot'

I lost it – you would!, that's typical of you!
je l'ai perdu – vraiment ! ça ne m'étonne pas de toi !

b) Pour exprimer des ordres, ou pour renforcer une affirmation :

you will do as you are told!
tu feras ce qu'on te dit de faire !

he will (damn well) do as he's told!
il fera bien ce qu'on lui dit de faire !

will you stop that right now!
veux-tu bien cesser cela tout de suite !

I will not tolerate this!
je ne tolèrerai pas ça !

c) Pour faire appel à la mémoire de quelqu'un ou à son savoir (dans un niveau de langue relativement soutenu) :

you will remember the point at which we left off last week's seminar
vous vous souviendrez où nous nous sommes arrêtés lors du séminaire de la semaine dernière

as you will all doubtless be aware, there have been rumours recently about . . .
comme vous en êtes tous certainement conscients, des rumeurs courent concernant . . .

d) Pour faire des suppositions :

there's someone at the door – that'll be Graham
il y a quelqu'un à la porte – ça doit être Graham

how old is he now? – he'll be about 45
quel âge a-t-il maintenant ? – il doit avoir à peu près 45 ans

e) Pour faire des propositions :

will you have another cup? – thank you, I will
en reprendrez-vous une autre tasse ? – oui, merci, je veux bien

won't you try one of these?
vous ne voulez pas essayer un de ceux-ci ?

did they ask you if you would like to try one?
est-ce qu'ils/elles vous ont demandé si vous vouliez en prendre un ?

f) Pour formuler des demandes :

will/would you move your car, please?
pourriez-vous déplacer votre voiture, s'il vous plaît ?

La forme **would** est plus polie, moins directe.

AUTRES AUXILIAIRES

vii) **USED TO**

Used to (pour exprimer un passé révolu) peut être considéré comme une sorte d'auxiliaire, puisque l'emploi de **do** est facultatif :

he used not to smoke so much
he didn't use to smoke so much
il ne fumait pas tant (autrefois)

did you use to know him?
est-ce que tu le connaissais ?

used you to know him?
le connaissais-tu ?

Dans les deux derniers exemples, la première forme est plus courante en anglais parlé.

viii) **DARE, NEED**

Ces verbes se comportent comme des verbes ordinaires ou comme des auxiliaires modaux. Comme auxiliaires, ils ne prennent pas de **-s** à la 3ème personne du singulier du présent ; **do** n'est pas employé dans les phrases interrogatives et négatives, et s'ils sont suivis d'un infinitif, on ne met pas **to** devant le radical.

a) Comme verbes ordinaires :

I don't dare to say anything
je n'ose rien dire

would/do you dare to ask him?
oseriez-vous/osez-vous lui demander ?

you don't need to ask first
tu n'as pas besoin de demander

do I need to sign it?
faut-il que je le signe ?

b) Comme auxiliaires modaux :

I daren't say anything je n'ose rien dire	**dare you ask him?** oses-tu le lui demander ?
you needn't ask first tu n'as pas besoin de demander	**need I sign it?** faut-il que je le signe ?

★ **Dare** peut aussi fonctionner comme un verbe ordinaire aux formes interrogative et négative (c.-à-d. avec **do**) et, comme les auxiliaires, être suivi d'un infinitif sans **to** :

I don't dare say anything
je n'ose rien dire

★ Dans les propositions principales qui ne sont ni interrogatives ni négatives, **need** se comporte toujours comme un verbe ordinaire :

I need to go to the toilet
j'ai besoin d'aller aux toilettes

ix) **HAVE, GET**

Have ou **get** peuvent être employés comme des "verbes de moyen", comme on le voit ici :

we're going to have/get the car resprayed
nous allons faire repeindre la voiture

I can't do it myself but I can have/get it done for you
je ne peux pas le faire moi-même, mais je peux le faire faire pour vous

L'action n'est pas accomplie par le locuteur, mais il la fait faire par quelqu'un d'autre.

Quand **have/get** sont suivis d'un infinitif à la voix active le **to** est omis après **have** mais il est maintenu après **get** :

I'll have the porter bring them up for you
I'll get the porter to bring them up for you
je les ferai monter par le portier

16 Exprimer le Présent

i) Le présent simple est employé :

a) Pour exprimer des événements généraux ou habituels ou un état de choses :

I have a shower in the mornings
je prends une douche le matin

she works for an insurance company
elle travaille dans une compagnie d'assurances

where do you buy your shoes?
où achètes-tu tes chaussures ?

where do you come from?
d'où viens-tu ?

what do I do when the computer bleeps at me?
que dois-je faire quand l'ordinateur sonne ?

the earth goes round the sun
la terre tourne autour du soleil

b) Avec des verbes qui expriment un état d'esprit, une humeur, etc., comme le désir, le dégoût, un point de vue ou qui se réfèrent aux sens (odorat, goût, toucher, vue, ouïe) :

I (dis)like/love/hate/want that girl
j'aime/je n'aime pas/j'adore/je déteste/je veux cette fille

I believe/suppose/think/imagine he's right
je crois/je suppose/je pense/j'imagine qu'il a raison

we hear/see/feel/perceive the world around us
nous entendons/voyons/sentons/percevons le monde autour de nous

do I smell gas?
ça sent le gaz ?

ii) Le présent progressif est employé :

    a) Pour exprimer des événements ou des états qui se déroulent ou ont lieu au moment où l'on parle :

what are you doing up there?
qu'est-ce que tu fais là-haut ?

I'm trying to find my old passport I left here
j'essaie de trouver mon ancien passeport que j'ai laissé ici

at the moment it's being used as a bedroom
en ce moment, on s'en sert comme chambre

what are you thinking about?
à quoi penses-tu ?

    b) Pour exprimer une attitude (en général de mécontentement, d'ennui, d'amusement ou de surprise) envers quelque chose :

he's always mixing our names up (contrariété, amusement, etc.)
il confond toujours nos noms

he's always losing his car keys
il perd toujours les clés de sa voiture

you're always saying that!
tu dis toujours cela !

you're not going out looking like that!
tu ne vas pas sortir comme ça !

iii) Les différences du présent simple et du présent progressif :

I live in London (simple)
je vis à Londres

I'm living in London (progressif)
je vis (actuellement) à Londres

La seconde phrase implique que le locuteur n'habite pas d'une façon définitive à Londres, mais qu'il y est installé temporairement. La première phrase exprime un état de choses.

I have a shower every morning (simple)
je prends une douche tous les matins

I'm having a shower every morning (these days) (progressif)
je prends une douche tous les matins (en ce moment)

La seconde phrase implique que prendre une douche
régulièrement le matin n'est qu'un fait temporaire, quelque
chose que l'on fait à un certain moment (et qui peut ne pas
durer). La première phrase, au présent simple, n'implique pas
ces restrictions temporelles.

she works for an insurance company
elle travaille pour une compagnie d'assurances

she's working for an insurance company
elle travaille (actuellement) pour une compagnie d'assurances

La différence est moins apparente dans cet exemple. Mais la
première phrase ne pourrait pas faire référence à un état de
choses temporaire. La seconde phrase peut faire référence à un
état de choses temporaire ou définitif.

On trouve des cas dans lesquels il n'existe pas de différence
entre le présent simple et le présent progressif :

how are you feeling this morning?
how do you feel this morning?
comment te sens-tu ce matin ?

17 Exprimer le Passé

i) Le prétérit simple :

Il est employé pour exprimer des faits ou des états accomplis dans le passé :

he got up and left the room
il s'est levé et a quitté la pièce

broken again? – I only fixed it yesterday!
encore cassé ? – je l'ai réparé hier seulement !

in what year did the Rolling Stones have their first hit?
en quelle année les Rolling Stones ont-ils eu leur premier hit ?

ii) Used to/would :

Ces deux formes sont employées pour exprimer soit des faits ou des états qui se déroulaient ou qui avaient lieu régulièrement dans le passé, soit des habitudes du passé :

we always used to have fish on Fridays
nous mangions toujours du poisson le vendredi

on Fridays we would have fish
le vendredi nous mangions du poisson

iii) Le prétérit progressif :

Ce temps accentue le caractère de continuité, de durée d'une action ou d'un fait :

I was living in Germany when that happened
j'habitais l'Allemagne quand cela s'est passé

sorry, could you say that again? – I wasn't listening
pardon, pourriez-vous répéter ce que vous avez dit ? – je n'écoutais pas

what were you doing out in the garden last night?
que faisiez-vous dans le jardin hier soir ?

I was having supper when he came home
j'étais en train de dîner quand il est arrivé à la maison

Le prétérit simple et le prétérit progressif sont souvent
employés pour mettre en valeur le lien qui existe entre
deux faits du passé ou la façon par laquelle le locuteur veut
les présenter. Dans le dernier exemple ci-dessus, un fait
ponctuel (**he came home**) est opposé à un fait qui dure, qui
a lieu lorsque le fait ponctuel se produit (**I was having supper**).
Comparez cet exemple avec celui-ci :

I had supper when he was coming home
j'ai dîné pendant qu'il rentrait à la maison

Cette phrase est très différente. L'aspect de durée ou de
continuité a été transformé en **he was coming home**. **I had
supper** fait référence à quelque chose qui a lieu à un moment
précis pendant le déroulement de l'action plus longue de
coming home. Comparez aussi :

I was having supper while he was coming home
j'étais en train de dîner alors qu'il rentrait à la maison

Dans cette phrase, le point de vue a été transformé pour
présenter les deux événements comme deux événements qui
se déroulent parallèlement.

iv) Le present perfect :

a) Ce temps est employé pour les états ou actions du passé
qui ont un rapport avec le présent :

I've read nearly all of Somerset Maugham's books
j'ai lu presque tous les livres de Somerset Maugham

I have never read any of Somerset Maugham's books
je n'ai lu aucun des livres de Somerset Maugham

Dans ces deux exemples, on décrit ce qu'on a lu jusqu'à
maintenant des œuvres de Somerset Maugham.

Comparez ces exemples avec :

I read one of Maugham's novels on holiday last year
j'ai lu un des romans de Maugham en vacances l'année
dernière

Cette phrase décrit un événement totalement accompli
dans le passé.

Quelques comparaisons utiles :

have you seen him this morning? (dit quand c'est encore le matin)
did you see him this morning? (dit dans l'après-midi, ou dans la soirée)
est-ce que tu l'as vu, ce matin ?

b) La forme progressive peut être employée pour renforcer l'aspect de durée d'une action ou d'un état de choses :

what have you been reading recently?
qu'est-ce que tu as lu récemment ?

we haven't seen you for ages, where have you been keeping yourself?
nous ne vous avons pas vu depuis longtemps, où étiez-vous caché pendant toute cette période ?

what have you been saying to him to make him cry?
qu'est-ce que tu lui as dit pour le faire pleurer ?

I've been meaning to ask you something, doctor
je veux vous poser une question depuis un certain temps, docteur

Cependant parfois il y a peu de différence de sens entre le prétérit simple et le prétérit progressif :

I've been living here for 15 years (progressif)
I've lived here for 15 years (simple)
je vis ici depuis 15 ans

Remarquez l'emploi de **since** pour faire référence à une date précise du passé :

I've been living here since 1972
I've lived here since 1972
je vis ici depuis 1972

La différence d'emploi entre le prétérit simple et le prétérit progressif peut parfois être assez subtile :

I've been waiting for you here for a whole hour!
ça fait une bonne heure que je t'attends ici !

I've waited for you here for a whole hour!
je t'ai attendu ici une bonne heure !

Dans ce cas, on pourrait employer la phrase du premier exemple quand la personne attendue arrive, alors qu'on l'attend encore. Le second exemple ne pourrait pas être employé puisqu'il sous-entend que l'attente est terminée. (Mais on pourrait, par exemple, l'employer quand on parle au téléphone à la personne attendue).

v) Le plus-que-parfait :

a) Ce temps est employé pour décrire une action ou un état de choses du passé qui s'est déroulé ou avait cours avant d'autres événements du passé. Il fait référence à un moment du passé en relation à un autre moment du passé :

the fire had already been put out when they got there
l'incendie avait déjà été éteint quand ils sont arrivés

he searched the directory but the file had been erased the day before
il a cherché dans le répertoire, mais le fichier avait été effacé la veille

had you heard of him before you came here?
avais-tu entendu parler de lui avant de venir ici ?

they hadn't left anything in the fridge so I went out to eat
ils/elles n'avaient rien laissé dans le réfrigérateur, donc je suis allé manger en ville

Il peut être aussi employé pour indiquer l'arrêt d'un état de choses (particulièrement des états d'esprit, des humeurs, etc.) :

I had hoped to speak to him this morning
j'avais espéré lui parler ce matin

Ceci implique que la probabilité de pouvoir lui parler semble maintenant très faible ou qu'elle a disparu.

b) Pour accentuer la durée, le plus-que-parfait progressif peut être employé :

I'd been wanting to ask that question myself
je voulais moi aussi poser cette question

had you been waiting long before they arrived?
est-ce que tu as attendu longtemps avant qu'ils/elles
arrivent ?

Pour le plus-que-parfait dans les propositions qui expriment
la condition, voir page 45.

18 Exprimer le Futur

i) **Will** et **shall** :

a) Pour faire référence au futur à la première personne du singulier ou du pluriel, on emploie **will** ou **shall**. On peut contracter ces deux formes en **'ll**. **Shall**, cependant, est surtout une forme britannique :

I will/I'll/I shall let you know as soon as I can
je vous le ferai savoir aussi vite que possible

we won't/shan't need that many
nous n'en aurons pas besoin d'autant

b) On emploie **will** pour les autres personnes :

you'll be sorry!
tu vas le regretter !

lunch will take about another ten minutes
le déjeuner sera prêt dans à peu près 10 minutes

they'll just have to wait
ils/elles n'auront qu'à attendre

c) Si le locuteur fait une déclaration d'intention à la 2ème ou 3ème personne (par exemple une promesse ou une menace), on trouve parfois **shall**, mais il est devenu bien moins courant que **will** :

you shall be treated just like the others
tu seras traité comme les autres

they shall pay for this!
ils/elles vont le payer !

Si l'intention ou la volonté dont on parle ne dépend pas du locuteur, **will** (**'ll**) est employé :

he will/he'll do it, I'm sure
il le fera, j'en suis sûre

d) **Shall** est employé pour faire des propositions, des suggestions :

shall we make a start?
on commence ?

e) **Will** peut être employé pour exprimer la demande :

will you come with me please?
vous voulez bien venir avec moi, s'il vous plaît ?

f) Pour exprimer le futur immédiat :

Dans les exemples suivants, **will** est plus employé que **shall** (la forme contractée **'ll** demeurant la plus fréquente) :

that's OK, I'll do it
c'est d'accord, je le ferai

I'll have a beer please
je prendrai une bière, s'il vous plaît

that's the door bell – OK, I'll get it
on sonne à la porte – d'accord, j'y vais

ii) Le futur simple et le futur progressif :

a) **Will** et **shall** suivis par la forme progressive peuvent être employés pour accentuer la continuité d'une action :

what will (what'll) you be doing this time next year?
qu'est-ce que tu feras l'année prochaine à cette époque ?

b) Comparez les exemples suivants :

will you speak to him about it? (simple)
tu lui en parleras ?

will you be speaking to him about it? (progressif)
tu comptes lui en parler ?

L'emploi de la forme progressive dans le second exemple indique que le locuteur ne fait pas une demande directe (comme dans le premier exemple), mais qu'il demande simplement et objectivement si la personne à laquelle il s'adresse a l'intention de "lui en parler" (**speak to him about it**).

iii) **Be going to** :

a) Cette forme est souvent employée de la même manière que **will** :

will it ever stop raining?
is it ever going to stop raining?
va-t-il un jour s'arrêter de pleuvoir ?

b) **Be going to** est plus courant que **will** ou **shall** dans les déclarations d'intention :

I'm going to take them to court
je vais les mener devant le tribunal

they're going to buy a new car
ils vont s'acheter une nouvelle voiture

Mais dans une phrase plus longue contenant d'autres adverbes et d'autres propositions, on peut aussi employer **will** :

listen, what we'll do is this, we'll make him think that we've left, then we'll come back in through the back door and . . .
écoute, voilà ce que nous allons faire, nous lui ferons croire que nous sommes partis, puis nous reviendrons par la porte de derrière et . . .

c) **Be going to** est préféré à **will** quand les motifs de la déclaration faite à propos du futur dépendent directement du présent :

I know what he's going to say (because it's written all over his face)
je sais ce qu'il va dire (parce que c'est écrit sur son visage)

iv) Le présent simple :

a) Ce temps peut être employé pour faire référence au futur lorsqu'on fait allusion à un arrangement préalable d'événements :

when does the race start?
à quelle heure la course commence-t-elle ?

the match kicks off at 2.30
le match commence à 2 heures 30

Comme le second exemple le montre, il est très courant d'employer le présent simple avec un adverbe de temps :

we go on holiday tomorrow
nous partons en vacances demain

the plane leaves at 7.30
l'avion décolle à 7 heures et demie

b) Le présent simple est normalement employé dans des propositions circonstancielles de temps ou de condition :

you'll be surprised when you see her
vous serez surpris quand vous la verrez

if the sun shines, I'll be truly amazed
si le soleil brille, je serai vraiment étonné

Remarquez : ces propositions commençant par **when** ou **if** ne doivent pas être confondues avec des propositions interrogatives indirectes :

does he know when they're arriving? (when are they arriving?)
sait-il quand ils/elles arrivent ? (quand arrivent-ils/elles ?)

I don't know if he'll agree (will he agree?)
je ne sais pas s'il sera d'accord (sera-t-il d'accord ?)

v) Le présent progressif :

a) Le présent progressif est souvent employé d'une façon semblable à **be going to** pour exprimer l'intention :

I'm putting you in charge of exports (= I'm going to put you in charge of exports)
je vous donne la responsabilité du service des exportations (je vais vous donner . . .)

what are you doing for your holidays? (= what are you going to do for your holidays?)
qu'est-ce que tu fais pour tes vacances ? (qu'est-ce que tu vas faire . . . ?)

Mais remarquez une différence subtile entre les deux exemples suivants :

I'm taking him to court
je le mène devant le tribunal

I'm going to take him to court
je vais le mener devant le tribunal

Le premier exemple est plus précis que le second, moins sujet à doute ou à révision. Le second exemple donne un fait moins établi, moins sûr.

b) Le présent progressif peut aussi être employé pour signifier un arrangement préalable dans le futur, d'une façon semblable à **will** + infinitif progressif ou présent simple :

he's giving a concert tomorrow
il donne un concert demain

c) Il peut être employé comme le présent simple pour faire référence à des événements organisés dans le futur :

when are they coming?
quand arrivent-ils/elles ?

they're arriving at Heathrow at midnight
ils/elles arrivent à Heathrow à minuit

vi) **Be to** :

Be to est souvent employé pour exprimer des plans précis du futur, surtout des plans qui dépendent de la décision d'autres personnes ou du destin :

all the guests are to be present by 7.30
tous les invités doivent être présents avant 7 heures 30

I'm to report to a Mr Glover on Tuesday
je dois me présenter à un certain M. Glover mardi

are we ever to meet again, I wonder?
allons-nous nous rencontrer encore, je me le demande ?

vii) **Be about to** :

Cette forme est employée pour exprimer le futur imminent :

please take your seats, the play is about to begin
veuillez vous asseoir, la pièce va commencer

En anglais américain particulièrement, cette forme est employée pour exprimer les intentions futures d'une personne :

I'm not about to sign a contract like that!
je ne signerai pas un tel contrat !

En anglais britannique, on emploie plus volontiers **be going to** dans ce cas.

viii) Le futur antérieur :

a) Ce temps est employé pour exprimer un événement qui sera accompli à une certaine date du futur :

by the time you get there we will have finished dinner
quand vous arriverez là, nous aurons fini de dîner

b) Il est aussi employé pour faire des suppositions, des hypothèses :

I expect you'll have been wondering why I asked you here
je suppose que vous vous êtes demandé pourquoi je vous ai convoqué

19 Les Particules des Verbes Composés

Dans cette section, on s'intéresse aux particules des verbes. On distingue pour chacune de celles-ci les principaux usages résumés par une courte définition. Des exemples types correspondant à chaque sens sont donnés pour chaque définition.

ABOUT

1 indique un mouvement dans toutes les directions, parfois avec une idée de désordre, de confusion :

I felt about for the light switch; the pain of his wounds made him lash about (*c.-à-d. se débattre*); I was rushing about trying to get ready when the phone rang; people milled about in the streets (*c.-à-d. fourmiller*); I wish you would stop fussing about

2 indique l'inaction, l'oisiveté :

I hate standing about at street corners, so make sure you're on time; she always keeps me hanging about when we arrange to meet

3 autour de soi, dans les alentours :

make sure there's nobody about before you force the window; he looked about for a taxi; there's a lot of hay fever about at this time of year

4 au sujet de :

what do you think about his latest film?; they know a lot about antiques; are his books known about over here?; what's he rambling on about now? (*c.-à-d. raconter*)

ACROSS

1 d'un côté à l'autre :

we walked across the railway lines

2 de l'autre côté, souvent de la route :

always help old ladies across busy roads; I'm just popping across for a newspaper

3 indique un effort intellectuel, destiné à la compréhension :

he finds it hard to put his ideas across; how can I get it across to them that it's important to keep copies of all your files?

AFTER

1 en suivant, derrière :

the boy was running after his ball and just dashed out into the road; there she is at the corner – send someone after her

2 à la recherche de :

the police are after him; I'm after a book on butterflies

3 au sujet de :

nurse, if anyone calls to enquire after Mr Thompson, tell them he's resting comfortably

4 indique un lien ou une ressemblance entre membres d'une famille :

my niece takes after me; he's called after his grandfather

AGAINST

1 contre, en touchant :

the cat startled me, brushing against me in the dark hall

2 en opposition, contre :

I'm against capital punishment; she always kicked against the idea of marriage

3 indique que quelque chose protège :

fluoride is said to guard against tooth decay

4 indique que quelque chose porte préjudice à quelqu'un :

will the fact that he has a previous conviction go against him?

AHEAD

1   en face, devant :

> the favourite has got ahead now and looks likely to win; look straight ahead please

2   indique le mouvement vers le succès ou la réalisation, le progrès :

> you will never get ahead unless you are conscientious; why do you think you have kept ahead of the competition all these years?; the project is moving ahead nicely

3   dans le futur :

> looking ahead to the next budget . . .; it is essential to plan ahead

---

ALONG

1   le long de :

> he walked along the street in a daze; the road runs along the river bank

2   indique une action en cours, le progrès :

> we were driving along when suddenly . . .; we were tearing along at a hundred miles an hour; things are coming along nicely; how's she coming along at school?; the work is just chugging along at a pretty slow pace; how do old age pensioners manage to rub along on so little money? (*c.-à-d. se débrouiller*)

3   indique qu'on part, qu'on fait partir :

> I'll have to be hurrying along if I want to catch my train; I'll be getting along now then; the police told the crowd to move along; she told the children to run along and play

4   avec :

> why not bring your sister along?; he's going to have to drag his little brother along

5   vers un lieu qui n'est pas très loin et qui est souvent dans la même rue :

> my mother sent me along to see how you were

APART

1 indique une séparation :

> the two fighters had to be dragged apart; I saw them draw apart as I entered the room; I can't get these two pieces apart

2 en morceaux, en différentes parties, sens dessus dessous :

> he says it just came apart in his hands; the police pulled the flat apart looking for drugs

3 de côté, à part :

> the doctor drew the parents apart; joking apart, what do you really think?

4 indique qu'on se distingue du reste, qu'on n'est pas compris dans un groupe :

> what sets her apart from all the other children in my class is . . .; he stands apart from the others because of his very placid temperament

---

AROUND
(voir aussi **round**)

1 en différents endroits, autour de soi :

> you have to search around for that kind of information; I'm hunting around for a pen that works

2 dans les alentours :

> he's around somewhere – have you looked in the kitchen?; where's that umbrella? – it must be lying around somewhere

3 indique qu'on n'a rien à faire :

> how much longer do we have to wait around before he arrives?

ASIDE

1 de côté, sur le côté :

please step aside and let us pass; they moved the old wardrobe aside to reveal . . .

2 dans le but de créer une certaine intimité :

the teacher called him aside to ask how his father was; he drew her aside for a moment

3 indique qu'on met quelque chose de côté pour y revenir ou s'en servir plus tard :

leaving that question aside for the moment . . .; could you lay that aside and work on this instead?; I have some money put aside if you need it

---

AT

1 à un certain endroit :

I called at our mother's this morning but she wasn't in *(c.-à-d. aller chez quelqu'un)*; this train will call at Preston and Carlisle *(c.-à-d. desservir)*; how many stations did you stop at?

2 vers, dans la direction de :

the explorers worked their way through the jungle, chopping at the undergrowth with their machetes; don't clutch at my hand like that; the birds were picking at the crumbs; he hinted at the possibility of a promotion

---

AWAY

1 indique une absence ou un départ :

I'm sorry but he has been called away on some important business; he drove away in a taxi; he ran away into the crowd

2 indique qu'on prend de la distance ou qu'on s'éloigne :

the child backed away from the dog; something must be done to get her away from their influence; why do you move away whenever I touch you?

3 indique qu'on continue quelque chose pour un certain temps :

let the mixture boil away for five minutes; teenagers chewing away at gum . . .; she's pegging away at her maths (*c.-à-d. travailler avec détermination*); well, keep asking away until you get an answer; there he was, snoring away on the sofa; they just sat there giggling away; she was in the bath, singing away; he lay groaning away on the ground

4 pour enlever quelque chose, pour se débarrasser de :

I want you to brush those leaves away from the path; maybe someone with a van could take the wardrobe away; she rubbed the dirt away from the window; if you don't want it throw it away

5 pour mettre à l'abri, de réserve :

lock it away where it'll be safe; he keeps it stored away in the attic; I wouldn't be surprised if he had salted away a fair bit in his time (*c.-à-d. mettre de l'argent de côté pour plus tard*)

6 jusqu'à disparaître :

the water has all boiled away; he is wasting away with grief; the water gradually trickled away down the slope; he slowly rubbed the old paint away

7 épuiser quelque chose :

he has drunk his entire wages away

8 indique le début d'une action :

could I ask some questions? – sure, fire away

BACK

1 en arrière, vers l'arrière :

> she flung back her hair; move your men back, Lieutenant; thinking back . . .

2 pour donner l'idée de retour :

> flood waters are receding and people are beginning to filter back to their homes; it's so cold I think I'll head back; she's being moved back to Personnel Department; I'll send it back to you in the post; she asked her secretary to read the letter back (*c.-à-d. lire à haute voir, pour un texte dicté*)

3 de nouveau :

> we've bought back our old house; could you play that bit back? (*c.-à-d. rejouer sur une bande magnétique*)

4 indique l'idée de faire retraite :

> the intense heat forced them back; the plant will die back in autumn but give you a lovely show again in summer

5 indique qu'on ralentit une allure, etc. :

> rein your horse back or you'll be in trouble; the pilot throttled the engines back and came in to land

6 indique qu'on réduit, qu'on coupe quelque chose :

> this old rose bush needs to be chopped back; we'll have to cut back on our expenses; we trimmed back the hedge a bit

7 indique qu'on retient ou qu'on réprime quelque chose :

> I forced back my tears; what are you keeping back from us?

BEHIND

1 derrière :

the wall they were hiding behind gave way; his wife always walks behind

2 en retard :

the landlady says we're getting behind with the rent; if you're slipping behind with the payments/your work . . .; you're dropping badly behind with your work

3 indique qu'on reste en arrière, qu'on est laissé en arrière :

do you mind being left behind to look after the children?; that's OK, you go on ahead, I'll stay behind

BY

1 indique le mouvement, le passage :

we had to push by a lot of people; the cars raced by; time goes by so fast, doesn't it?

2 indique qu'on se réfère à quelque chose :

my mother swears by castor oil; which theory do you go by?

3 indique qu'on fait une visite ou un arrêt rapide :

I've just dropped by for a minute; come by some time; I'll pop by to see you one day; we stopped by at the art gallery on the way home

DOWN

1   indique un mouvement de haut en bas :

the sun blazed down on their bare heads; call Tom down for tea (*c.-à-d. d'en haut*); she dropped down from the tree; pass me down that big plate from the top shelf

2   indique un mouvement vers le sol ou vers le bas :

I bent down to pick up the old man's stick; the hurricane blew down hundreds of mature trees; he drew her down beside him on the couch; draw the blinds down

3   indique qu'on prend en note, pour s'y référer plus tard :

could someone write down the main points?; I've got it down in my notebook; I could see him scribbling something down

4   indique qu'on met une fin à quelque chose :

the audience hooted the proposal down; it was voted down; they all shouted the speaker down

5   indique qu'on attache quelque chose serré ou qu'on l'assure :

we have to chain the garden furniture down or it would vanish overnight; screw the lid down properly; they tied him down on the ground; glue it down

6   indique qu'on arrête un véhicule :

we waved a taxi down

7   indique qu'on transmet quelque chose d'une génération à une autre :

the necklace has been passed down from mother to daughter for centuries; an old folksong which has come down though the centuries

8   indique une réduction ou une diminution :

all the prices in the shop have been marked down; thin the sauce down with a little milk if necessary; you're going too fast, slow down; the pilot eased down on the throttle

9 indique que quelque chose ne marche pas comme il devrait, a une panne :

> the computer is down again; she broke down and wept

10 indique une action punitive imposée par une autorité :

> the police are clamping down on licence-dodgers; the teacher really came down on me for not having learnt the dates properly; the court is going to hand down its sentence tomorrow

11 indique qu'on consomme, qu'on avale de la nourriture ou des boissons :

> if you don't force some food down you'll collapse; the dog gobbled it all down in a second; she absolutely wolfed her dinner down; come on now, drink this down

---

FOR

1 indique le but, l'objectif :

> with all this overtime she's doing, she must be bucking for promotion; she felt in her bag for the keys; stop fishing for compliments!; the qualities looked for in candidates are . . .

2 indique qu'on est en faveur de quelque chose :

> he argued strongly for a return to the traditional methods of teaching grammar; the points of view argued for in this paper

FORTH

1   en avant, surtout pour affronter un adversaire :

> the Saracens sallied forth to engage the infidel in hand to hand combat (*dans cet emploi, vieilli*); he sallied forth to face the waiting fans (*emploi humoristique*)

2   donne une idée de naissance, de mise au monde, de production :

> Mary brought forth a son (*emploi vieilli ou biblique*); the tree puts forth the most gloriously scented blossom

3   indique que la personne qui parle le fait pendant un long moment et parfois d'une manière pompeuse :

> he is always holding forth about something; she spouted forth about the benefits of free enterprise

FORWARD

1   en avant, droit devant :

> please come forward one by one as I call your names; the cat edged forward to the corner of the lawn where the bird was sitting; bring your chair forward

2   en parlant du futur, en anticipant :

> we're really looking forward to seeing them again; that's something I am definitely not looking forward to; looking forward to hearing from you (*formule de fin de lettre polie*)

3   pour une date, en avance :

> the chairman has decided to bring the board meeting forward a week

4   pour quelque chose que l'on suggère, que l'on propose :

> does anyone have any other suggestions they wish to bring forward?; the theory that he puts forward in his book

FROM

de, depuis :

> we'll be flying from Heathrow; where did you fly from?;
> where did you spring from? (*c.-à-d. sortir, apparaître tout à
> coup*); where do babies come from?; they come from Ghana
> (*c.-à-d. ils sont Ghanéens*); they will be coming from Ghana
> next week (*c.-à-d. arriver de*)

HOME

1   à la maison, là où on habite :

> who is taking you home?; I'll see you home safely; go home

**2   indique qu'on met quelque chose à sa place, qu'on l'enfonce
aussi profond que possible :**

> make sure you hammer the nails home; is the plug pushed
> home properly?

**3   indique qu'on fait comprendre quelque chose à quelqu'un ou
qu'on lui fait apprécier quelque chose :**

> did you drive it home to them that they must be back by
> midnight?; the recent accident brought home to them very
> forcefully the need for insurance; that comment really hit
> home (*c.-à-d. faire son effet*)

IN

1   indique un mouvement de l'extérieur vers l'intérieur :

> we opened the door and the cat just wandered in; there's
> no need to burst in like that; we crept in so as not to disturb
> you; don't stand so close to the edge of the pool – you
> might fall in

2   indique la localisation dans un lieu, quelque part :

> I think it was a bad idea to leave that bit in the letter; you
> shouldn't have left it in; I'm going to the bank to pay these
> cheques in; the car's pretty full but we could squeeze one
> more in

3   indique qu'on est enfermé ou que quelque chose est fermé :

when the police arrived they found he had barricaded
himself in; women at home with children often feel fenced
in; help! I'm locked in!; the old doorway was bricked in

4   indique qu'on ajoute quelque chose à autre chose :

fold in the flour; rake in some fertiliser; these extra ideas
which the director of the film built in are not found in the
original novel; a new character was then written in to
the series

5   indique qu'on s'approche ou que quelque chose approche :

members of the orchestra eventually began to filter in;
when the train pulled in; as I looked out of the window I
saw a car drive in

6   indique qu'on remplit ou qu'on complète quelque chose :

fill in this form; the artist then drew in the remaining
features

7   chez soi ou chez quelqu'un :

I'm staying in this evening to wash my hair; you've bought
in enough tins to last a lifetime; let's invite the people next
door in for a drink

8   indique la reddition de quelque chose :

the wanted man handed himself in to the police; give your
essays in tomorrow; when do you need this work in by?

9   indique qu'on termine ou qu'on arrête quelque chose ou que quelque chose s'arrête :

I'm jacking my job in (*c.-à-d. plaquer*); pack that noise
in!; the engine's packed in

10   indique qu'on détruit totalement quelque chose :

they had to beat the door in since nobody had a key; the
roof fell in, showering the firemen with debris

11   indique qu'on diminue ou qu'on rétrécit quelque chose :

I asked my dressmaker to take the sleeves in; pull the rope
in a bit to get rid of the slack; hold your stomach in

INTO

1   indique un mouvement de l'extérieur vers l'intérieur :

> don't just barge into the room – knock first; I could see
> into the room and there was nobody there; the operator cut
> into our conversation; the Fraud Squad is enquiring into
> the affair

2   indique qu'on utilise une partie de quelque chose, à contre-cœur le plus souvent :

> we're going to have to break into our savings to pay for the
> repairs to the roof; it cuts into our time too much

3   indique un contact physique, qu'on rentre dans quelqu'un ou quelque chose :

> if you looked where you were going you wouldn't keep
> barging into people; some idiot running for a train
> cannoned into me

OFF

1   indique qu'on enlève quelqu'un ou quelque chose :

> don't bite it off – use the scissors; it took ages to scrape the
> old paint off; he was taken off in a police car; we're going
> to have to force the lid off

2   donne une idée de départ :

> the car slowly moved off; the boys rushed off when they
> saw the local policeman approaching; don't hurry off –
> stay and have some tea; he just wandered off down the
> road and I never saw him again

3   indique le début de quelque chose, le commencement :

> let me start off by saying . . .; who's going to lead off with
> the first question?

4 indique qu'on quitte un moyen de transport, quel qu'il soit :

as the bus slowed, he jumped off; the doors opened and everyone got off; come on, hop off, let me have a go on your bike; she doesn't like riding because she keeps falling off

5 indique qu'on arrête quelque chose, qu'on éteint quelque chose :

put the lights off please; he choked off my screams with a gag; he has sworn off alcohol

6 indique que quelque chose a changé dans son volume, ses qualités premières, s'est dégradé :

don't touch the soup until it has cooled off a bit; this meat has gone off; attendances have fallen off

7 pour intensifier le sens d'un verbe :

the script writers have decided to kill this character off; the detective was bought off (*c.-à-d. acheté, corrompu*); most of the land has been sold off

8 indique un congé :

can I have next week off please?; they gave him a couple of days off

9 indique que quelque chose est inutilisable, condamné, qu'on l'a rendu inaccessible :

the street has been barricaded off because of a gas leak; for reasons of safety, that part of the road has been closed off; they have divided some of the rooms off in an attempt to save on heating costs; this part has been partitioned off from the rest of the room; the rubbish dump has been walled off

ON

1 indique la poursuite d'une action, qu'on continue quelque chose :

> read on to the end of the chapter; they just chatted on for hours; she worked on into the night; I think I'll work on a little longer; he ran on despite the cries for him to stop; shall we stroll on then?; they climbed on until the light failed; he slept on in spite of the noise around him

2 indique qu'on met quelque chose, qu'on enfile quelque chose :

> he whipped a dressing gown on and went to answer the door; the police clapped handcuffs on the thief; what did he have on?; it was too small, I couldn't get it on

3 indique un état de marche pour un appareil électrique ou quelque chose de semblable :

> do you know that you've left the headlights on?; turn the TV on, would you?

4 indique qu'on utilise quelque chose comme une base :

> what do the animals feed (up)on in winter?; all cars should run on unleaded petrol; what sort on fuel does it run on?; she thrives (up)on hard work; that wasn't something I'd planned on

5 à bord d'un moyen de transport, quel qu'il soit :

> the train stopped and everybody got on; they couldn't get any more passengers on; how many passengers are allowed on?

6 indique que quelque chose s'adapte :

> the lid hooks on; where does this bit fit on?; he latches on to anyone who looks rich (*c.-à-d. s'accrocher à*)

7 indique l'acceptation :

> it seemed like an excellent idea and we seized (up)on it immediately

8 indique qu'on fait avancer :

the jockey's having to whip the horse on; the crowd is clapping her on as she reaches the last mile (*c.-à-d. encourager par des applaudissements*); he wanted to look in the car showroom but I hurried him on (*c.-à-d. faire avancer*)

9 indique que quelque chose est arrangé ou prévu :

I've got something on every night next week; what's on TV tonight?

10 donne l'idée de transmission, de passage d'une personne à une autre :

she handed your book on to me; could you pass the news on?

OUT

1 indique qu'on sort d'un endroit :

they bolted out of the door; she drove out of the garage; he said a few words and then hurried out; I'm popping out to the library

2 indique une privation ou une exclusion :

that tree will have to come down, it's blocking out all the sun; I've thrown out that old jacket of yours; deal me out of this game, it's about time I went home; heavy floods have driven thousands of people out of their homes; go and rout him out of bed; they have a habit of freezing out people they don't like; I feel a bit left out

3 indique qu'on part :

the train had only just pulled out when . . .; he walked out on his wife and kids (*c.-à-d. plaquer*); I've had enough of this relationship, I'm getting out

4 indique qu'on distribue :

we need volunteers to hand out leaflets; who's going to deal out the cards?

5 indique qu'on étend ou étire quelque chose :

> he held out his hand in a pleading gesture; reach out your glass; you can pull the elastic out to twice its length

6 indique qu'on enlève, qu'on fait sortir :

> is it time to take the cake out? (*c.-à-d. hors du four*); don't push me out of the way; a lot of the pages have been ripped out; we had a bit of an argument about it but I finally screwed some money out of him

7 indique qu'on veut résoudre ou qu'on résoud un problème :

> I couldn't get the equation to work out; things just didn't pan out between us (*c.-à-d. marcher*); it all came out right in the end

8 indique qu'on se tire d'une situation difficile ou qu'on s'en échappe souvent avec difficulté :

> how did you get out of doing your homework?; I wish I could wriggle out of this visit to my in-laws

9 indique un bruit fort :

> stop barking out orders like a sergeant-major; the loudspeakers were blaring out the candidate's message; she cried out in pain; speak out clearly please

10 indique que quelque chose s'éteint :

> the fire has gone out; he butted his cigar out in the ashtray; switch the light out in the garage; the champion was knocked out in the first round (*c.-à-d. être mis K.O.*)

11 à l'extérieur, hors de la maison :

> the soldiers camped out in the fields; it was such a beautiful night we said the children could sleep out (*c.-à-d. dehors*); I've been invited out for lunch; is he in or is he out?

12 indique qu'on élargit ou qu'on rallonge quelque chose :

> I left the dress to be let out at the seams; your essay needs to be fleshed out (*c.-à-d. développer*); the speech was rounded out with some statistics on the company's performance in the last year

OVER

1 en allant d'un côté à l'autre, en traversant :

> she walked over the railway bridge; he saw me on the other pavement and hurried over; hey, move over, there's room for two in this bed!; I'll fly over and see you; they plan to bring witnesses over from France to testify

2 en parcourant une courte distance :

> I'll drive over and see you soon; our neighbours are having us over for dinner on Saturday night (*c.-à-d. chez eux*)

3 indique qu'on passe de quelque chose à autre chose, qu'on fait un transfert :

> we've switched over to another paper; I don't like this programme, could you change over?

4 indique qu'on retourne quelque chose :

> he folded over the letter so that I couldn't see the signature; fork the ground over thoroughly before planting

5 indique qu'on transmet un sentiment ou une intention, une impression, etc. :

> it is very difficult to get over to men how women feel about rape; they need to find a better way of putting their company image over; they come over as being rather arrogant; how did they come over to you?

6 au-dessus de :

> he bent over the balcony for a better look; with this threat hanging over him . . .

7 indique l'idée de couvrir :

> skies are expected to cloud over later in the day; the lake rarely freezes over; the door was papered over many years ago; the beautiful old floorboards have been carpeted over; the horrible realization that I was not alone crept over me

8 indique que l'on fait durer quelque chose ou qu'il reste quelque chose :

> the film has proved so popular that it is being held over for another two weeks; there's quite a lot left over

9 indique que l'on fait quelque chose complètement ou que l'on finit quelque chose :

> the party was over by midnight; just check over the names on the guest list; be sure to read your essay over before handing it in

10 indique que quelque chose déborde de ses limites :

> the milk has boiled over; the river flooded over into the streets; the water was all spilling over

11 indique qu'on est renversé, qu'on tombe :

> she was knocked over by a bus; she tumbled over; over he went with a crash!

PAST

indique le passage :

> he brushed past me in the street; we had just gone past the shop when . . .; cars raced past; time just flies past; he just casually strolled on past

ROUND
(surtout en anglais britannique)

1 indique un mouvement circulaire, en rond :

thoughts were spinning round in her head; you must hand your sweets round

2 dans un rond, en formant un rond :

a crowd gathered round to watch; they all crowded round

3 indique qu'on fait le tour de quelque chose, autour de soi :

we went round the art gallery; would you like to see round the house?; were you able to see round?; I'll phone round and see if anyone else knows about it; could you ask round?

4 indique qu'on fait changer de place, qu'on déplace quelque chose :

I've been bumping into things ever since your mother changed all the furniture round; he turned the car round and went home (*c-à-d. il a fait demi-tour*)

5 chez soi, pour les gens qui ne vivent ou ne travaillent pas très loin :

could you call round tomorrow morning, doctor?; they always go out when their son has some of his friends round; drop round some time; let's invite them round

THROUGH

1 à travers, indique le passage :

we arrived at Ipswich and just drove straight through; the door flew open and the policeman came bursting through, gun at the ready; he looked through me as if I didn't exist; we're not stopping here, just passing through

2 en pénétrant quelque chose :

the crowd broke through the barriers; the sun is expected to break through sometime this morning; supplies are filtering through; you're wearing your jumper through at the elbows; the soles of my boots are almost worn through

3 indique le succès :

she brought all of us through the exam; his teachers pushed him through; we'll just have to muddle through without her (*c.-à-d. se débrouiller*); he was very ill but he's pulled through now; against all the odds they fought through

4 indique qu'on fait quelque chose complètement, de fond en comble, du début à la fin :

they went through everyone's hand luggage; will you read through my speech and give me your opinion?; I'll be up all night wading through this paperwork; have these bags been looked through yet?; it has to be read through twice; it had obviously been checked through in some detail; the plan hasn't been properly thought through

5 indique la fin :

I'm through with men!; let me know when you get through with what you're doing

TO

1 indique le mouvement vers un lieu :

name the foreign countries you've travelled to

2 indique que l'on ramène à la conscience :

when do you think they'll have brought him to?

3 indique le rapport, la relation :

what do you say to this suggestion?; who are you talking to?; has your letter been replied to yet?; are you being attended to, madam?

4 indique une fermeture :

could you push the door to a little?

TOGETHER

ensemble, comme un tout :

we always gathered together for morning prayers; let's collect some of the neighbours together and talk about it; you must keep the group together and not let people wander off on their own; what were just vague ideas are coming together into a definite proposal; he's really got it together (*c.-à-d. avoir du succès, réaliser ses ambitions personnelles*)

TOWARDS
(anglais américain **toward**)

1 dans la direction de, vers :

> he started walking towards the bridge; my husband wants a holiday in Spain but I'm leaning towards France

2 en face de, sur :

> the castle looks towards the sea; the street which it looks towards

3 envers, à propos de, au sujet de :

> how does she really feel towards him?

4 indique qu'on fait quelque chose ou qu'on utilise quelque chose dans un but :

> I'd like to start saving towards my retirement; put that money towards a new car

---

UNDER

1 sous :

> when the sirens sounded, we always used to get under the table; fold the edges under; the sides of the carpet are folded back and tacked under with staples

2 en vertu de, indique que quelque chose relève de quelque chose :

> under the terms of the new law . . .; that information comes under the Official Secrets Act; who do you come under?

3 indique qu'on réprime, qu'on maintient quelque chose dans un état d'ordre apparent :

> a military government held the country under for many years; the government is doing its best to keep the rebels under

4 indique qu'on désigne une certaine catégorie :

> I'm looking for books on garden design – what subject do they come under in the catalogue?; what should I look under? – vegetables or fruit?

UP

1 indique un mouvement vers le haut :

> hand that hammer up so I don't have to get off the step
> ladder; pass the suitcases up; the climbers struggled slowly
> on up; bet you can't lift that up; she hitched up her skirt
> and started to run; I'll just finish pinning up the hem of this
> dress; hold your head up

2 à l'étage supérieur :

> carry this tray up to your father; do you know where his
> room is or do you want me to see you up?; let's invite our
> neighbours up for coffee

3 indique qu'on se lève ou qu'on redresse quelque chose :

> I jumped up to protest; they all stood up; the old man sat
> up in bed with a start; don't slouch, straighten up your
> shoulders

4 indique que quelque chose s'approche :

> old age has crept up; the manager of the shop rushed up to
> ask if he could be of assistance; he wandered up to us

5 indique qu'un état s'améliore :

> business is looking up; the weather has cleared up

**6 indique une augmentation ou une hausse pour un prix, une
quantité, un volume, etc. :**

> this has forced house prices up; turn the television up, I
> must be going deaf; he's souping up the engine of his car
> (*c.-à-d. rendre plus puissant*); the fire blazed up, catching
> them by surprise; let me plump up your pillows; why did
> they do the pub up? – I liked the old-style décor they had
> before

7 indique qu'on rassemble ou qu'on cherche quelque chose :

> she bundled up her clothes and beat a hasty retreat; I'm
> going to have to gen up on the latest fashions; he wants me
> to hunt up his ancestors; where can I pick up a taxi?; do
> you think you can rake up enough money for the deposit?;
> where did you dig up that story?

8 indique le support :

a street of shored-up buildings; what's it held up by?; can anyone back your story up?

9 indique la fin d'une action :

that wraps up our programme for this week; she bust up the marriage, not him; come on, drink up; they ate up and went

10 indique que l'on fait quelque chose à fond ou complètement :

she's in big trouble for smashing up the company car; you've fouled our plans up; should actors black up or not to play Othello? (*c.-à-d. se noircir le visage, etc.*); it helps soften the material up; tighten this screw up; when the mixture has hardened up sufficiently

11 indique qu'on finit par arriver quelque part, après une suite d'actions :

we ended up in the pub of course; we're going to land up in hospital if you don't slow down

12 indique que quelque chose est enfermé, retenu à l'intérieur :

he'll be locked up for several years; why don't you talk about your problems instead of bottling things up?; they've bricked the old doorway up

13 indique que quelque chose est réduit en morceaux :

chop the meat up for me; I hate the noise the waste disposal unit makes as it crunches everything up; slice it up into smaller pieces

14 indique qu'on sort quelque chose :

you owe me money, so fork up: he has been coughing up a lot of phlegm

UPON

parfois interchangeable avec "on" (voir ON) mais d'un usage souvent plus soutenu

WITH

1 avec, chez :

> who did you stay with?; who did he come with?; their kids have nobody to play with

2 indique ce qu'on utilise :

> what was it painted with?; you can have the ones I've finished with

20 Les Types de Verbes Composés

Dans le Dictionnaire des Verbes Composés de ce livre, les
verbes ont été classifiés en :

vi, vic, vtsép, vtsép*, vtts, vttsc

VI (verbe intransitif)

> **get off: he got off at Victoria Station**
> il descendit à la gare Victoria

> **listen in: do you mind if I listen in while you talk?**
> ça vous dérange si j'écoute pendant que vous parlez ?

VIC (verbe intransitif à complémentation)

Ces verbes sont des verbes intransitifs construits avec une
particule qui peut ou doit être suivie d'un complément :

> **join in: they all joined in the chorus** (le complément **the
> chorus** peut être omis)
> ils se mirent tous à chanter (en chœur)

> **come across: where did you come across that word?** (le
> complément **word** est nécessaire)
> où avez-vous trouvé ce mot ?

Surtout dans le second cas, cette construction ressemble à
celle d'un verbe transitif, et il existe parfois une forme
passive :

> **a type of virus which had never been come across before**
> un genre de virus qui n'avait jamais été rencontré
> auparavant

VTSEP (verbe transitif, séparable)

Les deux parties du verbe peuvent être séparées :

dig up: they're digging the road up; they're digging up the road
ils font des travaux sur la route

Il existe une forme passive :

the road is being dug up again
la route est une fois de plus en travaux

Si le complément du verbe est un pronom personnel (ou **it**), alors on DOIT séparer les deux parties du verbe :

look up: I'll look him up when I'm in Paris
je le contacterai quand je serai à Paris

VTSEP*

Ce sont des verbes transitifs séparables qui peuvent se construire aussi avec un complément après la préposition :

knock over: she knocked the coffee over (vtsép)
she knocked the coffee over the carpet (vtsép*)
elle renversa le café (sur le tapis)

(Remarque : les compléments comme **£10** dans **they've put the price up £10** *ils ont augmenté le prix de 10 £* ne sont pas inclus dans cette classification; le * ne concernera parfois qu'une seule catégorie sémantique du verbe).

VTTS (verbe transitif, toujours séparé)

take back: the old song really took Grandpa back
cette vieille chanson replongeait Grand-père dans le passé

Le complément ne peut PAS se placer après la particule. La forme passive est possible :

Grandpa was really taken back by the old song
Grand-père était replongé dans le passé quand il entendait cette vieille chanson

VTTSC (verbe transitif, toujours séparé, à complémentation)

La particule doit toujours être séparée du verbe ET l'on DOIT placer un complément après le verbe et après la particule :

let in for: do you realize what you could be letting yourself in for?; he's let me in for a lot of extra work
tu te rends compte dans quoi tu t'es fourré ? ; par sa faute, je suis forcé de faire du travail supplémentaire

Dictionnaire des
Verbes Composés

Les abréviations suivantes ont été utilisées dans le Dictionnaire des Verbes Composés :

Am	anglais américain
Br	anglais britannique
Fam	style familier
Fig	sens figuré
Pop	style populaire
qn	quelqu'un

Les abréviations des types de verbes sont :

vi	verbe intransitif
vic	verbe intransitif à complémentation
vtsép(*)	verbe transitif séparable
vtts	verbe transitif toujours séparé
vttsc	verbe transitif toujours séparé, à complémentation

Voir les explications précises de ces catégories aux pages 111-113.

A

abide by *vic* (*se conformer à, suivre*) you'll have to abide by the rules

account for *vic* **(a)** (*rendre compte de, justifier*) how did they account for their absence?; there's no accounting for taste I suppose, but have you seen what they've done with their front room?
(b) (*retrouver, localiser*) the firemen did not need to enter the building since all the occupants were accounted for **(c)** (*détruire, éliminer*) in recent action, the rebels have accounted for a great many government troops; those two will account for as many sweets as all the other kids put together (*c.-à-d. vont consommer*) **(d)** (*être la source de, la cause de*) shop-lifting accounts for most of the store's losses

act (up)on *vic* **(a)** (*agir sur*) rust is caused by salt acting on metal
(b) (*suivre, pour un conseil, etc.*) acting on her lawyer's advice, she has decided not to sue

act out *vtsép* (*concrétiser, réaliser*) he treats his patients for neuroses by having them act out their fantasies

act up *vi* (*se conduire mal*) that child acts up every time her mother goes out without her; (*marcher mal*) the photocopier is acting up again

add in *vtsép** (*ajouter*) add in a little salt and the mixture is complete

add on *vtsép** (*ajouter*) we're thinking about adding on a conservatory; should we add something on as a tip?

add up 1 *vi* **(a)** (*compter*) I'd have thought that at your age you could add up by now! **(b)** (*s'expliquer*) it's all beginning to add up; it's a mystery, it just doesn't add up
2 *vtsép* (*ajouter, dans un calcul*) if you add all the figures up the total is surprisingly large

add up to *vic* **(a)** (*s'élever à*) how much does it all add up to?
(b) (*faire, finir par faire, pour une suite d'actions*) is that all you've done? – it doesn't add up to much, does it?; if you put all the facts together it adds up to quite an interesting case

adhere to *vic* (*suivre*) I don't adhere to that philosophy at all

admit to *vic* (*confesser, avouer*) he admitted to a slight feeling of apprehension

agree on *vic* (*se mettre d'accord sur, décider de*) they cannot agree on a name for the baby; well, that's agreed on then

agree to *vic* (*accepter*) she felt she could not agree to my terms; they agreed to their son taking the job

agree with *vic* **(a)** (*être d'accord avec, approuver*) I am afraid I cannot agree with you; she doesn't agree with all this psychoanalytic treatment for child molesters **(b)** (*réussir à, convenir à*) seafood doesn't agree with me

allow for *vic* (*prendre en considération, tenir compte de*) when calculating how much material you'll need, always allow for some wastage; I suppose I should allow for his inexperience; has that been allowed for in your figures?

allow out *vtsép* (*autoriser à sortir*) the curfew meant that nobody was allowed out after dark; some prisoners are allowed out at weekends

angle for *vic* (*chercher, pour des compliments, etc.*) he was angling for promotion so he developed a sudden interest in the boss's daughter; never angle for compliments

answer back 1 *vi* **(a)** (*répondre avec insolence*) don't answer back, young man! **(b)** (*répliquer*) she's the boss, so I can't answer back **2** *vtsép* (*répondre à, avec insolence*) that child will answer anyone back

answer for *vic* (*répondre de, garantir*) if he keeps on at me like this, I won't answer for my actions; (*être responsable de*) the people who elected him in have a great deal to answer for

answer to *vic* **(a)** (*avoir affaire à, rendre des comptes à*) if you lay one finger on him you'll have me to answer to; who do you answer to in your job? **(b)** (*répondre à, pour une description*) a woman answering to the description has been seen in the area

argue away 1 *vtsép* (*diminuer l'importance de, avec des arguments*) you cannot argue the facts away – ozone depletion is a serious problem

2 *vi* (*se disputer sans arrêt*) they've been arguing away all morning

argue for/against *vic* (*débattre le pour/le contre de*) the speakers will argue for and against unilateral disarmament

argue out *vtsép* (*discuter de, avec l'intention d'arriver à une conclusion*) I'll leave you to argue it out between you

ask after *vic* (*demander des nouvelles de*) let your grandfather know I was asking after him

ask around 1 *vi* (*demander, se renseigner, autour de soi*) I'll ask around at work and see if anyone else is interested
2 *vtsép* (*inviter chez soi*) why don't we ask them around for dinner one night

ask back *vtsép* (*inviter chez soi, après une sortie ensemble*) do you want to ask them back for a drink after the theatre?

ask in *vtsép* (*inviter chez soi, quand la personne invitée se trouve tout près*) I would ask you in for tea but my husband's not very well

ask out *vtsép* (*inviter à sortir*) he's asked her out so many times she must be running out of excuses by now; when he finally summoned up the courage to ask her out . . .

ask up *vtsép* (*inviter à monter chez soi*) don't get too excited if she asks you up for coffee – her mother lives with her!

attend to *vic* **(a)** (*s'occuper de*) are you being attended to, Madam?; I'll attend to this **(b)** (*observer*) now attend to the experiment very closely, I'll be asking you questions later

auction off *vtsép* (*mettre aux enchères*) they auctioned off all the family silver to raise some money

average out 1 *vtsép* (*faire la moyenne de*) I've averaged out how much I spend a week, and it's frightening
2 *vi* (*faire une moyenne*) over a full year it averages out quite differently

average out at *vic* (*faire . . . en moyenne*) how much does that average out at a year?

B

babble away/on *vi* (*bredouiller, raconter*) you were babbling away in your sleep last night; I have no idea what you're babbling on about

back down *vi* (*se rendre, se dégonfler*) he takes pride in never backing down, however strong the opposition's case

back on to *vic* (*donner par derrière sur*) the house backs on to a lane

back out 1 *vi* **(a)** (*reculer, sortir en marche arrière*) he backed out of the drive **(b)** (*se dérober, se retirer, pour un engagement*) they can't back out from the deal now!
  2 *vtsép* (*sortir en marche arrière*) I'm not very good at backing the car out – will you do it?

back up 1 *vi* (*reculer, pour faire de la place*) all the cars had to back up to let the ambulance past
  2 *vtsép* **(a)** (*appuyer, supporter*) he'll need to back up his claim to the estate with something stronger than that; I doubt if the electors will back them up **(b)** (*ramener en marche arrière*) the driver had to back his lorry up all the way to the service station **(c)** *Am* (*immobiliser*) the accident backed traffic up all the way to the turnpike

bail out *vtsép* **(a)** (*libérer contre caution*) their lawyer bailed them out **(b)** (*aider, tirer d'affaire*) I'm not bailing you out again – you're on your own this time

balance out 1 *vi* (*correspondre*) the figures don't balance out
  2 *vtsép* (*compléter*) he cooks and she knows a lot about wine, so they balance each other out very nicely

bale out 1 *vi* **(a)** (*sauter en parachute en cas d'urgence*) Dad never tires of telling how he had to bale out over the Channel during a dogfight **(b)** (*écoper l'eau*) she's taking on a lot of water – start baling out
  2 *vtsép* (*écoper*) we'll have to bale the water out first

band together *vi* (*s'unir*) if we band together we can do something about this problem

bandy about/around *vtsép** (*utiliser souvent, pour des mots, des* noms, *etc.*) "decentralization" is a word the government bandies about a lot; (*faire du bruit à propos de*) the newspapers have been bandying that story around for weeks now

bank (up)on *vic* (*compter sur*) him turn up on time? – I wouldn't bank on it if I were you

bargain for *vic* (*s'attendre à*) if she marries him she'll get more than she bargained for; I didn't bargain for your kid brother coming as well

bash about *vtsép* Fam* (**frapper, tabasser*) her husband bashes her about something awful; (*maltraiter, abîmer*) you can always rely on baggage handlers bashing your suitcases about

bash on *vi Fam* (*continuer, surtout malgré des difficultés, etc.*) the weather forecast was bad but they decided to bash on with their plans for a picnic

battle on *vi* (*continuer à lutter, surtout malgré des difficultés, etc.*) he has fallen very far behind the other runners but he's still battling on; just battle on as best you can in the circumstances

bawl out *vtsép* **(a)** (*hurler*) please don't bawl out my name **(b)** (*crier après, engueuler*) the boss really bawled us out for that mistake

bear down 1 *vi* **(a)** (*pousser, pour une femme en travail*) if that obstetrics nurse had said "bear down, dear" one more time, I would have screamed **(b)** (*foncer sur, s'approcher d'une manière menaçante*) the crew of the fishing boat jumped overboard as they saw the liner bearing down on them; the boys scattered as the headmaster bore down on them
　2 *vtsép* (*accabler*) the Third World is borne down by the burden of poverty

bear out *vtsép* (*confirmer*) onlookers bore out her statement to the police; he feels that the report bears him out in his estimates of radiation levels in the area

bear up *vi* (*tenir bon, ne pas se laisser abattre*) Mother found it difficult to bear up when there was still no news after the second day; bear up! – just one more day to the weekend

bear (up)on *vic* (*avoir un rapport avec*) I don't see how that bears on what I am supposed to be doing

bear with *vic* (*supporter patiemment, faire preuve de patience envers*) the old lady asked the salesman to bear with her while she looked for her glasses

beat back *vtsép* (*repousser, pour des assaillants*) they beat back the attackers three times but were eventually overrun

beat down 1 *vi* (*tomber dru*) the rain was beating down so fast it was difficult to see the road
    2 *vtsép* **(a)** (*faire baisser le prix à qn*) I felt quite proud of myself for beating him down so much **(b)** (*détruire*) the drunk threatened to beat the door down if they didn't open up; hailstorms have beaten down the county's entire barley crop

beat off *vtsép* (*repousser*) the tourists tried unsuccessfully to beat off all the people trying to sell them things

beat out *vtsép* **(a)** (*frapper pour éteindre*) desperate sheep-farmers were beating out the brush fires with their bare hands **(b)** (*battre*) she beat out the rhythm on the table **(c)** (*débosseler*) the car door panel will have to be beaten out

beat up *vtsép* **(a)** (*agresser et battre*) beating up old ladies is his speciality **(b)** (*mélanger en battant, pour une préparation*) just beat up a few eggs for an omelette

beaver away *vi Fam* (*travailler, bosser*) he's still beavering away at his studies

belt out *vtsép Fam* (*jouer fort ou chanter à tue-tête*) he really belted that song out

belt up *vi* **(a)** *Pop* (*se la boucler*) I wish you would belt up **(b)** (*attacher sa ceinture de sécurité*) I'm not starting this car until you belt up

bind over *vtsép* (*relaxer sous condition de ne pas troubler l'ordre public*) he's the kind of judge who will bind people over rather than send them to prison; the drunk was bound over for three months to keep the peace

black out 1 *vi* (*perdre conscience*) she was alright until she saw the blood and then she blacked out
    2 *vtsép* **(a)** (*obscurcir, rendre obscur*) the impact of the scene is heightened when they black the stage out **(b)** (*empêcher la*

retransmission de) we regret that industrial action has blacked out this evening's programmes

blast off *vi* (*décoller, pour un engin spatial*) the latest space shuttle blasted off at 5 am local time today

blaze away *vi* **(a)** (*maintenir un tir nourri*) the troops blazed away at the target **(b)** (*flamber, pour un feu*) the fire is blazing away merrily in the grate

blink at *vic* (*fermer les yeux sur*) his wife blinks at his affairs

blink away *vtsép* (*refouler, pour des larmes, battre des cils pour faire partir*) I blinked my tears away

block in *vtsép* (*bloquer, coincer, surtout pour une voiture*) that man next door has blocked me in again

block off *vtsép* (*barricader, fermer*) the street will be blocked off until the wreckage is cleared

block up *vtsép* **(a)** (*boucher*) don't throw the tea leaves down the sink or you'll block it up; the worst thing about a cold is that your nose gets all blocked up **(b)** (*barrer*) they've blocked up the entry

blossom out *vi* (*se métamorphoser*) she's blossoming out into quite a beautiful young woman

blot out *vtsép* (*effacer*) a word has been blotted out here; you must try to remember and come to terms with the past, not blot it out; (*masquer*) the mist has blotted out the view

blow in 1 *vi* **(a)** (*être détruit par une poussée d'air*) all the windows blew in because of the explosion **(b)** (*entrer, sous la force du vent*) shut the door – the dust is blowing in **(c)** *Fam* (*débarquer, arriver à l'imprévu*) when did you blow in?
   2 *vtsép* **(a)** (*détruire, pour une poussée d'air*) the blast blew all the windows in **(b)** (*faire entrer, pour de l'air*) blow some more air in

blow off 1 *vi* (*être emporté par le vent*) some of the roof tiles have blown off
   2 *vtsép** **(a)** (**emporter, pour le vent*) the high winds blew the tiles off the roof **(b)** (*arracher, pour une explosion, faire sauter par un coup de feu*) the gunman threatened to blow their heads off

blow out 1 *vi* **(a)** (*s'éteindre*) the candles have blown out **(b)** (*exploser*)
the rear tyre blew out
    2 *vtsép* **(a)** (*éteindre*) be sure to blow the match out properly
(*calmer*) the storm soon blew itself out **(b)** (*locution*) to blow
someone's brains out *faire sauter la cervelle à qn*

blow over 1 *vi* **(a)** (*tomber, s'effondrer*) the garage must have blown
over in high winds last night **(b)** (*se calmer, se dissiper, pour des
disputes, etc.*) it will soon blow over and you'll be friends again;
the storm will blow over soon
    2 *vtsép* (*renverser, faire tomber, pour le vent, etc.*) did the wind
blow anything over?

blow up 1 *vi* **(a)** (*sauter, exploser*) the ammunitions depot blew up
(b) (*se mettre en colère*) do you often blow up like that?
(c) (*éclater, pour une dispute, etc.*) the argument blew up out of
nowhere
    2 *vtsép* **(a)** (*détruire, faire sauter*) terrorists have blown up the
presidential palace **(b)** (*gonfler*) do the tyres need blowing up?
(c) (*agrandir, pour des documents, etc.*) I'd like this photograph
blown up **(d)** (*exagérer*) you're blowing this up out of all
proportion

bluff out *vtsép* (*se sortir d'une situation difficile par la ruse,
l'intelligence, etc.*) when the police get here we'll just have to
bluff it out; she can bluff her way out of anything

board in/up *vtsép* (*barricader, fermer*) the windows and doors have all
been boarded up to stop tramps getting in

bog down *vtsép habituellement au passif* (*être coincé, s'embourber*)
the car is bogged down in the mud; the important thing is not to
get bogged down in details

boil down to *vi* (*se résumer à*) what his claim boils down to then is . . .

boil up 1 *vtsép* (*faire bouillir*) the doctor wants you to boil up some
water
    2 *vi Fam* (*bouillir*) I could feel the anger boiling up inside me

bolt down 1 *vic* (*dévaler*) she bolted down the stairs and into the street
    2 *vtsép* (*manger vite, avaler*) don't bolt your food down like that

bone up on *vic Fam* (*potasser, chiader*) you'll have to bone up on your
history if you want to pass that test next week

book in 1 *vi* (*faire enregistrer une arrivée à l'hôtel*) do we have to book in by a certain time?
  2 *vtsép** (*faire une réservation pour*) I've booked them in to the best hotel in town

book out 1 *vi* (*faire enregistrer son départ*) when do we have to book out by?
  2 *vtsép* (*enregistrer le départ de*) the receptionist booked them out before noon

book up 1 *vi* (*réserver*) have you booked up for a holiday?
  2 *vtsép habituellement au passif* (*être complet*) the hotel is all booked up

boot up 1 *vtsép* (*amorcer, en informatique*) use this diskette to boot the computer up
  2 *vi* (*amorcer, pour un ordinateur*) for some odd reason the computer is refusing to boot up

bottle up *vtsép* (*ne pas exprimer, pour des sentiments, etc.*) it does no good to bottle your feelings up

bottom out *vi Fam* (*toucher le fond*) the government hopes that unemployment has finally bottomed out

bow out *vi Fam* (*prendre congé*) when the company brought in computers, old Mr Parsons decided the time had come to bow out

bowl out *vtsép* (*au cricket, éliminer*) we bowled him out for ten

bowl over *vtsép* **(a)** (*renverser*) the old lady was bowled over by a boy on a bike **(b)** (*renverser, couper bras et jambes à*) I was bowled over by winning first prize

box in *vtsép* **(a)** (*cerner, encercler*) the defence seem to have him boxed in **(b)** (*encastrer*) we're boxing in the sink; (*enfermer*) don't you feel boxed in in such a small room?

branch off *vi* (*s'embrancher*) the road branches off to the left

branch out *vi* (*se diversifier*) the company intends to branch out into a new area of business

brazen out *vtsép* (*se montrer insolent, crâner, payer d'effronterie*) *couramment 'to brazen it out'* when they accused him of gate crashing the party, he brazened it out and refused to admit he hadn't been invited

break away *vi* **(a)** (*échapper à*) she broke away from the guards who were escorting her to hospital **(b)** (*se détacher, rompre*) when did you break away from your family?; it was the year France broke away from NATO **(c)** (*s'effondrer*) the merest touch and the surface breaks away

break down 1 *vi* **(a)** (*tomber en panne*) the car broke down on the motorway; (*ne pas tenir debout*) that's where your argument breaks down **(b)** (*échouer*) their marriage seems to be breaking down; talks between the two sides have broken down; (*éclater, pour une crise de nerfs, etc.*) I broke down in tears **(c)** (*se décomposer*) the compound breaks down into a number of components
  2 *vtsép* **(a)** (*détruire, abattre*) the firemen had to break down the door to rescue the children **(b)** (*vaincre*) she was unable to break down her parents' opposition to her plans **(c)** (*détailler, décomposer*) we really need to break the figures down a bit further

break in 1 *vi* **(a)** (*faire une interruption, pendant une conversation, etc.*) I really must break in at this point **(b)** (*entrer par effraction*) when did you realize that someone had broken in?
  2 *vtsép* **(a)** (*détruire*) the thieves broke the door in **(b)** (*dresser, pour un cheval*) she's good at breaking in horses; (*assouplir, faire, pour des chaussures*) I hate having to break new shoes in

break into *vic* **(a)** (*entrer par effraction dans*) thieves broke into a number of houses on the street last night **(b)** (*utiliser une partie de*) I'll have to break into my holiday money to pay for the repairs to my car **(c)** (*interrompre*) why did you break into the conversation like that? **(d)** (*se mettre à . . .*) I broke into a cold sweat when I realized how high up I was; he often breaks into song in the shower

break off 1 *vi* **(a)** (*se détacher net*) it just broke off in my hand, honestly **(b)** (*s'arrêter*) can we break off for the rest of the day? **(c)** (*s'interrompre*) he broke off when the chairman entered the room
  2 *vtsép* **(a)** (**détacher, casser*) break off two pieces of chocolate for you and your brother **(b)** (*suspendre, arrêter*) talks have been broken off **(c)** (*rompre, pour une relation amoureuse*)

it wouldn't surprise me if they broke it off soon; they've broken off the engagement

break out *vi* **(a)** *(éclater, prendre)* fires have broken out all over the city **(b)** *(avoir une éruption)* the baby is breaking out in a rash **(c)** *(s'évader)* the prisoners broke out late last night **(d)** *(dire tout à coup)* "I don't agree", she broke out **(e)** *(ouvrir, habituellement une bouteille)* let's break out another bottle

break up 1 *vi* **(a)** *(craquer, se briser)* the ice on the river is breaking up at last; *(se briser)* their marriage is breaking up; *(locution)* I just broke up *j'ai éclaté de rire* **(b)** *(se terminer)* when did the party finally break up?; the schools will be breaking up for summer soon **(c)** *(se séparer, pour un couple)* I've heard that they're breaking up

  2 *vtsép* **(a)** *(mettre en morceaux)* you'll have to break the earth up before you can plant anything **(b)** *(arrêter)* the warder broke up the fight between the prisoners; *(détruire)* it was his drinking that broke the marriage up

bring about *vtsép* *(causer)* what brought this about?

bring back *vtsép* **(a)** *(ramener chez soi)* Mum told me to bring you back for supper **(b)** *(ramener à, pour un état)* a couple of days in bed will bring him back to normal; *(réélire)* it will be up to the electors to decide whether to bring back the previous government **(c)** *(rappeler, pour des souvenirs, etc.)* that song brings back memories

bring down *vtsép* **(a)** *(faire crouler)* if that boy doesn't stop jumping up and down like that he's going to bring the house down about our ears; *(locution)* their jokes always bring the house down *leurs blagues connaissent toujours un succès triomphant* **(b)** *(descendre, abattre)* the spy plane was brought down by a missile **(c)** *(faire atterrir)* the badly damaged plane was brought down with no loss of life **(d)** *(faire tomber)* it was really the students who brought down the government; he brought him down with a rugby tackle **(e)** *(se faire remarquer, par une autorité)* stop making so much noise or you'll bring the headmaster down on us **(f)** *(baisser)* this new drug will bring his temperature down; she would have brought the price down even further if you'd gone on bargaining

bring in *vtsép* **(a)** *(faire entrer, amener)* I've brought Mrs Jones in to see you **(b)** *(introduire)* new tax legislation will be brought in next year **(c)** (*faire appel à, faire intervenir*) the company is bringing consultants in to see if the problems can be solved; this argument is between you two – why bring me in? **(d)** (*fêter, pour le Nouvel An*) to bring in the New Year **(e)** (*gagner*) how much money is your eldest son bringing in? **(f)** (*rendre, pour un jugement*) the jury brought in a verdict of not guilty

bring off *vtsép** **(a)** (*sauver ou récupérer d'un bateau, etc.*) the bodies are being brought off the ship today **(b)** (*réussir, pour une affaire*) did you bring the deal off?

bring on *vtsép* **(a)** (*faire entrer*) please bring on our next contestant **(b)** (*causer, entraîner, faire apparaître*) damp days always bring on my arthritis; what brought this on? **(c)** (*faire pousser*) this mild weather will bring the roses on nicely **(d)** (*locution*) I brought it on myself *je n'ai personne à blâmer*

bring out *vtsép* **(a)** (*faire sortir, conduire à l'extérieur*) they brought the man out under armed guard **(b)** (*faire sortir de ses réserves*) his grand-daughter is about the only one who can bring him out (of himself) **(c)** (*faire sortir, faire apparaître*) the sun has brought out all the bulbs; disasters bring out the best – and worst – in people; they're bringing out the new models very soon; (*provoquer chez, pour une allergie*) strawberries bring her out in a rash

bring round *vtsép* **(a)** (*emmener ou porter chez qn*) I'll bring him round to meet you some time **(b)** (*persuader*) you'll never bring my dad round to that way of thinking **(c)** (*ranimer*) they brought her round quite quickly after she fainted **(d)** (*ramener à*) I finally managed to bring the conversation round to what I wanted to talk about

bring up *vtsép* **(a)** (*élever*) we've brought four kids up **(b)** (*mentionner, soulever*) Madam Chairwoman, I wish to bring up the question of travel expenses **(c)** (*vomir*) everything she swallows she brings up ten minutes later

brown off *vtsép Fam* (*ennuyer, embêter*) I'm browned off with always having to do the dishes; you're all looking a bit browned off – what's wrong?; he's very browned off with you because you didn't go to the party (*il est fâché*)

brush aside *vtsép* (*écarter, repousser*) the Minister brushed aside the reporters; she won't listen – just brushes our objections aside

brush up *vtsép* **(a)** *(ramasser avec une brosse)* I want all those crumbs brushed up off the floor **(b)** *(rafraîchir, travailler)* he'll have to brush up his Spanish

buck up 1 *vi* **(a)** *(se dépêcher)* buck up or we'll be late **(b)** *(s'égayer, prendre courage)* I wish he would buck up a little
  2 *vtsép* **(a)** *(remonter le moral à)* the good news bucked me up no end **(b)** *(locution)* to buck up one's ideas *se reprendre*

bucket down *vi Fam* *(pleuvoir des cordes)* it's bucketing down

buckle down/to *vi* *(se mettre à, pour une tâche, s'y mettre)* I suppose I had better buckle down if I want to finish the housework this morning; if you don't buckle down to your piano practice . . .; he buckled to and finished cleaning the car

build on 1 *vtsép** *(ajouter)* next door are building on a conservatory
  2 *vic* *(s'appuyer sur, développer à partir de)* the company is building on its earlier success

build up 1 *vi* *(s'accumuler, augmenter)* pressure on the government is building up
  2 *vtsép* **(a)** *(augmenter, accumuler)* I wouldn't build my hopes up if I were you; we're trying to build up our savings so we can buy a house soon **(b)** *(créer)* his father built that company up from nothing; you've built up quite a reputation for yourself **(c)** *(donner de la force à)* the children need some vitamins to build them up **(d)** *habituellement au passif* *(construire)* the area has become quite built up **(e)** *(faire connaître par la publicité)* the play has been so built up that it's impossible to get tickets for it

bump into *vic* **(a)** *(rentrer dans, se cogner contre)* I was so engrossed in my thoughts that I bumped into a lamp post **(b)** *(rencontrer par hasard)* he's always bumping into people he knows

bump off *vtsép Fam* *(assassiner, tuer)* his job was bumping people off for a fee

bump up *vtsép Fam* *(augmenter)* they've bumped up the price of beer again

bundle off *vtsép** *(envoyer sans plus attendre, d'urgence)* the baby was bundled off to hospital in an ambulance

bung up *vtsép Fam* *(boucher)* who bunged the sink up?; I'm/my nose is all bunged up

burn down 1 *vi* (*être détruit par le feu*) the theatre burned down; (*devenir moins fort, pour un feu*) the fire is burning down
    2 *vtsép* (*incendier, brûler*) vandals have burned down a number of derelict buildings in the area

burn out 1 *vi* (*s'éteindre*) the fire is burning out; *Fig* (*perdre son enthousiasme, etc.*) social workers frequently burn out at an early age
    2 *vtsép* **(a)** (*rendre sans abri, pour un incendie*) they were burned out **(b)** (*éteindre*) the fire has burnt itself out

burn up 1 *vi* (*se consumer*) the rocket burned up in the atmosphere
    2 *vtsép* (*consommer, brûler*) children burn up a lot of energy playing; this stove burns up a lot of wood

burst into *vic* **(a)** (*faire irruption dans*) she burst into the room **(b)** (*éclater en, se mettre à*) he burst into tears; then they all burst into song

burst out *vi* **(a)** (*éclater de*) I burst out laughing; (*s'écrier*) "where were you last night?", he burst out **(b)** (*sortir précipitamment*) they all burst out of the room

butt in *vi* (*se mêler à la conversation, etc.*) we were just having a cosy chat when she butted in; is this a private argument or can anybody butt in?

buy into *vic* (*acheter des actions dans*) he has bought into his neighbour's business

buy off *vtsép Fam* (*acheter, donner des pots-de-vin à*) the councillor was bought off with an all-expenses paid holiday in the south of France

buy out *vtsép* (*acheter toutes les actions ou les valeurs immobilières de*) all the other shareholders have been bought out

buy up *vtsép* (*dévaliser, rafler*) look at all those parcels – she must have bought up the entire store!; (*acheter en grande quantité*) because of the threatened shortage people have been buying up toilet paper

buzz off *vi Fam* (*s'en aller, se casser*) tell that kid brother of yours to buzz off; just buzz off and leave me alone

C

call back 1 *vi* **(a)** (*revenir*) I'll call back later to see her **(b)** (*rappeler, au téléphone*) if you'd like to call back in an hour . . .
   2 *vtsép* **(a)** (*rappeler, au téléphone*) he said he would call you back **(b)** (*rappeler, faire revenir*) I know she's on holiday but she'll have to be called back to deal with this; I think the last pair should be called back for another audition

call for *vic* **(a)** (*demander, réclamer*) the Opposition is calling for her resignation **(b)** (*passer prendre*) would it be too much of a rush if I called for you at seven? **(c)** (*nécessiter, demander*) this is the kind of job that calls for brains rather than brawn; that's wonderful news – it calls for a celebration

call in 1 *vi* **(a)** (*rendre visite*) the social worker is going to call in later **(b)** (*téléphoner*) off-duty nurses called in and offered to help; prison officers are not actually on strike but a great many of them are calling in sick
   2 *vtsép* **(a)** (*faire venir*) they've finally decided to call the doctor in **(b)** (*retirer de la circulation*) the bank has called in its loans

call off *vtsép* **(a)** (*annuler, résilier*) the meeting will have to be called off; does this mean we'll have to call our holiday off?; they've called it off (*c.-à-d. fiançailles ou mariage*) **(b)** (**rappeler*) call your dog off!

call out 1 *vi* (*crier, hurler*) don't call out in the street like that
   2 *vtsép* **(a)** (*crier*) the master of ceremonies called out the names of the prizewinners **(b)** (*appeler, faire venir*) call out the guard!; I don't like calling the doctor out at this time of night **(c)** (*donner la consigne de grève*) the men were called out (on strike) halfway through the morning shift

call up *vtsép* **(a)** (*faire venir*) the situation looked dangerous and the lieutenant decided to call up reinforcements **(b)** (*appeler sous les drapeaux*) Dad was called up in 1940 **(c)** (*téléphoner à*) please don't call me up at midnight **(d)** (*évoquer*) the speech called up thoughts of the past

call (up)on *vic* **(a)** (*rendre visite à*) gentlemen used to ask permission to call on young ladies **(b)** (*exhorter, sommer*) the opposition called on the government to make its position clear

calm down 1 *vi* (*se calmer*) getting hysterical won't help, just calm down; I want you all to calm down now, children
    2 *vtsép* (*calmer*) leave it to Mum, she'll calm him down

care for *vic* **(a)** (*soigner, s'occuper de*) she has spent years caring for her invalid mother **(b)** (*aimer*) you know I don't care for that kind of language; I don't believe he ever cared for you or he wouldn't have treated you the way he did

carry away *vtsép* (*emporter, pour des sentiments*) he let his enthusiasm carry him away; she gets carried away by the sound of her own voice; take it easy, don't get carried away! (*c.-à-d. ne t'emporte pas*)

carry forward *vtsép* **(a)** (*remettre, pour une date*) can I carry my leave forward and have six weeks next summer? **(b)** (*reporter, pour des chiffres*) this amount should have been carried forward to the next page

carry off *vtsép* **(a)** (*remporter*) she carried off the prizes for Latin and French **(b)** (*réussir*) it wasn't the easiest of speeches to make but you carried it off very well **(c)** (*tuer, pour une épidémie*) tuberculosis carried off a great many people in the last century

carry on 1 *vi* **(a)** (*continuer*) just carry on with what you were doing **(b)** *Fam* (*faire une scène*) he carried on just because his wife wanted an evening out; what a way to carry on! **(c)** *Fam* (*avoir une liaison*) have you been carrying on behind my back?
    2 *vtsép* (*poursuivre*) grandfather wants me to carry on the business after he dies; (*entretenir*) we have carried on a correspondence for years

carry out *vtsép* **(a)** (*porter à l'extérieur*) they had to carry him out since he couldn't walk **(b)** (*tenir, pour une promesse*) never make a promise that you cannot carry out; (*mener, pour une enquête*) the coast guard is carrying out a search for the missing crew members

carry through *vtsép* (*mener à sa fin*) the plan has to be carried through to the last detail

carve out *vtsép* **(a)** (*tailler, sculpter*) he has now carved out twenty or so statues **(b)** *Fig* (*se tailler*) the company plans to carve out its own niche in the market

carve up *vtsép* **(a)** (*découper, surtout pour la viande*) ask the butcher to carve the meat up for you **(b)** (*diviser, partager*) they just carved up the land among themselves with no regard for the native inhabitants **(c)** *Fam* (*doubler dangereusement sur la route*) did you see how that fool carved me up?

cash in 1 *vtsép* (*encaisser, échanger contre de l'argent*) are you going to cash in your premium bonds?
2 *vic* (*tirer avantage de, profiter de*) she's cashing in on the fact that her father knows a lot of influential people

cast away *vtsép* (*abandonner comme naufragé*) Robinson Crusoe was cast away on his desert island for a great many years

cast back *vtsép* (*ramener dans le passé*) if you cast your mind back a week, you will recall that . . .

cast off 1 *vtsép* **(a)** (*arrêter, pour un tricot*) cast off the remaining stitches **(b)** (*larguer les amarres de*) we cast the launch off at dawn
2 *vi* **(a)** (*arrêter les mailles*) cast off when only four stitches remain **(b)** (*larguer les amarres*) they will cast off shortly

cast on 1 *vi* (*monter les mailles*) I usually cast on with my thumb
2 *vtsép* (*monter, pour un tricot*) cast on 80 stitches; have you cast the sleeve on yet?

catch at *vic* (*avancer la main vers, essayer d'attraper*) she caught at his sleeve and asked for help

catch on *vi* **(a)** (*prendre, s'imposer, pour une mode*) I remember you saying that the Beatles would never catch on **(b)** *Fam* (*piger*) she's so naive she didn't catch on

catch out *vtsép* **(a)** (*coincer, prendre par défaut*) the police caught him out by asking for a description of the programme he said he was watching **(b)** (*au cricket, éliminer*) he was caught out very early on

catch up 1 *vi* (*gagner du terrain, rattraper la distance*) the runners behind are catching up; (*rattraper*) I wish I could catch up with my work/sleep
2 *vtsép* **(a)** (*rattraper*) you go ahead and I'll catch you up
(b) (*coincer*) they were caught up in a traffic jam for hours

cave in *vi* (*s'effondrer*) the walls and roof caved in under the force of the blast

centre on *vic* (*se concentrer sur*) the play centres on the idea of survivor guilt

chain up *vtsép* (*mettre à la chaîne*) I hope he chains that brute of a dog up at night; in those days people could be chained up in prison for years

chalk up *vtsép Fam* **(a)** (*marquer*) the team chalked up another win today **(b)** (*mettre sur un compte*) chalk it up, will you, and I'll pay next week **(c)** (*locution*) she'll just have to chalk it up to experience *elle n'aura qu'à le mettre sur le compte de l'expérience*

chance on *vic* (*tomber sur, par hasard*) I chanced on this piece of Meissen in a grubby little second-hand shop

change down *vi* (*rétrograder, en voiture*) traffic lights coming up – change down

change over *vi* **(a)** (*se convertir*) is it a good idea to change over entirely to electricity? **(b)** (*échanger*) let's change over and you wash while I dry; (*changer de chaîne*) as soon as opera or ballet comes on the TV, he changes over

change up *vi* (*passer en vitesse supérieure*) you have to change up faster than that

chase up *vtsép* (*trouver avec difficulté*) we finally chased her up in the library; why not ask one of the big stores to chase up the pattern for you?

chat up *vtsép Fam* (*draguer, baratiner*) he's just chatting you up; I wish I could chat up men the way she does

cheat on *vic* **(a)** (*être infidèle à*) why didn't you tell me he was cheating on me? **(b)** (*tricher sur*) it's not a good idea to cheat on your expenses

check in 1 *vi* (*enregistrer son arrivée à l'hôtel, à l'aéroport*) have you checked in?
    2 *vtsép* **(a)** (*prendre l'enregistrement de l'arrivée de*) they must be here – I checked them in myself **(b)** (*prendre une réservation pour*) she's quite high-powered, so check her into a four-star hotel

check out 1 *vi* **(a)** (*quitter l'hôtel*) they checked out last night
(b) *Pop* (*correspondre, coller*) it doesn't check out
2 *vtsép* **(a)** (*s'informer sur*) we've checked her out and she's who she says she is **(b)** (*enregistrer le départ de*) the reception clerk will check you out

check through *vtsép* **(a)** (*examiner, fouiller*) they checked through everyone's hand luggage **(b)** (*envoyer par avion*) I have to change at Geneva – can my bags be checked right through to London?

cheer on *vtsép* (*encourager*) he's there every Saturday to cheer his team on

cheer up 1 *vi* (*reprendre le moral*) I hate it when people tell you to cheer up
2 *vtsép* **(a)** (*rendre son entrain à*) a visit to the pub will cheer him up **(b)** (*donner de la gaieté à, raviver*) the new curtains really do cheer the room up

chew on *vic* **(a)** (*mâchonner, mordre*) he chewed on his pipe stem for a bit and then said . . . **(b)** (*méditer, ruminer sur*) how much longer do you need to chew on it?

chew over *vtsép* (*méditer, réfléchir à*) I have been chewing this little problem over in my mind, Watson, and . . .

chew up *vtsép* **(a)** (*mâcher*) chew your food up well before swallowing **(b)** (*détruire*) your machine has chewed up my bank card; it's those heavy lorries that are chewing up the road

chicken out *vi Fam* (*se dégonfler*) I arranged a blind date with Annabel for my brother but he chickened out at the last minute; don't chicken out on us; (*se défiler*) he chickened out of his dental appointment

chip in *Fam* **1** *vi* **(a)** (*intervenir, dire son mot*) if I can chip in for a moment . . . **(b)** (*contribuer*) we've all chipped in for a present for her
2 *vtsép* (*contribuer*) how much is everyone else chipping in?

chip off 1 *vi* (*s'écailler*) the paint is chipping off
2 *vtsép** (*ébrécher*) be careful with those plates – I don't want any pieces chipped off; (*faire partir au couteau, écailler*) we slowly chipped off the old paintwork

choke back *vtsép* (*refouler, contenir*) looking at these pictures, I find it hard to choke back my tears/anger

choke up *vtsép* (*boucher, bloquer*) the drain is all choked up with leaves

chuck in/up *vtsép Fam* (*laisser tomber*) you're surely not thinking of chucking up your job?; one day I'm going to chuck all this in and buy a farm; he's chucked his latest girlfriend in

chug along *vi Fam* (*aller doucement*) Dad always chugs along at about 35, even on the motorway

clam up *vi* (*se taire, rester muet*) don't clam up on me, talk to me!

clamp down *vi* (*serrer la vis, se durcir*) the police are clamping down this Christmas so don't drink and drive

clamp down on *vic* (*serrer la vis sur*) the authorities are clamping down on misleading advertising

clean out *vtsép* **(a)** (*ranger et nettoyer*) I'll clean out a few cupboards today I think **(b)** *Fam* (*nettoyer de son argent*) the casino cleaned him out **(c)** *Fam* (*faire main basse sur*) someone has cleaned the shop out of sugar

clean up 1 *vtsép* **(a)** (*nettoyer, laver*) when are you going to clean this place up – it's a mess; the kids need to be cleaned up before we go to your mother's **(b)** (*nettoyer, épurer*) I like those old cowboy films where the sheriff always says "I'm going to clean up this town"
   2 *vi Fam* (*faire son beurre*) she really cleaned up at the roulette table

clear away I *vtsép* (*enlever, débarrasser*) workmen were clearing away the debris; it's your turn to clear the dishes away
   2 *vi* (*disparaître*) the clouds have all cleared away

clear off 1 *vtsép** (*enlever*) clear all those papers off the table
   2 *vi* (*s'en aller, décamper*) clear off!; the boys cleared off when they saw the headmaster coming down the street

clear up 1 *vtsép* **(a)** (*éclaircir, clarifier*) I'd like to clear up a point or two; we have some problems that need to be cleared up
   (b) (*nettoyer*) I can't come out – I have to clear up my room
   (c) (*guérir*) the doctor said this cream would clear up the acne

2 vi **(a)** (*s'améliorer, s'éclaircir, pour la météo*) it's clearing up **(b)** (*disparaître*) don't worry – that rash will soon clear up

climb down vi **(a)** (*descendre*) it took the climbers three hours to climb down **(b)** (*admettre qu'on a tort*) she'll never climb down, however strong the arguments against her

clock in 1 vi **(a)** (*faire un temps de*) the last of the marathon runners clocked in at six hours **(b)** (*pointer, au travail*) I have to clock in; you clocked in 10 minutes late
 2 vtsép (*pointer pour, à l'arrivée du travail*) do you think just this once you could clock me in?

clock off 1 vi (*pointer, à la sortie du travail*) when did you clock off?
 2 vtsép (*pointer pour, à la sortie du travail*) I'll clock you off if you like

clock up vtsép **(a)** (*faire, réaliser*) he clocked up a faster time than any of his rivals in the race **(b)** *Fam* (*remporter*) the team has clocked up another victory

close down 1 vi **(a)** (*fermer définitivement*) the factory is closing down next month; we're closing down soon **(b)** (*terminer les programmes*) television closes down a lot later than it used to
 2 vtsép (*fermer définitivement*) they closed the restaurant down because of health code violations

close in 1 vi **(a)** (*raccourcir*) the days are closing in **(b)** (*se rapprocher*) winter is closing in; (*cerner*) government troops are said to be closing in on the rebels
 2 vtsép (*boucher, fermer*) they're thinking of closing the porch in

close up 1 vi (*se rapprocher*) the photographer asked the people in the front line to close up so he could get them all in
 2 vtsép (*fermer*) they must have gone away for some time – the house is all closed up; the opening in the fence has been closed up to prevent similar tragedies in the future

cloud up 1 vi (*se couvrir, pour le ciel*) it's clouding up; (*se couvrir de buée*) the mirror has clouded up
 2 vtsép (*couvrir de buée*) the bathroom is poorly ventilated – steam always clouds the windows up

club together vi (*se cotiser*) if we club together, we can get one big present instead of lots of small ones

cobble together *vtsép* (*faire mal, expédier, bâcler*) my speech won't be very good I'm afraid – I cobbled it together on the train

collect up *vtsép* (*rassembler*) I began to collect up my parcels

comb through *vic* (*passer au peigne fin*) I've combed through the entire book and haven't found any reference to him

come across 1 *vi* (*faire une impression*) how did her story come across?; they come across as (being) rather nice people
  2 *vic* (*trouver par hasard*) I came across this when I was tidying up – is it yours?

come across with *vic Fam* (*fournir*) if we don't come across with the money, they say they'll kill him

come along *vi* **(a)** (*se dépêcher*) come along children, please!
  (b) (*avancer, progresser*) my speech was coming along rather well until yesterday **(c)** (*arriver*) everything was peaceful until you came along **(d)** (*venir aussi*) can I come along?

come apart *vi* (*se casser*) honestly, I don't know how it happened – it just came apart in my hands; (*s'écrouler*) she feels her life is coming apart at the seams

come at *vic* (*attaquer, agresser*) the pair of them came at me with a baseball bat

come away *vi* **(a)** (*partir*) why not come away with me to Paris for the weekend?; (*s'éloigner*) come away from that cat – it's got fleas **(b)** (*se détacher*) the handle has come away from the knife

come back *vi* **(a)** (*revenir*) I've forgotten your name but it will come back eventually **(b)** (*remonter, revenir en vogue, après avoir été dans une position basse*) we thought the fight was all over but he's coming back very strongly now; short hair is coming back **(c)** (*répliquer*) then she came back with one of her usual cutting remarks

come by 1 *vic* (*se faire*) how did your brother come by all those bruises?; (*trouver, dégoter*) I wonder where he came by all that money
  2 *vi* (*rendre visite*) I'll come by next week if that suits

come down *vi* **(a)** (*baisser*) oil prices have been coming down; her

temperature came down overnight **(b)** (*réduire de*) he'll come
down a few pounds if you bargain **(c)** (*disparaître, être enlevé*)
that disgusting poster is coming down right now – or else
(d) (*en être réduit à*) this is what we've come down to – selling
the family silver **(e)** (*revenir au problème de, se ramener à*) it all
comes down to money **(f)** (*descendre, atteindre*) the curtains
should come right down to the floor **(g)** (*parvenir à, par
héritage*) the necklace came down to her from her great-aunt

come down on *vic* **(a)** (*tomber sur le dos de*) one mistake and he'll
come down on you like a ton of bricks **(b)** (*décider pour*) he'll
wait and see what happens and then come down on the winning
side

come down with *vic* (*attraper, pour une maladie*) I always come down
with a cold at this time of year

come forward *vi* (*se présenter*) the police have appealed for witnesses
to come forward

come in *vi* **(a)** (*arriver*) our new stock will not come in until next week
(b) (*entrer en caisse, pour des sommes*) I don't have much
coming in at the moment – can you wait a bit? **(c)** (*avoir affaire*)
where does she come in in all this?; (*être, s'avérer*) an extra pair
of hands always comes in useful **(d)** (*contacter par radio*) are
you receiving me? come in, please

come in for *vic* (*recevoir*) the government is coming in for a lot of
criticism over its latest proposals; he came in for a lot of adverse
publicity when he was younger

come in on *vic* (*entrer dans*) why should we let him come in on the
deal?

come into *vic* **(a)** (*hériter de*) she'll come into a tidy little sum when
her great-uncle dies **(b)** (*être concerné par, engagé dans*) wait a
minute – when did I come into this crazy scheme?; (*avoir à voir*)
ability doesn't come into it – it's who you know that matters
(c) (*locutions*) to come into blossom *fleurir*; to come into effect
entrer en application; would you mind explaining how the car
came into your possession, sir? *est-ce que vous pourriez me
dire comment cette voiture est entrée en votre possession,
monsieur ?*

come of vic **(a)** (*résulter de*) nothing will come of it; this is what comes of being too self-confident **(b)** (*venir de*) the mare comes of good stock **(c)** (*locution*) she inherited a fortune when she came of age (*c.-à-d. atteindre la majorité*)

come off 1 vi **(a)** (*s'enlever, se détacher*) could you fix my bike? – the chain has come off; I'm afraid the carpet is ruined – wine stains never come off **(b)** (*avoir lieu*) I shall be very surprised if that wedding ever comes off **(c)** (*réussir*) yet another attempt to beat the record that hasn't come off **(d)** (*s'en tirer*) considering what he's done, he has come off very lightly; it could have been a serious accident, but they all came off without a scratch **(e)** (*s'en sortir, s'en tirer*) we came off very badly in the debate on capital punishment **(f)** *Pop* (*jouir*) he did eventually come off but it was a long wait

2 vic **(a)** (*partir de, s'en aller de, pour des taches, etc.*) that kind of mark never comes off silk **(b)** (*se détacher*) the handle has come off the knife; (*abandonner*) they're threatening to come off the gold standard **(c)** (*exclamation marquant l'impatience, l'incrédulité : ça va !, ça suffit !*) come off it – I've heard that line before

come on vi **(a)** (*se dépêcher*) come on, or we'll miss the start **(b)** (*progresser, avancer*) how's the work coming on? **(c)** (*commencer*) the rain came on about six; I have a sore throat coming on; when does that programme you want to watch come on? **(d)** (*entrer en scène*) the character he plays doesn't come on until halfway through the first act **(e)** *Pop* (*faire son/sa. . .*) she tried to come on like a femme fatale but soon gave it up; he was coming on a bit too macho

come out vi **(a)** (*sortir*) the magazine comes out on a Wednesday; when do you expect your latest film to come out?; now that the sun has come out maybe I'll get my washing dried; next door's roses always come out early **(b)** (*être connu*) the election results came out a few hours ago; the truth will come out eventually **(c)** (*faire la grève*) nurses all over the country have come out in protest **(d)** (*avoir, pour une éruption cutanée*) the baby has come out in a rash **(e)** (*bien sortir pour des photos*) they're pleased that their holiday photographs have come out so well **(f)** (*partir, pour des taches, etc.*) I've had this coat cleaned three times and the stain still hasn't come out **(g)** (*sortir d'hôpital, de prison*) she'll be coming out soon **(h)** (*se résoudre, pour un* *calcul*) of course the equation hasn't come out – you copied the figures down wrongly **(i)** (*se déclarer*) we've come out against the idea of moving; the committee came out in her favour **(j)** (*se sortir d'une situation*) she came out of that looking rather silly, don't you think?

come out with *vic* (*sortir, déballer, en général quelque chose que l'on n'attend pas*) I'm always on the edge of my seat wondering what he'll come out with next; she finally came out with what was bothering her

come over 1 *vi* **(a)** (*se ranger à*) I doubt if I will ever come over to your way of thinking **(b)** (*donner l'impression de*) he comes over as (being) a bit pompous, but in fact he's rather shy **(c)** (*se sentir, devenir*) Granny says she came over all funny in the supermarket
  2 *vic* (*prendre à, pour des sautes d'humeur*) I don't know what's come over her – she's usually such a quiet little thing

come round *vi* **(a)** (*revenir à d'autres sentiments*) give him time – he'll come round eventually; (*se ranger à*) I'm sure they'll come round to our point of view in the end **(b)** (*reprendre conscience*) imagine that poor woman coming round and seeing all those faces staring at her **(c)** (*revenir périodiquement*) he swears birthdays come round more often after you're 40

come through 1 *vi* **(a)** (*arriver, pour des documents officiels, etc.*) he's very annoyed because his visa is taking so long to come through **(b)** (*survivre*) it must have been a terrifying experience but they have come through all right
  2 *vic* **(a)** (*réussir*) their daughter has come through her law exams with flying colours **(b)** (*survivre à, se tirer indemne de*) I am sure you will come through this ordeal; very few people came through the First World War unscarred either physically or mentally

come to 1 *vi* (*reprendre conscience*) she came to in a hospital bed
  2 *vic* **(a)** (*revenir à*) the bill came to much more than I could afford; (*parvenir à*) that nephew of his will never come to anything; (*en être réduit à*) has it come to this, that we must leave a house our family has lived in for 400 years?
  (b) (*être question de*) when it comes to buying a car, find yourself a reputable dealer **(c)** (*aller jusqu'à*) if it comes to a malpractice suit, the surgeon is in trouble; when does the case

come to trial? (*c.-à-d. être entendu*); (*en venir à*) I do wish she would come to the point **(d)** (*locution*) come to that, where were you last night? *à propos, où étais-tu hier soir ?*

come up *vi* (*être entendu, pour des affaires juridiques, un procès*) when does her case come up (for trial)?; (*être soulevé*) he beat a hasty retreat when the subject of fee-paying schools came up; (*sortir, être posé*) do you think this question will come up in the exam?; (*être prochainement*) two other houses in our street are coming up for sale soon; (*sortir*) my number never comes up in the draw; the bulbs are starting to come up; (*arriver, se passer*) call me if anything comes up that you can't handle

come up against *vic* (*rencontrer, pour des obstacles, etc.*) you realize that you'll come up against some pretty strong opposition on this?; who does she come up against in the next round?

come up to *vic* **(a)** (*arriver à*) she's so tall that I only come up to her shoulder; we're coming up to the halfway mark now **(b)** (*répondre à*) his latest play does not come up to expectations

come up with *vic* (*trouver, concocter*) she's come up with a solution; he keeps coming up with these awful jokes; I'll let you know if I come up with anything that might help

conk out *vi Fam* **(a)** (*s'arrêter de marcher*) the radio has conked out on us **(b)** (*perdre conscience*) he's conked out – better send for a doctor

cool down 1 *vi* **(a)** (*se calmer*) we'll talk about it once you've cooled down **(b)** (*se rafraîchir, refroidir*) it has cooled down quite a bit since yesterday; let the soup cool down a bit; things have cooled down between them (*c.-à-d. la passion commence à disparaître*) **2** *vtsép* **(a)** (*calmer*) I'll try to cool her down but I don't think I'll have much success **(b)** (*rafraîchir*) how about a beer to cool you down after all that hard work?

cotton on *vi Fam* (*piger*) I never did cotton on

cough up 1 *vtsép* **(a)** (*cracher en toussant*) if you can cough the phlegm up, you'll soon feel better; people with tuberculosis cough up blood **(b)** *Fam* (*payer*) I've got to cough up another £50 **2** *vi Fam* (*payer*) he coughed up for the meal

count in *vtsép* (*inclure*) have you counted the neighbours in?; anybody want to go out for lunch? – count me in!

count on *vic* (*compter sur*) we can always count on you to be late; he counted on me and I let him down

count out *vtsép* **(a)** (*compter*) if you want to know how much money you have, count it out **(b)** (*faire le compte, en boxe*) his opponent is on the canvas and being counted out **(c)** (*exclure*) he's teetotal, so count him out of the pub crawl; (*ne pas compter sur*) a weekend camping out in the snow? – no thanks, count me out!

count up *vtsép* (*faire l'addition de*) I've counted these figures up time and time again and get a different answer every time

cover up 1 *vi* (*dissimuler*) don't try to cover up – I know it was you; the government was accused of covering up; (*couvrir pour protéger*) the architects and builders are covering up for each other **2** *vtsép* **(a)** (*couvrir*) that dress is much too low – cover yourself up a bit **(b)** (*cacher, dissimuler*) it's highly unlikely that he meant to cover things up

crack down *vi* (*devenir plus strict*) in view of the increase in drunk driving the police are going to crack down

crack down on *vic* (*devenir plus strict envers*) they're going to crack down on drunk drivers

crack up *vi* **1 (a)** (*craquer*) the ice on the pond is cracking up **(b)** (*s'effondrer, craquer*) if he doesn't take a holiday soon, he'll crack up; do you think their marriage is cracking up?; she cracked up under the pressure **(c)** (*éclater de rire*) I cracked up when he said that **2** *vtsép* *Fam* (*locution*) foreign holidays are not what they're cracked up to be *les vacances à l'étranger ne sont pas à la hauteur de leur réputation*

cream off *vtsép* (*écrémer, prendre le meilleur de*) the oldest universities cream off the best candidates

cross off *vtsép** (*rayer*) cross his name off the list

cross out *vtsép* (*barrer*) cross your mistakes out neatly, please

cry off *vi* (*se décommander*) I hate it when people cry off at the last minute

cry out *vi* **(a)** (*crier de douleur*) the pain made her cry out
(b) (*avoir grand besoin de*) that room is just crying out for red velvet curtains

cuddle up *vi* (*se pelotonner*) cuddle up if you're cold; the little girl cuddled up to her grandmother

curl up *vi* **(a)** (*s'installer confortablement*) I like to curl up in bed with a good book **(b)** (*s'enrouler*) hedgehogs curl up into a ball for protection

cut across *vic* **(a)** (*couper à travers*) we cut across the playing field **(b)** (*dépasser, transcender*) concern for the environment cuts across party lines

cut back 1 *vi* (*faire des économies*) we're definitely going to have to cut back
2 *vtsép* (*tailler*) now is the time to cut your raspberries back; (*réduire*) the company is cutting back production until the seamen's strike is over

cut down 1 *vtsép* **(a)** (*couper*) they're cutting down the trees that were damaged in the storm **(b)** (*tuer, abattre*) he was cut down by machine-gun fire
2 *vi* (*réduire la consommation*) if you won't stop smoking then at least cut down

cut in 1 *vi* **(a)** (*interrompre*) the interviewer cut in to ask a question **(b)** (*faire une queue de poisson*) that idiot will cause an accident cutting in in front of people like that
2 *vtsép* (*faire participer*) can you cut me in on one of your deals?

cut off *vtsép* **(a)** (**découper, couper*) they had to cut his clothes off in the emergency room; cut off his head! **(b)** (*couper, isoler*) the town has been cut off by floods; don't you feel cut off living in the country? **(c)** (*couper, pour l'électricité et le téléphone*) we'd hardly said hello before we were cut off; it's dreadful to think how many people have their electricity cut off because they can't afford to pay the bills **(d)** (*déshériter*) the old man cut his son off without the proverbial penny

cut out 1 *vi* (*caler, pour un moteur*) will you have a look at the engine – it keeps cutting out
2 *vtsép* **(a)** (*découper*) I cut this magazine article out for you

(b) (*couper*) the worst bit is cutting the dress out **(c)** (*éliminer*) cut out starchy food for a couple of weeks **(d)** *Fam* (*arrêter*) I've told you already to cut out the silly jokes

cut out for *vttsc Fig habituellement au passif* (*être fait pour*) I'm not cut out for all these late nights

cut up *vtsép* **(a)** (*couper*) cut the meat up quite small
(b) *habituellement au passif* (*affecter, froisser*) he was definitely a bit cut up about not being invited

D

dash off 1 *vi* (*partir précipitamment*) she was sorry she missed you but she had to dash off
    2 *vtsép* (*rédiger en vitesse*) I dashed off an answer yesterday; (*faire en un tour de main*) he says he dashes these paintings off in his spare time

deal with *vic* **(a)** (*traiter avec, avoir affaire à*) armament manufacturers will deal with anybody **(b)** (*s'occuper de, prendre en charge*) she dealt with that problem very well; the case wasn't very professionally dealt with **(c)** (*traiter de*) the play deals with euthanasia

die away *vi* (*s'éteindre, mourir*) the noise of the car engine died away

die down *vi* (*s'apaiser, diminuer*) he had to wait for the applause to die down

die off *vi* (*mourir les uns après les autres*) by the time he was in his twenties, his relatives had all died off; their livestock is dying off as the drought intensifies

die out *vi* (*s'éteindre, disparaître*) entire species are dying out as their habitat is destroyed

dig in 1 *vi* **(a)** (*creuser des tranchées*) the first thing the troops had to do when they got to the front was to dig in **(b)** *Fam* (*commencer à manger, attaquer le repas*) dig in – there's lots more where that came from
    2 *vtsép* (*mélanger à la pelle*) before planting, dig in a couple of handfuls of fertilizer

dig into *vic* **(a)** *Fam* (*entamer sérieusement*) dig into that pie as much as you like – I made two **(b)** (*fouiller dans*) they want us to dig into her past

dig out *vtsép* **(a)** (*déterrer*) dig out the roots **(b)** (*dégager, pour des catastrophes, etc.*) they hope to have the remaining survivors dug out by nightfall **(c)** (*dénicher, trouver*) have you dug those files out yet?; we want more information on the company's early days, so see what you can dig out

dig up *vtsép* **(a)** (*déterrer*) this rose bush will have to be dug up and moved **(b)** (*trouver, dénicher*) we're hoping to dig up some items to show that there was a Roman encampment here; I've dug something up that might prove he's been lying to us

dip into *vic* **(a)** (*tremper rapidement dans*) she dipped her toes into the bath water to test it **(b)** (*puiser dans, utiliser une partie de*) she doesn't want to dip into her savings if she can help it **(c)** (*feuilleter, lire par petits morceaux*) this is the kind of anthology to be dipped into rather than read all at once

dish out *vtsép* **(a)** (*servir*) Mum's dishing supper out now **(b)** (*donner, sortir, pour des ordres ou des conseils qui ne sont pas désirés*) you're always dishing out advice!

dish up 1 *vtsép* (*servir*) somebody dish up the soup
2 *vi* (*servir*) when will you be dishing up?

dispense with *vic* (*se passer de*) he called it "dispensing with my services" – I call it getting the sack

dispose of *vic* **(a)** (*se débarrasser de*) dispose of your waste paper here **(b)** *Fam* (*tuer, liquider*) we have to dispose of him before he talks **(c)** (*se débarrasser de, régler son compte à*) so far she has disposed of six opponents who want to take the title away from her

divide out *vtsép* (*distribuer*) they divided the food out

divide up *vtsép* (*diviser, répartir*) contestants will be divided up into groups of four

do away with *vic* **(a)** (*abolir*) they should do away with school **(b)** (*supprimer, tuer*) he has threatened to do away with himself

do by *vic* *Fam* (*traiter*) the company did very badly by its employees;

she did very well by her grand-daughter at Christmas; he'll feel very hard done by if you don't at least send him a birthday card

do down *vtsép* **(a)** (*duper, rouler*) why did you let the salesman do you down? **(b)** (*dire du mal de*) there's always someone ready to do you down

do for *vic Fam* **(a)** (*tuer*) if he keeps on treating her this way, she'll do for him **(b)** (*épuiser, flanquer en l'air*) it was that last hill that did for me **(c)** (*faire le ménage pour*) who does for you?

do in *vtsép Fam* **(a)** (*tuer, supprimer*) somebody on our street was done in last night **(b)** (*épuiser, éreinter*) Christmas shopping always does me in

do out *vtsép* (*nettoyer, faire*) will you do the kitchen out tomorrow please, Mrs Jones?

do out of *vttsc Fam* (*escroquer pour*) he always maintained that he had been done out of his inheritance; they did him out of his share of the money

do over *vtsép* **(a)** (*redécorer*) the whole house needs doing over **(b)** *Fam* (*tabasser*) the other gang did him over **(c)** *Am* (*refaire*) the teacher said I had to do my project over

do up 1 *vi* (*se fermer, se boutonner*) clothes that do up at the front pose fewer problems for people in wheelchairs
2 *vtsép* **(a)** (*attacher, fermer*) do your buttons up
(b) (*envelopper*) it seems a pity to open it when it's done up so nicely **(c)** (*remettre à neuf*) they're doing up all the buildings on the street; (*mettre sur son trente et un*) you've really done yourself up – what's the occasion?

do with *vic* **(a)** *utilisé avec 'could'* (*avoir besoin de*) you could do with a haircut; what I could be doing with right now is a hot bath
(b) (*être en relation avec, avoir affaire avec*) he has something to do with computers; it sounds very fishy to me and you should have nothing to do with it; that's got nothing to do with it!; it has to do with your mother, I'm afraid; my business has nothing to do with you **(c)** (*finir de*) I've done with trying to help people; (*en finir avec*) he says it's all over – he's done with her
(d) (*finir d'utiliser*) if you've done with the hammer, put it back where it belongs

do without 1 *vic* (*se passer de*) we can do without the sarcasm
   2 *vi* (*se passer*) if you don't find anything you like in here then you'll have to do without

double back 1 *vi* (*revenir sur ses pas*) they felt they ought to double back since they didn't recognize any landmarks
   2 *vtsép* (*replier*) double back the bedclothes and let the mattress air

double over/up *vi* (*se plier, se tordre*) the pain struck again and she doubled over; the joke made me double up

double up *vi* (*partager un lit, une chambre, etc.*) with so many guests coming, some of them are going to have to double up; do you mind doubling up with me?

drag behind 1 *vtsép** (*tirer, traîner*) I made for the bus stop, dragging my cases behind me
   2 *vi* (*être à la traîne, être en retard*) you're dragging behind in maths

drag in *vtsép* **(a)** (*tirer à l'intérieur*) the trunk is too heavy to lift – let's just drag it in **(b)** *Fam* (*tenir à placer, ramener dans la conversation*) why do you have to drag in the one mistake I made?

drag on *vi* (*s'éterniser*) the play dragged on and on

drag out *vtsép* (*faire durer, faire traîner*) I had to drag my presentation out to fill the time allotted to me

drag up *vtsép* **(a)** (**monter en tirant*) drag it up the stairs
   (b) *Fam* (*amener*) you dragged me up to London for this?
   (c) (*remettre sur le tapis*) there's no need to drag up the past
   (d) *Fam* (*élever tant bien que mal*) those children are being dragged up, not brought up; where were you dragged up?

draw alongside 1 *vi* (*se mettre côte à côte*) then this big Mercedes drew alongside . . .
   2 *vic* (*se mettre côte à côte avec*) the Customs launch drew alongside the liner

draw away 1 *vi* **(a)** (*partir*) we waved as the car drew away
   (b) (*prendre de l'avance, se détacher*) the first half dozen runners are now beginning to draw away **(c)** (*s'écarter*) I can't help drawing away when he touches me

    2 *vtsép* (*écarter, éloigner, mettre à part*) she drew us away
from the other guests

draw back 1 *vi* (*reculer*) she drew back from the edge of the cliff
    2 *vtsép* **(a)** (*ramener*) what drew you back to music?
(b) (*ouvrir, tirer*) he draw back the curtains and light flooded
into the room

draw in 1 *vi* **(a)** (*arriver*) the train will be drawing in soon; the car
drew in to the drive **(b)** (*raccourcir, pour des jours et des nuits*)
the days have started to draw in again
    2 *vtsép* **(a)** (*amener*) fresh air from outside is drawn in by these
ventilators **(b)** (*impliquer*) they were arguing again and I left
because I didn't want to be drawn in

draw on 1 *vi* **(a)** (*approcher*) as summer drew on . . . **(b)** (*s'avancer,
pour le temps*) as the day gradually drew on
    2 *vic* (*faire appel à, utiliser*) for this essay, I want you to draw
on your own childhood memories
    3 *vtsép* (*enfiler*) she drew on a pair of long white gloves

draw out 1 *vi* **(a)** (*partir*) they waved as the train drew out
(b) (*allonger, pour des jours et des nuits*) after Christmas, the
days start to draw out
    2 *vtsép* **(a)** (*sortir*) she drew out a gun; (*retirer, pour de
l'argent*) I've drawn out all my savings **(b)** (*prolonger*) they
drew the meeting out on purpose **(c)** (*faire parler*) I managed to
draw her out on her plans

draw up 1 *vi* (*s'arrêter, en voiture*) he drew up with a squeal of brakes
    2 *vtsép* **(a)** (*établir, mettre au point*) I think we should draw up
a plan of action; (*formuler*) the old lady drew up a new will
(b) (*approcher*) draw up a chair and join us

dream away *vtsép* (*passer en rêvant*) he'll dream his whole life away
at this rate

dream up *vtsép* (*concevoir, pour des projets irréels, etc.*) they've
dreamed up some scheme that they say will make us all rich

dredge up *vtsép* **(a)** (*draguer*) the barges are dredging up silt
(b) (*ressortir*) where did you dredge that old scandal up?

dress up 1 *vi* **(a)** (*s'habiller, avec élégance*) for that special occasion
when you want to dress up . . . **(b)** (*se déguiser*) it's a

Hallowe'en party and everybody has to dress up
2 *vtsép* **(a)** (*habiller, avec élégance*) she dressed herself up for
the wedding **(b)** (*déguiser*) you could dress yourself up as
Pierrot

drink down *vtsép* (*avaler*) drink this down and you'll soon feel better

drink in *vtsép* (*boire*) these plants will drink in as much water as you
care to give them; *Fig* (*boire, pour des paroles, etc.*) I'm
drinking in your every word

drink up 1 *vi* (*finir son verre, etc.*) drink up and I'll get the next round
2 *vtsép* (*finir*) have you drunk up your tea?

drive at *vic* (*vouloir dire*) I'm sorry, but I really don't see what you're
driving at; did you think she was driving at something when she
said she couldn't afford a holiday this year?

drive back 1 *vi* (*rentrer en voiture*) are you driving back or taking the
train?
2 *vtsép* **(a)** (*ramener en voiture*) George will drive you back to
your hotel **(b)** (*repousser*) the soldiers did not have the strength
to drive back another attack

drive home *vtsép* **(a)** (*enfoncer à fond*) once you have driven the
screws home . . . **(b)** (*faire comprendre*) I tried to drive it home
to them that this was not an isolated incident

drive off 1 *vi* (*partir en voiture*) he drove off about an hour ago
2 *vtsép* **(a)** (*emmener en voiture*) all three of them were driven
off in an unmarked police car **(b)** (*repousser, refouler*) the
attackers were driven off when reinforcements arrived

drive on 1 *vi* (*poursuivre sa route, en voiture*) he decided to drive on
rather than stop there for the night
2 *vtsép* (*inciter, pousser*) her friends drove her on to sue

drive up *vi* (*arriver, pour une voiture*) a car/he has just driven up

drop back *vi* (*prendre du retard*) he has dropped back and it looks as if
he's given up the race

drop behind 1 *vi* (*prendre du retard, se laisser dépasser*) you're
dropping behind – do try to keep up
2 *vic* (*se laisser distancer par*) that last lap exhausted her and
now she's dropping behind the leaders

drop in 1 *vi* (*passer, faire un court arrêt*) I'll drop in and see mother tomorrow; would you drop in at the supermarket on your way home?

    2 *vtsép** (*déposer*) drop this in (the night safe) for me, will you?

drop off 1 *vi* **(a)** (*tomber*) with all this heavy shopping to carry, I feel as if my arms are going to drop off **(b)** (*s'endormir*) it was 4 am before she dropped off; why don't you go to bed instead of dropping off in the chair? **(c)** (*diminuer*) church attendance has been dropping off for many years

    2 *vtsép* (*déposer*) drop these books off at the library; (*déposer, en voiture*) where do you want to be dropped off?

drop out *vi* **(a)** (*tomber*) there's a hole in your pocket and the keys must have dropped out **(b)** *Fam* (*arrêter ses études, un cours, etc.*) he dropped out at the age of 14; so many have dropped out that the course may be cancelled; (*choisir de vivre en marge de la société*) in the sixties a lot of people dropped out (of society) and went off to places like India

drum into *vttsc* (*seriner à, répéter à*) drum it into the children that they mustn't take sweets from strangers

drum up *vtsép* (*trouver, décrocher*) how are you drumming up support for the campaign?; we must drum up some more business

dry off 1 *vi* (*sécher*) don't touch the varnish while it's drying off

    2 *vtsép* (*sécher*) come and dry yourself off in front of the fire

dry out 1 *vi* **(a)** (*sécher*) leave your wet things in the bathroom to dry out **(b)** (*se désintoxiquer, pour l'alcool*) I think she's somewhere drying out

    2 *vtsép* (*assécher, rendre sec*) soap can dry your skin out

dry up 1 *vi* **(a)** (*s'assécher*) streams and rivers are drying up because of this long heat wave **(b)** (*rester sec, avoir un trou de mémoire*) she was haunted by the thought that she might dry up in the middle of her big speech in the second act **(c)** *Pop* (*se taire*) why don't you dry up?

    2 *vtsép* (*essuyer*) dry the bathroom floor up

dwell (up)on *vic* (*penser à, s'appesantir sur*) get on with your life instead of dwelling on what might have been

E

ease off/up *vi* (*calmer le rythme, ralentir*) he's been told to ease off if he doesn't want a heart attack; ease up – there's a 30 mile an hour limit here

eat away *vtsép* (*éroder, ronger*) the action of the waves is eating the coastline away

eat in *vi* (*prendre ses repas chez soi*) I'm tired of eating in all the time

eat into *vic* (*diminuer*) long term unemployment eats into people's self-confidence; (*entamer*) it's silly to eat into your savings when you could get a bank loan

eat out 1 *vi* (*aller au restaurant*) let's eat out tonight
   2 *vtsép* (*locution*) the child is eating her heart out for a pony *l'enfant meurt d'envie d'avoir un poney*

eat up 1 *vtsép* **(a)** (*finir*) eat up your spinach **(b)** *Fig* (*dévorer*) jealousy is eating him up
   2 *vi* (*finir son repas*) eat up, the taxi's waiting; eat up, there's lots more (*c.-à-d. régale-toi, il y en a beaucoup*)

edge out 1 *vi* (*sortir avec une extrême prudence*) I opened the window and cautiously edged out
   2 *vtsép* **(a)** (*aller avec une extrême prudence*) she edged her way out on to the ledge **(b)** (*démettre de ses fonctions petit à petit*) there's a move to edge him out of the chairmanship

egg on *vtsép* (*encourager*) it was sickening to hear the crowd egg the boxers on; I wish I hadn't let you egg me on to accept

end up *vi* (*finir*) no one ever thought she would end up in prison; how did the film end up?; I ended up telling him in no uncertain terms what I thought

enter into *vic* **(a)** (*passer, pour un marché, etc.*) we entered into this contract with our eyes open **(b)** (*avoir affaire avec*) morality rarely enters into foreign policy

enter (up)on *vic* (*commencer, débuter*) she has entered on a new career

even out 1 *vi* (*tourner autour de, pour des sommes, des quantités, etc.*) production figures are evening out at about 5,000 per week

2 *vtsép (partager d'une façon égale)* we have to even out the burden of caring for the handicapped

even up *vtsép* **(a)** *(égaliser)* that last goal evened up the score; if you pay for the meal, that will even things up **(b)** *(arrondir à une somme supérieure)* I hate these odd pennies – just even it up to a pound

explain away *vtsép (justifier, d'une façon peu plausible)* he tried to explain away his absence from the last meeting; explain this away if you can

eye up *vtsép Fam (regarder, lorgner)* I passed the time eyeing up all the men; he eyed up every one of the women at the party

F

face up to *vic* **(a)** *(accepter, pour une réalité)* we'll have to face up to the fact that we're not getting any younger **(b)** *(affronter)* it might help if she faced up to her fears of rejection

fade away *vi (s'éteindre)* the sound of the procession faded away; *(disparaître)* old soldiers never die, they merely fade away

fade in 1 *vi (monter, apparaître progressivement, dans un film)* the music faded in
    2 *vtsép (faire apparaître en fondu, dans un film)* fade in the crowd scenes

fade out 1 *vi (disparaître progressivement, dans un film)* the music fades out for the last few seconds
    2 *vtsép (faire disparaître en fondu, dans un film)* fade out the crowd scenes

fall about *vi (se tordre de rire)* her scripts always make me fall about

fall away *vi* **(a)** *(descendre en pente)* be careful – the ground falls away here **(b)** *(baisser, diminuer)* attendance at committee meetings has been falling away recently

fall back *vi (reculer)* the demonstrators fell back when they saw the water cannon

fall back on *vic* (*utiliser en cas d'urgence*) I suppose we can always fall back on temporary staff

fall behind *vi* **(a)** (*se laisser distancer*) he began well but now seems to be falling behind **(b)** (*prendre du retard*) you mustn't fall behind with the payments

fall down *vi* **(a)** (*tomber par terre*) he fell down and bumped his head **(b)** (*s'écrouler*) why don't they demolish that old building instead of letting it fall down? **(c)** (*achopper, échouer*) that's where their argument falls down; if you fall down on this, she won't give you another chance

fall for *vic* **(a)** (*être attiré par, en pincer pour*) he has fallen for the girl next door; I've really fallen for that Victorian chair in the antique shop **(b)** (*se laisser tromper par*) you didn't fall for that old story, did you?

fall in with *vic* **(a)** (*finir par accepter*) I fell in with the plans for a picnic because the children were so keen **(b)** (*s'associer à, fréquenter*) the teenager next door has fallen in with a bad crowd

fall off *vi* **(a)** (*tomber*) I was terrified of falling off and clung to the chimney for dear life **(b)** (*diminuer*) enrolment is falling off

fall on *vic* **(a)** (*retomber sur*) if anything goes wrong you can be sure that the blame will not fall on him **(b)** (*attaquer*) they fell on the meal as if they hadn't eaten for days

fall out *vi* **(a)** (*tomber*) the window is open so be careful you don't fall out **(b)** (*se disputer*) my sister and I have fallen out

fall over 1 *vi* (*tomber, basculer*) the vase is top-heavy, that's why it keeps falling over
2 *vic* **(a)** (*trébucher sur*) move your suitcase before someone falls over it **(b)** (*vouloir à tout prix*) he was falling over himself to buy the woman a drink

fall through *vi* (*échouer*) their plans for a skiing holiday have fallen through

farm out *vtsép* (*donner en sous-traitance*) if deadlines are to be met then some of the work will have to be farmed out; (*confier, donner à garder*) those two next door are always farming their kids out

feed in *vtsép** (*entrer, dans un ordinateur*) the keyboarders feed the data in

feed up *vtsép* (*faire manger plus que la normale, gaver*) Mum always wants to feed us up when we come home for the weekend

feel up *vtsép Fam* (*toucher sans permission, peloter*) I slapped his face for feeling me up

feel up to *vic* (*se sentir capable de*) I don't feel up to cooking a big meal tonight – let's go out; he suggested a long walk but she didn't feel up to it; do you feel up to a visit from my mother?

fetch up 1 *vi* (*se retrouver*) we eventually fetched up in a tiny little village in the middle of nowhere; the road was very icy and they fetched up in a ditch
2 *vtsép* (*vomir*) he fetched up his dinner

fiddle about/around *vi* **(a)** (*bricoler*) he fiddled about for ages and still couldn't get the car to go **(b)** (*perdre son temps*) why don't you stop fiddling about and get down to some work?

fight back 1 *vi* **(a)** (*rendre les coups*) everybody encounters a bully at some time – you must learn to fight back **(b)** (*recouvrir*) he has been ill but is now fighting back
2 *vtsép* (*refouler*) I fought back my anger and tried to answer calmly

fight down *vtsép* (*se battre contre*) you must fight down these fears

fight off *vtsép* (*repousser*) government troops have fought off a number of attacks; his bodyguards had to fight off over-eager fans

fight on *vi* (*poursuivre le combat*) she regards this as merely a setback and is determined to fight on

fight out *vtsép* (*régler, en se battant ou se disputant*) you'll have to fight this one out; I left them to fight it out

figure on *vic* (*compter sur*) I didn't figure on your mother coming too; he didn't figure on a woman for the position

figure out *vtsép* **(a)** (*comprendre*) she can't figure you out at all **(b)** (*arriver à comprendre*) how did you figure it out that he was the culprit?; the dog figured out how to open the door; (*calculer*) we figured out that they must be paying three times as much rent as we are

fill in 1 *vi* (*faire un remplacement temporaire*) this isn't her normal job – she's just filling in; who'll be filling in for you while you're on holiday?

    2 *vtsép* **(a)** (*boucher, mettre à niveau*) workmen are filling those potholes in at last **(b)** (*remplir*) I must have filled in twenty forms **(c)** (*informer*) will someone please fill us in on what's been happening? **(d)** (*faire passer, pour le temps*) are you busy or just filling in time?

fill out 1 *vi* (*prendre du poids, s'arrondir*) he's beginning to fill out at last after his long illness

    2 *vtsép* (*remplir*) will you fill out this form please?

fill up 1 *vi* (*se remplir*) the room was filling up

    2 *vtsép* **(a)** (*faire le plein d'essence dans une voiture par exemple*) fill her up; (*remplir, pour un récipient*) let me fill your glass up **(b)** (*remplir, pour un formulaire*) there are one or two forms to be filled up first

filter out 1 *vi* (*quitter lentement*) mourners filtered out of the church; (*sortir lentement*) information is beginning to filter out that . . .

    2 *vtsép* (*filtrer*) filter out the impurities

find out 1 *vtsép* (*trouver, découvrir*) I could have found that out for myself

    2 *vi* (*découvrir ce qui était caché, secret*) has your wife found out yet?

finish off 1 *vtsép* **(a)** (*finir*) let me just finish this chapter off; finish off your lunch; you can finish off the cream if you like **(b)** (*épuiser*) all that heavy digging has finished him off **(c)** (*tuer, abattre*) the men were finished off with a bullet through the skull

    2 *vi* (*finir*) what did you have to finish off with?

finish up 1 *vtsép* (*finir*) finish up your lunch; don't finish up the pie

    2 *vi* (*se retrouver, finir*) we finished up in the pub down the road; he'll finish up in court; (*finir par devenir*) any more of this uncertainty and I'll finish up a nervous wreck

fire away *vi Fam* (*commencer, surtout à parler ou à poser des questions*) fire away – I'm all ears

fish out *vtsép* **(a)** (*sortir, repêcher*) they fished him out of the river **(b)** (*sortir, extirper*) just let me fish the keys out

fish up *vtsép* (*sortir*) she fished her purse up from the bottom of the bag

fit in 1 *vtsép** (*trouver la place pour, coincer*) could you fit this pair of shoes in the case?; (*trouver une place dans un planning, prendre*) the hairdresser says she can fit me in tomorrow
    2 *vi* **(a)** (*rentrer*) there's not enough room, the books won't fit in **(b)** (*concorder*) that doesn't fit in with what I was told **(c)** (*s'arranger*) how does that fit in with your plans?; (*être à sa place, s'intégrer*) I hate parties like this – I never feel that I fit in

fix on 1 *vtsép** (*attacher*) he fixed the handle on for me
    2 *vic* (*choisir, décider de*) have you fixed on a date yet?

fix up 1 *vtsép* **(a)** (*monter*) the marquee will be fixed up on their front lawn **(b)** (*arranger, prendre*) I've fixed up a blind date for you **(c)** (*fournir*) our in-laws will fix us up with a bed **(d)** (*arranger, spécialement l'apparence*) they're busy fixing up the house; if you're going out, don't you think you should fix yourself up a bit first?
    2 *vi* (*décider, prévoir*) I'm sorry but I've already fixed up to go out

fizzle out *vi* (*diminuer, tomber, pour des sentiments, etc.*) people's enthusiasm is starting to fizzle out; (*ne pas aboutir, s'en aller à vau-l'eau*) all those big plans we had have just fizzled out

flag down *vtsép* (*arrêter*) it's impossible to flag a taxi down when it's raining; I was cycling along when a policeman flagged me down

flake out *vi Fam* (*s'endormir, tomber comme une masse, tomber dans les pommes*) six late nights in succession – no wonder you flaked out; I just want to flake out on the couch

flare up *vi* **(a)** (*s'embraser, prendre*) the fire flared up, turning night into day **(b)** (*éclater*) the argument flared up when she said something about favouritism; (*se mettre en colère*) he flares up at the least little thing

flip over 1 *vtsép* (*retourner*) do you want your egg flipped over?; (*feuilleter*) she was flipping over the pages of a magazine
    2 *vi* (*se retourner, d'un coup*) the plane just seemed to flip over

float (a)round *vi* **(a)** (*circuler*) rumours have been floating around about your resignation **(b)** (*traîner*) I'm just floating around until my sister comes out of the hairdresser's

flood in *vi* (*entrer à flots, affluer*) when she opened the door water
flooded in; people are flooding in to see this film; light flooded
in through the windows

flood out *vtsép habituellement au passif* (*être forcé à partir à cause
des inondations*) thousands of people in Bangladesh have been
flooded out

fly in 1 *vi* (*arriver par avion*) the royal visitors will fly in tomorrow
2 *vtsép* (*amener par avion*) the army will fly troops in if
necessary

fly off *vi* **(a)** (*partir par avion, voler*) they flew off in a helicopter
(b) (*s'envoler*) his toupee flew off in the wind

fly out 1 *vi* (*partir par avion*) the President flew out this morning;
which airport are you flying out of?
2 *vtsép* (*amener par avion, faire voyager par avion*) troops are
being flown out as quickly as possible; the company is flying her
out to be with her husband

fly past 1 *vic* (*survoler*) the squadron will fly past the airfield at
precisely two o'clock
2 *vi* (*s'envoler*) the weekend has just flown past

fold away 1 *vi* (*se plier*) does this table fold away?
2 *vtsép* (*plier et ranger*) fold your clothes away neatly; she
folded the tablecloth away

follow on *vi* **(a)** (*suivre*) you go ahead – we'll follow on **(b)** (*continuer*)
how did the story follow on? **(c)** (*résulter*) it follows on from
this that . . .

follow out *vtsép* (*exécuter*) he followed out his plans

follow through 1 *vtsép* (*poursuivre jusqu'au bout*) she firmly intends
to follow the idea through
2 *vi* (*accompagner son coup, sa balle*) the problem is that
you're not following through after you hit the ball

follow up 1 *vtsép* **(a)** (*poursuivre, suivre*) the police are following up a
number of leads; I want you to follow the matter up
(b) (*appuyer, compléter*) he followed up his complaint to the
shop with an angry letter to the manufacturer
2 *vi* (*poursuivre l'action*) he followed up with a right to the jaw

fool around *vi* **(a)** (*perdre son temps*) he spent too much time just fooling around **(b)** (*faire l'imbécile*) don't fool around with that glue or you'll get it all over you **(c)** *Fam* (*avoir une liaison*) she thinks her husband is fooling around

fork out *Fam* **1** *vtsép* (*fournir, à contre-cœur*) I suppose Daddy forked out the cash for the repairs to your new Porsche
    2 *vi* (*payer, surtout à contre-cœur*) we're all going to have to fork out

freak out *vi Pop* (*se mettre en colère*) Mum will freak out when she sees that you've dyed your hair blue

frighten away/off *vtsép* (*effrayer*) we keep a couple of Dobermanns to frighten off potential burglars; don't look so grim or you'll frighten people away

frown on *vic* (*désapprouver*) they all frowned on my suggestion; her parents frowned on her marriage to a man so much younger

G

gain on *vic* (*rattraper*) they're gaining on us

gear up **1** *vi* (*se préparer*) the shops are already gearing up for Christmas
    2 *vtsép* (*préparer*) businesses are getting geared up for 1992

get about *vi* **(a)** (*se déplacer, sortir de chez soi*) he doesn't get about much these days **(b)** (*se répandre*) a rumour has got about that you're leaving

get across **1** *vi* **(a)** (*traverser*) there are no traffic lights there so I found it difficult to get across **(b)** (*communiquer, se faire comprendre*) she can't get across to her audience
    2 *vtts* **(a)** (*faire traverser*) because of flooding, they will be unable to get much needed supplies across the river
    (b) (*faire comprendre*) did you get it across to her just how important it was?

get along *vi* **(a)** (*partir*) I must be getting along **(b)** (*s'entendre bien*) I wish I got along better with my neighbours **(c)** how are you getting along in the new house? (*c.-à-d. comment ça se passe ?*)

get around 1 *vi* **(a)** (*se déplacer, avoir une vie sociale importante*) handicapped people who find it hard to get around; that young man really gets around! **(b)** (*se répandre*) I wonder how that story got around
    2 *vic* (*éviter, contourner*) there's no getting around it, you'll have to tell him what happened; can we get around this difficulty?

get at *vic* **(a)** (*arriver à*) their house is very easy to get at **(b)** (*découvrir*) he intends to get at the truth **(c)** (*vouloir dire*) do you mind telling me what you're getting at? **(d)** (*critiquer, faire des remarques à*) his father is always getting at him for the length of his hair **(e)** *Fam* (*influencer, par des menaces*) the trial could not continue because a number of witnesses had been got at and refused to testify

get away 1 *vi* **(a)** (*partir*) I usually get away by six; will they manage to get away this year? **(b)** (*s'enfuir*) the terrorists got away in a stolen car
    2 *vtts* (*prendre, arracher des mains*) the policeman managed to get the gun away

get away with *vic* **(a)** (*s'enfuir avec*) the thieves got away with the old lady's life savings **(b)** (*s'en sortir avec*) he got away with a small fine of £10 **(c)** (*locution*) that child gets away with murder! *il tuerait père et mère qu'on lui pardonnerait!*

get back 1 *vi* **(a)** (*rentrer, revenir*) when did you get back?; I must be getting back soon **(b)** (*reculer*) get back from the edge of the cliff!
    2 *vtsép* **(a)** (*faire revenir*) the priest got the distraught woman back from the window ledge by promising that something would be done **(b)** (*obtenir le retour de*) I'll get it back from him tomorrow **(c)** (*rendre*) get the file back to me as soon as you can

get back at *vic* (*se venger de*) I'll get back at you for that

get back to *vic* **(a)** (*se remettre à, reprendre*) I must get back to work soon **(b)** (*revenir à, pour une information*) can we get back to you on that point later?

get behind 1 *vi* (*prendre du retard*) I've got so behind that I'm working late every night this week

    2 *vic* (*se cacher derrière*) get behind that tree

get by 1 *vi* **(a)** (*passer*) the car could not get by because of the roadworks **(b)** (*s'en sortir, se débrouiller*) he thinks he'll get by without studying; it must be difficult getting by on so little money; do you think I'll get by in Greece without speaking the language?

    2 *vic* **(a)** (*dépasser*) can I get by you? **(b)** (*échapper à l'attention de*) his latest book did not get by the censor

get down 1 *vi* **(a)** (*descendre, d'un mur, d'un arbre, etc.*) get down at once! **(b)** (*se coucher, se cacher*) get down or she'll see us **(c)** (*sortir de table*) may I get down?

    2 *vtsép* **(a)** (*descendre*) will you get my case down for me? **(b)** (*faire baisser*) the doctors have got his temperature down at last **(c)** (*prendre note de*) I'll get that down if you'll give me a moment

    3 *vtts* **(a)** (*déprimer*) this kind of weather gets everybody down **(b)** (*avaler*) her throat is so swollen she can't get anything down; get this soup down and you'll soon feel better

get down to *vic* (*se mettre à*) when are you going to get down to your homework?

get in 1 *vtsép* **(a)** (*appeler, faire venir*) I was so worried about the baby that I got the doctor in **(b)** (**rentrer, faire rentrer*) just let me get the washing in before the rain starts; farmers are only now getting their crops in **(c)** (*planter, mettre en terre*) you should get your bulbs in earlier than this **(d)** (*pouvoir faire*) she got some last-minute revision in the night before the exam **(e)** (*placer, caser*) she was talking so much I couldn't get a word in

    2 *vtts* **(a)** (*faire entrer, donner accès à, particulièrement une université*) these excellent exam results will get you in anywhere **(b)** (*assurer l'élection de*) it was the government's mistakes that got the opposition in

    3 *vic* (*entrer dans*) get in the car!; the smoke from the camp fire got in their eyes

    4 *vi* **(a)** (*arriver*) when does the train get in?; he got in before I did **(b)** (*entrer*) if they didn't have a key, how did they get in? **(c)** (*être élu*) she got in with a very small majority

get in on *vic* (*prendre part à*) they'd all like to get in on the deal

get into 1 *vic* **(a)** (*rentrer dans*) she hasn't been able to get into any of her clothes since the baby was born **(b)** (*arriver à, pour des sautes d'humeur*) I don't know what's got into her these days **(c)** (*locutions*) there's no need to get into a panic *ce n'est pas la peine de paniquer*; you'll get into trouble for that *tu vas avoir des ennuis à cause de ça*; they've got badly into debt *ils se sont sérieusement endettés* **(d)** (*apprendre, pour des habitudes, etc.*) she'll soon get into our ways **(e)** (*s'intéresser à, se laisser prendre par*) everyone says this is an excellent book, but I just can't get into it **(f)** (*être reçu à*) only a small percentage of candidates get into university; (*entrer dans*) the thieves got into the house through an open window

2 *vttsc* **(a)** (*mettre dans, fourrer dans*) did you manage to get everything into the suitcase?; you got me into this mess, now get me out **(b)** (*mettre de*) she knows just what to do to get her father into a good mood; don't get her into one of her rages

get in with *vic* **(a)** (*se mettre bien avec*) if you want to get in with him, tell him how much you enjoyed his singing **(b)** (*fréquenter*) she's worried about her daughter getting in with a bad crowd

get off 1 *vi* **(a)** (*descendre, d'un véhicule*) he got off at the traffic lights **(b)** (*quitter le bureau, sortir*) I'd like to get off early tomorrow **(c)** (*s'en tirer*) he shouldn't have got off; you got off lightly! (*c.-à-d. à bon compte*) **(d)** (*s'endormir*) I couldn't get off at all last night

2 *vtts* **(a)** (*envoyer*) it's time to get the children off to bed; I must get this letter off in time to catch the last post **(b)** (*enlever de*) get your hands off that child; get those football boots off the chair; you should have got that off your desk by now (*c.-à-d. tu aurais dû t'en occuper*) **(c)** (*sauver d'une peine, pour un avocat*) he has a reputation for always getting his clients off **(d)** (*prendre, comme congé*) maybe I could get the afternoon off **(e)** (*avoir de, obtenir de*) I got it off the woman next door **(f)** (*libérer de, dispenser de*) the burns were not very serious but they got him off work **(g)** (*endormir*) it always takes ages to get her off

get off with *vic* **(a)** (*avoir une touche avec, flirter avec*) trust her to get off with the only decent looking chap here **(b)** (*s'en sortir avec*) he got off with just a fine

get on 1 *vi* **(a)** (*monter, dans un bus, un train*) where did you get on? **(b)** (*progresser*) if he wants to get on, the best thing he can do is work hard **(c)** (*prendre de l'âge*) my grandmother is getting on **(d)** (*devenir tard*) time is getting on **(e)** (*s'entendre bien*) we don't get on **(f)** (*se débrouiller*) how is the old man going to get on without his dog?; how did you get on at the dentist's? (*c.-à-d. comment ça s'est passé . . .?*)

   2 *vtsép** (*mettre, poser, enfiler*) I can't get the lid on; once you get your coat on, will you start the car?; (*faire monter dans, mettre dans*) you won't be able to get that on the bus, it's far too big; I got her on (the train) with seconds to spare

get on for *vic* (*approcher*) she must be getting on for 90 but she's very active; it's getting on for four o'clock; there were getting on for 500 guests at the wedding

get on to *vic* **(a)** (*trouver, trouver le nom de*) how did you get on to me? **(b)** (*contacter*) I'll get on to the bank about it **(c)** (*en venir à*) I'd like to get on to the question of expenses

get on with *vic* **(a)** (*continuer, poursuivre*) please get on with what you are supposed to be doing; I would like to get on with my reading; that will do to be going on with (*c.-à-d. ça ira pour le moment*) **(b)** how are you getting on with the painting? (*c.-à-d. comment ça progresse, le/la . . .?*) **(c)** (*s'entendre bien avec*) I don't get on with my parents

get out 1 *vi* **(a)** (*partir*) I told her to get out **(b)** (*être libéré, sortir*) when does he get out? **(c)** (*sortir de chez soi ou socialement*) she doesn't get out much; he ought to get out more **(d)** (*s'ébruiter*) how did the news get out?

   2 *vtsép* **(a)** (*sortir*) I got my purse out to pay the milkman; get your books out and turn to page 54 **(b)** (*libérer*) our prime concern must be to get the hostages out **(c)** (*dire, sortir*) he couldn't get a word out when they told him his wife had had triplets; (*donner, publier*) we have to get this report out by Monday **(d)** (*éliminer, dans un match de cricket*) John got their best batsman out for ten

get out of 1 *vic* **(a)** (*échapper à*) he always gets out of the washing up **(b)** (*perdre, pour une habitude*) I've got out of the habit of studying; she has got out of the way of doing dishes without a dishwasher **(c)** (*partir de, sortir de*) let's get out of here; he got out of the country before the police came looking for him; the children get out of school at about three o'clock

   2 *vttsc* **(a)** (*tirer, pour une satisfaction, etc.*) I don't see what pleasure he gets out of all this studying; she really gets the most out of life, doesn't she? **(b)** (*sortir de*) get the big pot out of the cupboard; (*tirer de, obtenir de*) the detective finally got the truth out of the suspect

get over 1 *vi* **(a)** (*traverser, enjamber*) you get over first
(b) (*communiquer*) she cannot get over to her audience
2 *vic* **(a)** (*se remettre de*) he hasn't got over the shock of his wife's death yet; I'm getting over it gradually **(b)** (*surmonter*) she gave an excellent speech once she got over her difficulties with the microphone; you must get over these silly fears
3 *vtts* (*faire passer de l'autre côté de*) it's not easy getting fifty children over a busy road
4 *vtsép* (*faire passer, pour une opinion, un argument, etc.*) you got your point over very well

get over with *vtts* (*en finir avec*) once I got my appointment with the dentist over with, I thoroughly enjoyed my day off; can we get this over with quickly.

get round 1 *vi* **(a)** (*arriver chez quelqu'un*) the vet said she'll get round as soon as she can **(b)** (*se répandre*) the news is getting round
2 *vic* **(a)** (*échapper à, contourner*) there's no getting round it – you'll have to own up; how did they get round the export regulations? **(b)** (*cajoler*) I can always get round my father
3 *vtts* (*persuader*) you've got me round to your way of thinking

get round to *vic* (*s'occuper de, en finir avec, pour quelque chose de difficile ou d'ennuyeux*) I'll get round to it eventually, I promise

get through 1 *vi* **(a)** (*obtenir la communication téléphonique*) the lines must be down, I can't get through **(b)** (*passer, surtout malgré un obstacle*) will the message get through?; the cars could not get through because the pass was blocked with snow **(c)** *Am* (*finir*) the evening class does not usually get through until nine o'clock **(d)** (*réussir un examen, être reçu*) only three of the class didn't get through
2 *vic* **(a)** (*prendre, franchir, négocier*) you will not be able to get through the roadblock **(b)** (*réussir*) I got through my exams second time around **(c)** (*finir, achever*) will you get through your home work in time to come to the match? **(d)** (*utiliser*) he gets

through a dozen shirts a week; (*faire passer, pour le temps*) since she retired, she's been finding it difficult to get through the days

4 *vtts* **(a)** (*faire réussir un examen*) it was your essay that got you through **(b)** (*amener à bon port*) they got the food supplies through just in time **(c)** (*faire comprendre*) I finally got it through to him that I wasn't interested

get to *vic* **(a)** (*se rendre à*) how do we get to their house from here? **(b)** (*commencer à*) you know, I've got to wondering if maybe he isn't right after all **(c)** (*toucher au vif*) she really got to me with her sarcastic remarks; you shouldn't let it get to you (*c.-à-d. ne t'en fais pas*) **(d)** (*pouvoir, réussir à*) did you actually get to speak to the Prime Minister?

get together 1 *vi* (*se rencontrer*) when can we get together to discuss the project?; (*rencontrer*) he's getting together with the bank manager tomorrow

    2 *vtsép* (*rassembler*) get your things together

get up 1 *vi* **(a)** (*se lever*) it's time to get up (*c.-à-d. de son lit*); he got up to address the audience **(b)** (*se lever, se préparer*) there's a storm getting up

    2 *vtsép* **(a)** (*mettre, faire monter, augmenter*) we'll get up speed when we reach the motorway **(b)** (*organiser*) we've got up a petition to protest about the closure

    3 *vtts* **(a)** (*réveiller*) will you get me up early tomorrow? **(b)** (*monter*) help me get this up **(c)** (*s'habiller*) she's getting herself up as Cleopatra

get up to 1 *vic* **(a)** (*atteindre, arriver à*) it took ages to get up to the top **(b)** (*faire, pour des bêtises*) those children are always getting up to mischief; I don't want you getting up to anything while I'm out

    2 *vtts* (*monter à l'étage supérieur*) get this up to the top bedroom for me

give away *vtsép* **(a)** (*donner*) I gave it away to someone who needed it more **(b)** (*distribuer*) a former pupil is giving the prizes away **(c)** (*conduire à l'autel, pendant une cérémonie de mariage*) her uncle is to give her away **(d)** (*dénoncer*) who gave us away?; (*locution*) to give the game away *vendre la mèche*

give in 1 *vtsép* (*rendre*) give your homework in; I gave the wallet in to the police

2 *vi* (*céder*) Oscar Wilde said that the only way to get rid of temptation was to give in to it; (*donner sa langue au chat*) I give in – tell me what the answer is

give off *vtsép* (*produire, donner*) this fire gives off a lot of heat; something is giving off a bad smell

give on to *vic* (*donner sur*) the windows give on to the main road so it's a noisy flat

give out 1 *vtsép* **(a)** (*distribuer*) they were giving out leaflets about abortion **(b)** (*faire connaître*) the Chancellor gave out the trade figures today **(c)** (*produire*) the radiators are not giving out much heat
2 *vi* **(a)** (*s'épuiser*) supplies have given out; (*être à bout*) my patience is giving out **(b)** (*tomber en panne*) the radio has given out

give over 1 *vtsép* **(a)** (*consacrer*) they gave the entire evening over to a discussion of the film **(b)** (*mettre à la disposition de*) the vicar gave the hall over to the scouts
2 *vi* Fam (*arrêter*) give over, will you!

give up 1 *vtsép* **(a)** (*abandonner*) the climbers gave up hope of being found before nightfall; (*laisser tomber*) give it up as a bad job **(b)** (*arrêter*) she is giving up chocolate as part of her diet; I've given up trying **(c)** (*ne plus attendre*) we had almost given you up **(d)** (*considérer*) to give someone up as dead/lost **(e)** (*donner, céder*) I gave up my seat on the bus to a pregnant woman; (*rendre*) the escaped prisoner gave himself up after two days **(f)** (*consacrer*) I gave the entire week up to studying
2 *vi* (*se rendre*) don't shoot – we give up; (*donner sa langue au chat*) OK, tell me the answer then, I give up

give up on *vic* (*ne plus rien attendre de*) how can a mother give up on her daughter and say she's no good?

give way *vi* **(a)** (*céder*) his mother gave way to grief when she heard what had happened; (*céder le passage*) give way to oncoming traffic **(b)** (*se transformer*) my laughter gave way to tears; (*être remplacé*) natural fibres have given way to synthetics

gloss over *vtsép* **(a)** (*passer sur*) she very kindly glossed over my mistakes; I tend to gloss those things over **(b)** (*ne pas tout dire de, cacher*) he glosses over his past

go about 1 *vi* **(a)** (*circuler*) policemen always go about in pairs; there's a story going about that they've separated; there seems to be a virus going about; you can't go about saying things like that (*c.-à-d. ça ne se dit pas*) **(b)** (*sortir, fréquenter*) my son has been going about with her for a year now

   2 *vic* **(a)** (*s'y prendre*) what's the best way to go about buying a house? **(b)** (*s'occuper de*) just go about your business as usual

go after *vic* (*courir après, essayer d'obtenir*) go after them!; we are going after the big prize; she really goes after what she wants

go ahead *vi* **(a)** (*y aller*) if you have something to say to me, just go ahead!; (*poursuivre, mettre à exécution*) they have decided to go ahead with the wedding; he just went ahead and did it **(b)** (*avancer*) the project is going ahead quite satisfactorily **(c)** (*passer devant*) you go ahead, we'll follow later

go along *vi* **(a)** (*marcher le long de*) she met him as she was going along the road **(b)** (*progresser*) please check your punctuation as you go along **(c)** (*être d'accord*) I cannot go along with you on that; the specialist proposed therapy instead of surgery and his colleagues went along

go at *vic* (*attaquer*) he went at the wall with a hammer; the children went at the cakes with a will

go back *vi* **(a)** (*retourner*) let's go back some day **(b)** (*être rendu*) when do these library books go back?; the sheets you bought will have to go back because there is a flaw in them **(c)** (*être retardé, pour une montre, etc.*) don't forget that the clocks go back tomorrow **(d)** (*remonter*) the church has records going back to the 16th century

go back on *vic* (*revenir sur*) I cannot go back on my promise to her; he never goes back on his decisions

go by 1 *vi* **(a)** (*passer*) as the parade was going by . . .; many years have gone by since we met! **(b)** (*passer, filer*) don't let this opportunity go by

   2 *vic* **(a)** (*juger d'après, se fonder sur*) don't go by my opinion – I hate that kind of film; if you go by that clock, you'll miss the train **(b)** (*suivre*) he never goes by the rules; go by your brother's example **(c)** (*être connu sous*) she has been going by her maiden name since the divorce

go down *vi* **(a)** (*se coucher*) the sun is going down **(b)** (*couler*) the ship went down with all hands **(c)** (*baisser*) house prices may go down; flood waters are going down **(d)** (*s'incliner, être battu*) I won't go down without a fight **(e)** (*être reçu*) my suggestion did not go down very well; British television programmes always go down big in North America; how did your suggestion go down? **(f)** (*se boire*) this wine goes down very nicely, don't you think?; (*descendre*) some water will help the pill go down **(g)** (*déchoir*) my old neighbourhood has really gone down; his family has gone down in the world since losing all their money; (*tomber*) she went down in my estimation when I found out what really happened **(h)** (*rester, laisser son souvenir*) how will Ronald Reagan go down in history? **(i)** (*tomber malade*) trust me to go down with flu on the day of the exams

go for *vic* **(a)** (*attaquer*) what was I supposed to do when she went for me with a knife?; go for him, boy!; billiard players always go for the balls in a certain order **(b)** (*se battre pour*) if you really want it, go for it!; (*vouloir décrocher*) with his next jump, he's going for the gold **(c)** (*s'enticher de, s'attacher à*) I could go for you in a big way; she's always gone for the Scandinavian type

go in for *vic* **(a)** (*être candidat pour*) are you going in for the four hundred metres? **(b)** (*apprécier, faire par plaisir*) he doesn't go in for team sports; why do scientists go in for all that jargon?; my parents don't go in for pop music **(c)** (*s'adonner à*) they have decided to go in for catering

go into *vic* **(a)** (*entrer dans ou à*) our special training programme is now going into its third year; she has to go into hospital; he nearly went into hysterics at the thought of it (*c.-à-d. a piqué une crise*) **(b)** (*faire carrière dans*) she wants her daughter to go into teaching **(c)** (*aborder*) we won't go into that for the moment **(d)** (*s'embarquer dans*) my grandmother then went into a long and detailed description of her childhood **(e)** (*commencer à porter, pour des vêtements*) their son did not go into long trousers until he was fifteen

go off 1 *vi* **(a)** (*partir*) she has gone off with the man next door; he's gone off on some business of his own **(b)** (*pourrir, tourner*) the milk has gone off; (*se détériorer*) your work has gone off recently – is anything wrong? **(c)** (*sonner*) the alarm went off at the usual time; (*partir*) he said that the gun just went off in his hand **(d)** (*s'éteindre*) the lights went off all over the city last night **(e)** (*être reçu*) how did the play go off?; my presentation went off well/badly

  2 *vic* (*ne plus aimer*) I've gone off him since I found out what a male chauvinist pig he is; she says she has gone off Spain

go on 1 *vi* **(a)** (*continuer*) go on – what did he say then?; just go on with what you were doing; do we have enough coffee to be going on with or should I buy some more? **(b)** (*aller, pour un vêtement*) your coat won't go on unless you wear a different sweater **(c)** (*s'allumer, se mettre en marche*) the street lights go on when it gets dark **(d)** *Fam* (*ne pas cesser de parler*) once he starts, he goes on and on; (*s'en prendre à*) my aunt keeps going on at me about getting a job **(e)** (*se passer*) what's going on? **(f)** (*passer*) as time went on, I realized that . . .

  2 *vic* **(a)** (*commencer*) most people go on a diet at least once; he goes on unemployment benefit next week **(b)** *Fam* (*en pincer pour*) my sister is really gone on the boy next door **(c)** (*être guidé par*) I have nothing concrete to go on – I just don't trust him **(d)** (*approcher*) she's two years old, going on three

go out *vi* **(a)** (*sortir*) they were just about to go out **(b)** (*sortir de chez soi, quitter sa maison*) she doesn't go out much these days; we're going out for dinner **(c)** (*sortir, fréquenter*) she first went out with him six months ago **(d)** (*être battu*) I bet his team goes out in the first round **(e)** (*s'éteindre*) put some wood on the fire before it goes out; the lights went out **(f)** (*envoyer, partir par courrier, dans une société ou une organisation*) has that letter gone out? **(g)** (*locution*) I went out like a light *je me suis endormi tout d'un coup* **(h)** (*passer de mode*) the stores are betting on the miniskirt not going out for another year **(i)** (*descendre, pour la marée*) the tide has gone out

go over 1 *vi* **(a)** (*aller à un endroit précis*) I went over and tapped him on the shoulder **(b)** (*passer à, pour un changement*) they've gone over to the Conservative Party; he's thinking about going over to cigars **(c)** (*être reçu*) my suggestion didn't go over at all well

  2 *vic* **(a)** (*examiner*) we should go over the accounts **(b)** (*revoir, repasser*) let's go over your speech a second time **(c)** (*discuter de, parler de*) we must have gone over this point a dozen times already

go round 1 *vi* **(a)** (*tourner*) everything is going round
(b) (*faire un détour*) the policeman said we would have to go round **(c)** (*rendre visite*) you ought to go round and see him; she's gone round to her mother's **(d)** (*suffire*) there won't be enough to go round
2 *vic* **(a)** (*prendre, pour un chemin*) I went round the long way to be sure of not getting lost **(b)** (*visiter*) we must have gone round every museum in town; she went round the neighbourhood looking for her cat **(c)** (*suffire à*) is the roast big enough to go round everyone?

go through 1 *vi* (*prendre effet*) the deal has gone through; when does the divorce go through?
2 *vic* **(a)** (*souffrir*) she has gone through a lot **(b)** (*examiner, étudier*) the detective went through the witness's statement very carefully **(c)** (*fouiller dans*) I've gone through all the papers and I still can't find it **(d)** (*répéter*) how often do you have to go through your lines before you know them by heart? **(e)** (*user, utiliser*) children go through a lot of shoes; (*consommer*) we've gone through six pints of milk in two days

go through with *vic* (*aller jusqu'au bout de, réaliser, accomplir*) he decided at the last moment that he couldn't go through with the wedding; management went through with its threat to close the factory

go together *vi* **(a)** (*aller ensemble*) do these colours go together?
(b) (*se fréquenter, sortir ensemble*) we've been going together for a long time

go towards *vic* (*contribuer à*) the proceeds from the fête are going towards a new village hall

go under 1 *vi* **(a)** (*sombrer, couler*) it's too late – he's gone under
(b) (*couler, être en faillite*) his business is going under and there isn't much he can do about it
2 *vic* (*être connu sous*) since the divorce she's been going under her old name of Williams

go up *vi* **(a)** (*monter*) just go up – he's expecting you **(b)** (*monter, augmenter*) the patient's temperature had been going up and up; house prices are going up again **(c)** (*se lever*) the curtain will go up at eight o'clock **(d)** (*être détruit*) the building went up in flames; *Fig* (*partir en fumée*) his plans went up in smoke

go with *vic* **(a)** (*aller de pair avec*) mathematical skills usually go with an ability to play chess **(b)** (*aller avec, s'accorder avec*) change your tie – it doesn't go with that shirt **(c)** (*être compris dans le prix de*) do the carpets go with the house?

go without 1 *vi* (*s'en passer*) those are too dear – if you don't like any of the others you'll just have to go without
   2 *vic* (*se passer de*) I went without breakfast so I wouldn't be late

grow apart *vi* (*se détacher, pour des amis, des époux*) they have grown apart over the years

grow in *vi* (*repousser*) your hair will grow in soon

grow out of *vic* **(a)** (*devenir trop grand pour*) he has grown out of those shoes we bought just a few months ago **(b)** (*devenir trop mûr pour*) I've grown out of my friends; when are you going to grow out of biting your nails?

grow up *vi* **(a)** (*grandir, devenir adulte*) children grow up so fast nowadays **(b)** (*se comporter comme un adulte*) I wish you would grow up! **(c)** (*se développer*) a theory has grown up that . . .

guard against *vic* (*protéger de*) take vitamin C to guard against colds

H

hammer home *vtsép* **(a)** (*enfoncer au marteau*) be sure to hammer all the nails home **(b)** (*insister sur*) we hammered home the importance of wearing seat belts

hammer out *vtsép* **(a)** (*faire sortir au marteau, débosseler*) I'll have to hammer these dents out **(b)** (*mettre au point, avec des difficultés*) they have finally managed to hammer out an agreement on the withdrawal of troops

hand back *vtsép* (*retourner*) I'll hand it back to you as soon as I've finished

hand down *vtsép* **(a)** (*descendre, d'un endroit haut*) hand that plate down to me **(b)** (*transmettre, donner en héritage*) she handed the necklace down to her granddaughter **(c)** (*prononcer, pour une sentence*) the sentence will be handed down soon

hand in *vtsép* (*rendre à une autorité, etc.*) I want you to hand in your essays tomorrow

hand out *vtsép* **(a)** (*distribuer*) I've offered to hand leaflets out **(b)** (*donner, surtout pour des conseils, etc. qui ne sont pas désirés*) you can always rely on him to hand out advice

hand over 1 *vtsép* **(a)** (*remettre*) she handed the papers over to the lawyer for safekeeping **(b)** (*donner*) hand over your wallet **(c)** (*transmettre*) we now hand you over to our foreign affairs correspondent; he will be handing over the reins of power very soon
   2 *vi* **(a)** (*donner, rendre*) I know you have it, so hand over! **(b)** (*laisser la place à*) I now hand over to the weatherman; when will he be handing over to the new chairman?

hang about/around 1 *vi Fam* **(a)** (*attendre*) I had to hang about for ages before he finally arrived; now hang about, that isn't what she said! **(b)** (*traîner*) don't hang about or we'll never finish
   2 *vic* (*fréquenter, hanter*) I don't want you hanging about amusement arcades

hang back *vi* (*rester en arrière*) there's always one child who hangs back when Santa Claus is handing out the presents; if you have a contribution to make to the discussion, please don't hang back; (*se retenir de*) I hung back from saying anything because . . .

hang down *vi* (*tomber, pendre*) her hair hung down in ringlets

hang in *vi Pop* (*s'accrocher, tenir le coup*) hang in there, boys – we'll get you out soon; he'll just have to hang in until a better job comes along

hang on 1 *vi* **(a)** (*s'accrocher*) hang on tight **(b)** (*attendre*) can you hang on for a couple of minutes?
   2 *vic* **(a)** (*être suspendu à*) the audience was hanging on the speaker's every word **(b)** (*dépendre de*) the fate of the project hangs on the availability of supplies

hang on to *vic* **(a)** (*se cramponner à*) he hung on to the cliff face

    (b) (*conserver, garder*) I'd hang on to those documents if I were you

hang out *vi* **(a)** (*sortir, pendre*) your shirt tails are hanging out
    (b) *Fam* (*se trouver habituellement, traîner*) I'm looking for Bill – any idea where he hangs out? **(c)** *Fam* (*s'entêter, tenir bon pour obtenir*) I'm hanging out for a rise

hang together *vi* (*être plausible, tenir debout*) the plot of the film doesn't hang together

hang up 1 *vi* (*raccrocher, au téléphone*) don't hang up until you've heard what she has to say; hang up immediately
    2 *vtsép* (*accrocher, suspendre*) hang your coat up

happen along *vi* (*arriver par hasard*) then, thank goodness, a policeman happened along

hark back *vi* (*revenir, sur un sujet*) he keeps harking back to the Blitz

have around *vtts* **(a)** (*avoir à sa disposition*) it's always a good idea to have some candles around **(b)** (*inviter chez soi*) we must have them around for supper soon

have back 1 *vtsép* (*récupérer*) can I have it back?; I'll have my book back please (*c.-à-d. je voudrais que tu me rendes mon livre*)
    2 *vtts* (*inviter chez soi en retour*) we're having them back next Saturday

have in *vtts* **(a)** (*appeler, faire venir*) we'll have to have the plumber in to fix that leak **(b)** (*inviter chez soi*) the old ladies across the street like having people in for tea **(c)** (*locution*) to have it in for someone *avoir une dent contre quelqu'un*

have off *vtts* **(a)** (*enlever*) the doctor had the plaster off in no time at all **(b)** (*se faire enlever*) she's having the plaster off next week **(c)** *Pop* (*baiser*) those two look as if they have it off every night

have on 1 *vtsép* (*porter, pour des vêtements*) he looks totally different when he has something casual on
    2 *vtts* **(a)** *Fam* (*taquiner*) didn't you realize I was having you on? **(b)** (*avoir prévu, avoir . . . à faire*) she has a lot on this week; I have something else on, I'm afraid **(c)** (*avoir des informations sur*) he told the police they had nothing on him –

he'd been in hospital at the time **(d)** (*installer*) once we have the roofrack on, we'll be all set

have out *vtts* **(a)** (*se faire enlever*) he's in hospital having his appendix out **(b)** (*s'expliquer sur*) let's have this out once and for all

have up *vtts* **(a)** (*appeler en justice*) the two old tramps were had up for vagrancy **(b)** (*monter, installer*) they worked all night to have the exhibits up in time for the opening

head for *vic* **(a)** (*aller à, se rendre à*) where is he headed for?; let's head for home **(b)** (*aller vers*) she's heading for a disappointment if she thinks he's going to propose; the country is heading for civil war

head off *vtsép* **(a)** (*détourner l'attention de, occuper*) head Mum off for a couple of minutes while I finish wrapping her present **(b)** (*prévenir*) to head off accusations of favouritism . . .

head up *vtsép* (*présider, avoir la tête de*) how many committees does she head up?

hear of *vic habituellement au négatif* (*laisser*) I won't hear of you going to a hotel when we've got a spare room

hear out *vtsép* (*finir d'entendre, écouter jusqu'à la fin*) please hear me out; the committee heard her out before reaching a decision

heat up 1 *vi* **(a)** (*se réchauffer*) the room will soon heat up **(b)** (*s'animer*) the discussion heated up and turned into an argument **2** *vtsép* (*faire chauffer*) heat up some milk; (*réchauffer*) a bowl of soup will heat you up

hide out *vi* (*se cacher*) he's hiding out in some hotel to get away from his fans

hit back 1 *vi* (*riposter*) he has questioned my integrity and I firmly intend to hit back **2** *vtsép* (*frapper, renvoyer*) hit the ball back; (*frapper de retour*) he hit her so she hit him back

hit off *vtsép* **(a)** (*imiter*) he hits the prime minister off very well **(b)** (*locution*) we hit it off immediately *on s'est entendus tout de suite*

hit on *vic* (*découvrir, tomber sur*) I've hit on a possible solution

hit out *vi* **(a)** (*lancer des coups*) all of a sudden he started hitting out **(b)** (*attaquer*) all of the speakers at the conference hit out at the proposals

hive off 1 *vi* (*diversifier*) they're hiving off into the retail side of things **2** *vtsép* (*séparer*) my boss is furious that the company wants to hive off the research team

hold against *vttsc* (*reprocher à*) why do you hold my past against me?; I hold it against him that . . .

hold back 1 *vi* (*se retenir, rester silencieux*) I held back while the two of them discussed old times; he held back for a time but finally spoke his mind
2 *vtsép* **(a)** (*retenir*) marshals held the fans back; he held back his rage **(b)** (*maintenir en arrière*) it's your poor performance in maths that is holding you back **(c)** (*cacher, ne pas dire*) she's holding something back, I know she is; don't hold anything back

hold down *vtsép* **(a)** (*empêcher de monter*) the government must take action to hold down interest rates; (*maîtriser*) it took two of us to hold him down **(b)** (*avoir, occuper, pour un emploi*) she is holding down a fairly high-powered job in the City; (*garder, pour un emploi*) can he hold this job down?

hold forth *vi* (*disserter, pérorer*) she held forth at great length on the benefits of fresh air

hold in *vtsép* (*rentrer, retenir*) for heaven's sake, hold your stomach in; she shouldn't hold her emotions in

hold off 1 *vi* (*ne pas commencer*) the rain seems to be holding off **2** *vtsép* (*garder à distance*) the remaining men managed to hold off the attack until reinforcements arrived

hold out 1 *vi* **(a)** (*durer*) our supplies will not hold out for long **(b)** (*tenir le coup*) can you hold out until the doctor gets here? **2** *vtsép* **(a)** (*tendre*) she held out her hand **(b)** (*offrir, pour un espoir, une possibilité*) the doctor doesn't hold out much hope for a complete recovery

hold out on *vic* (*ne pas dire, cacher, pour une information*) you've been holding out on me – I didn't know you played the saxophone

hold to *vic* (*s'en tenir à*) he held to his decision

hold up 1 *vi* **(a)** (*tenir debout*) the centuries-old house continues to hold up **(b)** (*rester calme*) she held up magnificently under the strain
    2 *vtsép* **(a)** (*lever*) she held her face up to the sun **(b)** (*tenir debout*) what's holding the tent up? **(c)** (*retarder*) bad weather is holding the project up **(d)** (*faire un hold-up dans*) armed men held up another bank yesterday

hold with *vic* (*approuver*) I don't hold with all these fancy names for children

hole up *vi Fam* (*se terrer, se planquer*) the bank robbers decided to hole up for a while

home in on *vic* (*se diriger automatiquement sur*) the missiles can home in on the heat of aircraft engines; (*identifier*) she homed in on my one mistake

hook up 1 *vi* **(a)** (*s'agrafer*) the dress hooks up **(b)** (*faire un duplex, à la télévision*) we will be hooking up with European networks to bring you this very special programme
    2 *vtsép* (*agrafer, pour des vêtements*) hook me up

hot up *Fam* **1** *vi* (*chauffer, pour des paroles, le ton d'une conversation, etc.*) the argument hotted up when . . .; things are hotting up again on the labour relations front
    2 *vtsép* (*augmenter, hâter*) they are hotting up the pace

hunt down *vtsép* **(a)** (*rechercher*) they are being hunted down by state and federal police **(b)** (*dénicher, trouver*) he was finally hunted down

hunt out *vtsép* (*trouver, après des difficultés, dégoter*) I've hunted out those old family photographs you wanted to see

hurry along 1 *vi* (*se presser, se dépêcher*) hurry along please, the museum is now closed; you're hurrying along as if we were late
    2 *vtsép* (*dépêcher, accélérer*) I'm trying to hurry the project along but it's not easy; you can't hurry these things along

hurry up 1 *vi* (*se dépêcher*) do hurry up or we'll be late
    2 *vtsép* (*faire aller plus vite, accélérer*) I'll go and hurry them up; could you hurry things up a bit please – this is my lunch hour

I

ice over *vi* (*se recouvrir de glace, geler*) this river is too fast flowing to ever ice over

ice up *vi* (*givrer, geler*) the crash was attributed in part to the plane's wings having iced up; I can't get the key in – the lock must have iced up

improve on *vic* (*améliorer*) I told him you can't improve on perfection; she'll have to improve on that score with her next jump

iron out *vtsép* **(a)** (*faire disparaître au fer*) I'll iron out these creases in your shirt for you **(b)** (*résoudre*) there are one or two little problems that must be ironed out; (*faire disparaître*) have you ironed out your differences?

J

jack in *vtsép* Pop **(a)** (*abandonner, laisser tomber*) I'm going to jack this job in as soon as I can **(b)** (*arrêter*) jack it in!

jack up *vtsép* **(a)** (*soulever au cric*) he had to jack up the car to change the wheel **(b)** Fam (*faire grimper*) they've jacked up the price of petrol again

jam in(to) 1 *vtsép* (*coincer, serrer*) can you jam anything else in?
2 *vi* (*se coincer, se serrer, dans un endroit fermé*) hundreds of people jammed in to hear her speech

jam on *vtsép* (*appuyer à fond sur*) I had to jam on my brakes or I would have hit him; (**enfoncer complètement, à fond*) she jammed her hat on and marched out

jam up *vtsép* (*bloquer*) Sunday motorists in search of a good spot for a picnic have jammed up the roads

jar on *vic* (*irriter*) that constant banging is jarring on my nerves

jazz up *vtsép* Fam (*mettre de l'ambiance dans, animer*) it's very dull in here tonight – couldn't we jazz things up a bit?; (*égayer*) jazz up a plain dress with some costume jewellery

jockey for vtsép (*essayer d'obtenir, surtout pour des emplois, des fonctions*) everyone is jockeying for the position of chairperson

jockey into vttsc (*manœuvrer*) they jockeyed me into volunteering my services

jog along vi (*suivre son rythme*) the work is jogging along

join in 1 vi (*participer*) I want everyone to join in
    2 vic (*prendre part à*) I joined in the fun; they all joined in the chorus

join on 1 vi (*se fixer*) where does this bit join on?
    2 vtsép* (*attacher*) they've joined on another carriage

join up 1 vi **(a)** (*s'engager dans l'armée*) he joined up as soon as war was declared **(b)** (*se rencontrer*) the two groups will join up here
    2 vtsép (*connecter, mettre bout à bout*) join the ends up

jot down vtsép (*jeter prendre rapidement, pour des notes*) he jotted down a few notes for his speech; just jot it down

jump at vic (*sauter sur*) I jumped at the chance of a holiday in Spain; when he offered her the position she jumped at it

jump down 1 vi (*sauter du haut*) there aren't any steps – you'll have to jump down; he jumped down from the window
    2 vic (*locution*) to jump down someone's throat *sauter à la gorge de quelqu'un*

jump on 1 vi (*monter*) there was a bus sitting at the traffic lights so he decided to jump on
    2 vic Fam **(a)** (*attaquer, agresser*) the hooligans jumped on the old man at the corner of the street **(b)** (*critiquer*) he jumps on me for the least little thing

K

keel over vi **(a)** (*chavirer*) the lifeboat keeled over
    (b) (*s'évanouir, tomber*) he keels over at the sight of blood; the hat stand just keeled over

keep at 1 *vic* **(a)** (*continuer à travailler*) if he wants to get into university, he'll have to keep at his maths **(b)** (*harceler*) the pair of them kept at me, morning, noon and night

    2 *vttsc* (*obliger à travailler, faire travailler*) the boss kept us hard at it all morning

keep away 1 *vi* (*rester à une certaine distance*) I knew you had visitors so I kept away; (*ne pas succomber*) she can't keep away from chocolates

    2 *vtts* (*garder à l'écart, mettre à l'écart*) keep him away from me

keep back 1 *vi* (*rester en arrière*) a policeman was telling people to keep back

    2 *vtsép* **(a)** (*retenir, maintenir en arrière*) the marshals at the rock concert had a job keeping the fans back from the stage **(b)** (*refouler*) I couldn't keep back my tears; (*ne pas dire*) she's keeping something back from us **(c)** (*faire redoubler, pour un élève*) we do not like keeping children back but in this case feel we have no alternative **(d)** (*retarder*) am I keeping you back?

keep down 1 *vi* (*se baisser*) keep down or he'll see us

    2 *vtts* **(a)** (*baisser*) the policemen surrounding the house were told to keep their heads down; please keep your voice down – some people are trying to concentrate **(b)** (*ne pas garder, pour la nourriture*) the doctor was worried that her patient couldn't keep anything down

    3 *vtsép* **(a)** (*maîtriser*) it's a full-time job keeping the weeds down in this garden **(b)** (*maintenir à un bas niveau*) the government is not doing anything to keep inflation down; he's trying hard to keep his weight down but he's not having much success

keep from 1 *vttsc* **(a)** (*cacher à*) they kept the news from the old lady as long as possible; what are you keeping from me? **(b)** (*empêcher de*) the climber hung on to his partner's hand to keep him from falling over the edge **(c)** (*distraire de*) I mustn't keep you from your work **(d)** (*protéger de*) I'm trying to keep you from harm

    2 *vic* (*s'empêcher de*) he was such a boring speaker that I couldn't keep from nodding off

keep in with *vic* (*rester en bons termes avec*) if you want to keep in with him, just agree with everything he says

keep off 1 *vi* (*ne pas approcher*) that's my property – keep off!
    2 *vic* (*ne pas s'approcher de, ne pas marcher sur*) keep off the grass; (*ne pas aborder, éviter*) they tactfully kept off the subject of divorce; the doctor has ordered him to keep off the port and cigars
    3 *vttsc* (*maintenir à distance*) Mum said to keep our hands off the cakes
    4 *vtts* (*enlever, ne pas porter, pour un vêtement*) don't keep your coat off for long or you'll get cold

keep on 1 *vi* **(a)** (*continuer*) if they keep on like this much longer, I'm going to call the police; are you sure you told her she had to keep on past the war memorial? **(b)** (*faire des remontrances*) the headmaster keeps on at his pupils about their behaviour at the bus stop; it doesn't do any good to keep on about his drinking
    2 *vtsép* **(a)** (*garder, continuer à employer*) do you want to keep the cleaning woman on? **(b)** (**garder, continuer à porter*) make sure the baby keeps her gloves on

keep out 1 *vi* **(a)** (*ne pas entrer*) danger – keep out!; (*rester hors de, à l'abri de*) the poacher kept out of sight until the gamekeeper had finished his round **(b)** (*ne pas se mêler à*) I'm keeping out of this argument
    2 *vtsép* **(a)** (*empêcher d'entrer*) lock the door to keep people out; (*mettre hors de portée de*) keep plastic bags out of the reach of children; (*protéger de, empêcher d'entrer*) these boots are supposed to keep the rain out **(b)** (*ne pas mêler*) I'll do my best to keep you out of this

keep to 1 *vic* **(a)** (*honorer*) people should keep to their promises **(b)** (*garder*) she's keeping to the house on doctor's orders; keep to the right; (*respecter, suivre*) we must keep to the agenda and not go off at tangents all the time
    2 *vttsc* **(a)** (*faire tenir*) be sure to keep her to her promise; (*maintenir à un certain niveau*) we are endeavouring to keep delays to a minimum **(b)** (*locution*) to keep something to oneself *garder quelque chose pour soi*

keep up 1 *vi* **(a)** (*continuer*) if this snow keeps up much longer the roads will be blocked **(b)** (*suivre, pour une vitesse ou un rythme*) she dictated so quickly that her secretary couldn't keep up **(c)** (*rester en contact*) do you keep up with them?
    2 *vtsép* **(a)** (*maintenir, continuer*) we kept up a fairly regular exchange of letters until quite recently; it seems impossible for

him to keep this pace up; keep it up, you're doing fine
(b) (*entretenir*) her arthritis prevents her keeping up the garden
the way she would like **(c)** (*garder haut, empêcher de tomber*)
keep your spirits up; he has lost so much weight he finds it
difficult to keep his trousers up **(d)** (*garder éveillé*) our dinner
guests kept us up until three o'clock this morning

kick about/around 1 *vi Fam* (*traîner*) don't leave the paper kicking
about; find yourself something to do instead of kicking around
2 *vtsép* **(a)** (**pousser du pied, donner des coups de pied dans*)
they're not doing any harm kicking a ball around **(b)** (*marcher
sur les pieds à*) you've kicked me around long enough
(c) *Fam* (*débattre, mettre sur le tapis*) we kicked the proposal
around for a while but finally decided against it

kick in *vtsép* (*enfoncer à coups de pied*) the soldiers kicked the door in;
(*donner des coups dans*) I'll kick his teeth in!

kick off 1 *vi* **(a)** (*donner le coup d'envoi*) when do they kick off?
(b) *Fam* (*commencer*) our speaker will now answer questions –
who's going to kick off?; let's kick off with a situation report
2 *vtsép** **(a)** (*enlever à coups de pied*) it's always such a relief
to kick your shoes off **(b)** (*faire sortir de, expulser de*) they're
going to kick him off the team for misconduct

kick out 1 *vi* (*ruer*) the mules kicked out whenever anyone approached
2 *vtsép Fam* (*renvoyer, jeter*) his wife has kicked him out and
he's got nowhere to go

kick up *vtsép* (*faire, créer, pour des ennuis, des problèmes*) he'll kick
up an awful fuss when he finds out

knock about/around 1 *vi* = **kick about/around 1**
2 *vtts Fam* **(a)** (*battre*) he knocks her about regularly
(b) (*défoncer, abîmer*) the car was knocked about a good bit but
the driver is unharmed

knock back *vtsép* **(a)** (*descendre, pour une boisson*) he's knocking the
whisky back a bit, isn't he? **(b)** *Fam* (*coûter*) how much did that
knock you back?

knock down *vtsép* **(a)** (*démolir*) the council wants to knock those
houses down **(b)** (*renverser*) the car that knocked her down was
moving much too fast; the champion knocked his opponent down
in the first round **(c)** (*obliger de baisser le prix*) we're trying to

knock them down to something we can afford **(d)** (*baisser le prix de*) she knocked it down a fair bit **(e)** (*vendre, pendant une vente aux enchères*) both paintings were knocked down to dealers

knock off 1 *vi Fam* (*quitter le travail, s'arrêter de travailler*) I'll try to knock of early
   2 *vtsép* **(a)** (**renverser*) the cat must have knocked it off
(b) (**baisser de, pour un prix*) could you knock a pound or two off? **(c)** (*faire rapidement et sans effort*) she knocks those sketches off by the dozen **(d)** *Pop* (*voler, piquer*) those watches that he's trying to sell have probably been knocked off
(e) *Pop* (*tuer, descendre*) she's terrified he'll be knocked off for informing **(f)** *Pop* (*arrêter*) knock it off you two!

knock out *vtsép* **(a)** (*débourrer*) knocking his pipe out, he said . . .
(b) (*anesthésier, faire perdre conscience*) will they knock you out or just give you a local anaesthetic?; the challenger knocked the champion out with a single punch **(c)** (*éliminer, pour des candidats*) that's her knocked out of Wimbledon already!
(d) *Fam* (*crever, épuiser*) those children have knocked me out
(e) (*détruire*) the government jets knocked out two rebel encampments; the storm has knocked out power supplies to a great many homes **(f)** *Fam* (*plaire, remplir de joie*) his performance can hardly be described as knocking the critics out

knock over *vtsép* (*renverser*) he knocked several people over as he ran away; a bus knocked her over; *it wasn't me that knocked the ornament over

knock together 1 *vi* (*s'entrechoquer*) my knees were knocking together at the thought of the interview
   2 *vtsép* (*bricoler à la va-vite*) I've promised to knock a tree house together for the kids

knock up 1 *vi* (*se préparer à jouer*) the players are allowed two minutes to knock up
   2 *vtsép* **(a)** *Br* (*réveiller*) will you knock me up at six o'clock? **(b)** *Fam* (*faire un gosse à, mettre enceinte*) he's knocked her up **(c)** (*bricoler, préparer à la hâte*) if you don't mind leftovers, I'll knock a quick meal up for you

know of *vic* **(a)** (*savoir*) has Bill arrived? – not that I know of **(b)** (*connaître*) nothing is known of her whereabouts; I don't know him, I know of him (*c.-à-d. j'ai entendu parler de lui*)

knuckle under *vi* (*se rendre, céder*) I won't knuckle under to threats

L

lash down 1 *vtsép* (*arrimer*) the lorry driver lashed the tarpaulin down
  2 *vi* (*pleuvoir à verse*) it's lashing down

lash into *vic* **(a)** (*attaquer*) the two men lashed into each other
  (b) (*attaquer verbalement, critiquer*) I lashed into her for making such silly mistakes

lash out 1 *vi* **(a)** (*avoir un mouvement agressif*) he lashed out with a chain; she lashes out at anyone who opposes her
  (b) *Fam* (*dépenser de l'argent en somme importante*) I think I'll lash out and treat myself to a new coat
  2 *vtsép* (*claquer, pour de l'argent*) they lashed out a couple of thousand on that holiday to the States

last out 1 *vi* **(a)** (*survivre*) they can't last out for long in this weather unless they find shelter **(b)** (*suffire*) will our water last out?
  2 *vtsép* **(a)** (*survivre, passer*) she is not expected to last out the night **(b)** (*passer*) we have enough coal to last out the winter

laugh off *vtsép* (*se moquer de, rire de*) he laughed off all warnings

launch into *vic* (*commencer, plonger dans*) he launched into a glowing description of the car he had just bought

launch out *vi* **(a)** (*se diversifier, s'étendre*) the company is going to launch out and add textiles to its product range **(b)** (*locution*) to launch out on one's own *se lancer indépendamment*

lay about *vic* (*attaquer*) the old lady laid about him with her stick

lay down *vtsép* **(a)** (*poser*) he laid his glass down on the table
  (b) (*déposer, pour les armes*) the rebels have announced that they will lay down their arms; (*renoncer à*) she laid down her life for her beliefs **(c)** (*établir, stipuler*) it is laid down in the regulations; (*locution*) to lay down the law *faire la loi*

lay in *vtsép* (*amasser, faire entrer*) we have laid in enough canned goods to feed an army; you had better lay some wood in

lay off 1 *vi Fam* (*arrêter*) I've had as much criticism as I can take, so lay off
   2 *vic Fam* (*laisser tranquille*) my sister doesn't want to go out with you so lay off her
   3 *vtsép* (*licencier*) the company will be laying 350 employees off within the next few weeks

lay on *vtsép* (*fournir*) water and electricity are both laid on at the cottage; (*mettre en circulation*) extra buses will be laid on if necessary; (*offrir*) I'll lay on a meal for everyone

lay out *vtsép* **(a)** (*étendre*) lay the pattern out on the floor
   (b) (*préparer*) she always lays her clothes out the night before
   (c) (*préparer, pour un corps, pour un enterrement*) they laid Grandad out very nicely **(d)** (*aménager*) I don't like the way the office has been laid out **(e)** (*assommer*) he laid me out with one blow **(f)** (*dépenser, pour de l'argent*) your parents have laid out a considerable sum on your education

lay up *vtsép* **(a)** (*garder au lit, clouer au lit*) this flu has laid her up
   (b) (*immobiliser*) the severely damaged vessel will be laid up for repair

lead on 1 *vi* (*aller devant*) lead on!
   2 *vtsép* **(a)** (*tromper*) he led her on with promises of marriage; you led me on to believe that . . . **(b)** (*influencer*) it was those so-called friends of his that led him on to do it

lead up *vi* **(a)** (*précéder*) in the years leading up to the Declaration of Independence . . . **(b)** (*préparer à*) her opening remarks were plainly leading up to a full-scale attack on her critics; what's this leading up to?

lean on *vic* **(a)** (*dépendre de, compter sur*) his mother leans on him for advice **(b)** (*pousser, exercer une pression sur*) the company is leaning on her to take early retirement

leave behind *vtsép* **(a)** (*ne pas prendre*) drivers are advised to leave their cars behind and use public transport; I think we should leave the children behind **(b)** (*oublier, laisser*) I came out in such a rush that I left my keys behind **(c)** (*devancer*) when it comes to maths, she leaves most of the others far behind

leave off 1 *vtsép** (*ne pas mettre*) it was such a beautiful day I left my coat off; who keeps leaving the lid off the coffee jar?; she wants to leave most of her relations off the guest list
2 *vic* (*arrêter*) he has left off seeing her
3 *vi Fam* (*arrêter, pour quelque chose de pénible*) leave off, will you!

leave out *vtsép* **(a)** (*oublier, omettre*) you've left out an entire line; the old lady decided to leave her son-in-law out of her will **(b)** (*ne pas mêler*) leave me out of this **(c)** (*laisser sorti*) I'll leave out the instructions for the washing machine; do you want to leave the car out?

let down *vtsép* **(a)** (*descendre*) they let a rope down to the men stranded on the beach **(b)** (*décevoir*) you must stop letting people down like this **(c)** (*rallonger*) she always lets down the hem on her daughter's dresses **(d)** (*dégonfler*) the boys let his tyres down as a joke

let in 1 *vtsép* **(a)** (**laisser entrer*) these shoes are letting water in; don't let him in **(b)** (*mettre au courant*) they let me in on the secret
2 *vi* (*prendre l'eau, etc.*) are your boots letting in?

let in for *vttsc* (*causer*) your absence let us all in for a lot of extra work; (*s'engager dans*) he didn't realize what he was letting himself in for

let off *vtsép* **(a)** (*faire exploser*) animal rights activists have let off a number of bombs **(b)** (*produire*) the fire was letting off a lot of smoke **(c)** (*faire grâce à*) he was let off because of lack of evidence; the judge let him off with a fine **(d)** (*lâcher, libérer*) the teacher lets us off early on Fridays **(e)** (**déposer, d'un véhicule*) I asked the taxi driver to let me off at the corner

let on *vi* **(a)** (*dire, pour un secret*) I'm pregnant but don't you let on **(b)** (*prétendre, faire croire*) he likes to let on that he went to university

let out *vtsép* **(a)** (*libérer, relâcher*) they're letting him out on parole soon; (*faire sortir*) don't bother seeing me to the door, I'll let myself out **(b)** (*révéler, vendre la mèche pour*) who let it out about the party? **(c)** (*émettre*) she let out a yelp of pain **(d)** (*louer*) they let out rooms to students **(e)** (*élargir, pour des vêtements*) I'm either going to have to go on a diet or let all my clothes out

let up *vi* (*cesser, pour quelque chose qui a duré longtemps*) I wish this rain would let up; don't you ever let up?

lie back *vi* **(a)** (*s'allonger*) you lie back and rest **(b)** (*ne rien faire*) he just lay back and let the rest of us do the work

lie in *vi* (*faire la grasse matinée*) most people lie in on Sundays; I wish I could have lain in this morning

lie up *vi* **(a)** (*se reposer au lit*) the doctor says she's to lie up for a couple of days **(b)** (*se cacher*) the police are convinced that the wanted men are lying up somewhere **(c)** (*ne pas être utilisé*) that boat has been lying up for years

light up 1 *vi* **(a)** (*s'illuminer*) his face suddenly lit up; the room seemed to light up when she came in **(b)** (*allumer une cigarette, etc.*) he lit up and sighed with contentment
  2 *vtsép* **(a)** (*illuminer*) the fireworks lit up the sky
  (b) (*commencer à fumer*) they both lit up their pipes

line up 1 *vi* (*faire la queue*) people are already beginning to line up outside the cinema
  2 *vtsép* **(a)** (*mettre en rang*) the headmaster lined everybody up in the playground **(b)** (*prévoir, arranger*) I've lined a date up for you; he's got something else lined up for tomorrow

listen in *vi* (*écouter*) it's fascinating listening in on other people's conversations; do you mind if I listen in?

live down *vtsép* (*faire oublier*) we'll never live this scandal down; he won't let her live it down that she made one stupid mistake

live in/out *vi* (*vivre/ne pas vivre sur son lieu de travail ou d'étude*) they have at least three maids living in; I would rather live out than stay in a hall of residence

live off *vic* **(a)** (*vivre de*) that child would live off ice cream if he could; she lived off what she earned as a cleaner **(b)** (*vivre par, sur les ressources de*) his brother lives off him

live on *vi* (*durer*) the memory of their sacrifice will live on

live up to *vic* **(a)** (*être à la hauteur de, correspondre à*) nothing ever lives up to expectations **(b)** (*se montrer digne de*) there's no point in trying to live up to my sister's reputation

load down *vtsép* (*surcharger*) I'm loaded down with shopping

load up 1 *vi* (*charger*) there are a number of ships waiting to load up
   2 *vtsép* (*charger*) we loaded the car up with everything bar the kitchen sink

lock away *vtsép* (*mettre sous clé*) lock those papers away for the night; the police said they could lock him away for ten years

lock in *vtsép** (*emprisonner*) she is locked in a cell with three other women; (*enfermer, dans une chambre*) you almost locked me in

lock out *vtsép* (*enfermer dehors, fermer la porte à*) they've gone to bed and locked me out; the company has threatened to lock its employees out unless they return to work immediately

lock up 1 *vi* (*fermer la maison à clé*) you go to bed – I'll lock up
   2 *vtsép* (*mettre sous clé*) lock up your valuables; (*enfermer*) the dogs are locked up every night

long for *vic* (*mourir d'envie pour, attendre avec impatience*) I'm longing for the holidays

look after *vic* (*s'occuper de*) we've been looking after our grandchildren for the weekend; the car has been well looked after

look at *vic* **(a)** (*regarder*) look at those punks! **(b)** (*examiner*) I'll need to get someone in to look at that damp patch **(c)** (*considérer*) he doesn't look at it that way at all **(d)** (*considérer avec faveur*) he sent her the most beautiful flowers for her birthday but she still won't look at him

look back *vi* (*regarder en arrière*) he stopped and looked back; looking back over the last five years, do you have any regrets?

look down on *vic* (*mépriser*) he looks down on anyone who hasn't gone to university

look for *vic* (*chercher*) I'm really looking for something a bit bigger

look forward to *vic* (*attendre avec impatience*) you must be looking forward to their visit

look in *vi* (*passer, faire une courte visite*) I'll look in again tomorrow; they looked in for a minute

look into *vic* (*étudier, mener une enquête sur*) the company has promised that it will look into my complaint

look on 1 *vi* (*regarder*) a crowd looked on as firemen fought the blaze
   2 *vic* (*considérer*) they look on her as a daughter; I used to look on him with envy

look on to *vic* (*donner sur*) our house looks on to open fields

look out 1 *vi* **(a)** (*regarder vers l'extérieur*) she opened the window and looked out **(b)** (*faire attention*) look out – you're very close to the edge
   2 *vtsép* (*chercher, trouver*) look out a scarf for me; she has promised to look those letters out

look out for *vic* **(a)** (*ouvrir l'œil pour*) you could always ask the garage to look out for a second-hand car **(b)** (*s'occuper de*) he promised his parents he would always look out for his younger brother **(c)** (*faire attention à*) look out for the bones in this fish

look over *vtsép* (*visiter*) we're looking over a flat this evening; (*observer, regarder des pieds à la tête*) I'm sure I've been invited for the weekend just so his mother can look me over

look to *vic* (*compter sur*) you must stop looking to other people to solve your problems

look up 1 *vi* **(a)** (*lever la tête*) she looked up when I entered the room; looking up from his book **(b)** (*s'améliorer*) his business must be looking up if he's bought a new car
   2 *vtsép* **(a)** (*rendre visite à*) you must look us up again **(b)** (*chercher, dans un livre, etc.*) look it up in the encyclopaedia

look up to *vic* **(a)** (*regarder, en levant la tête*) he's so tall I have to look up to him **(b)** (*admirer*) everyone looks up to her for her courage

loosen up 1 *vtsép* (*relaxer, détendre*) some massage will loosen you up; (*assouplir*) they've promised to loosen up the rules
   2 *vi* (*s'échauffer*) the athletes take a couple of minutes loosening up

lose out *vi* (*être perdant*) you're the one who'll lose out; he lost out on a deal

louse up *vtsép Pop* (*gâcher, bousiller*) you're always lousing things up for me; he really loused that race up

M

make for *vic* **(a)** (*se diriger à, aller vers, se rendre à*) where are you making for? **(b)** (*encourager, contribuer à*) handling a complaint in that way does not make for good customer relations

make of *vic* **(a)** (*penser de*) well, what do you make of that? **(b)** (*accorder une certaine importance à*) you're making too much of this – I've known him since we were children; the Press isn't making much of this

make off *vi* (*se sauver*) the boys made off at a run when they saw the policeman

make off with *vic* (*prendre, voler*) who's made off with the scissors again?; don't leave your bag lying around – someone might make off with it

make out 1 *vtsép* **(a)** (*écrire, faire, pour un mandat, etc.*) make the cheque out to me **(b)** (*distinguer*) can you make out who it is? **(c)** (*déchiffrer*) he can't make out his own handwriting **(d)** (*comprendre*) I can't make her out at all
 2 *vi* (*se débrouiller*) how is she making out in her new job?
 3 *vic* (*faire paraître*) the insurance company is making out that I was negligent

make over *vtsép* (*céder*) she has made her entire estate over to her granddaughter

make up 1 *vtsép* **(a)** (*maquiller*) I must go and make my face up **(b)** (*mettre fin à, pour une dispute, etc.*) thank goodness they've made it up **(c)** (*rattraper, compenser*) he doesn't have to worry about making up any losses since he comes from a wealthy family; overtime will be necessary to make up the ground we lost because of the weather; sorry we had to cancel dinner, I promise I'll make it up to you **(d)** (*inventer*) she is making the whole thing up, it's not true **(e)** (*former*) would you make these up into three separate packages?; (*former, composer*) the community is made up primarily of old people

(f) (*augmenter*) for your birthday, I'll make your savings up to the price of a new bike
  2 *vi* **(a)** (*se réconcilier*) haven't you two made up yet?
  (b) (*rattraper*) he's making up on the leaders

make up for *vic* (*se faire pardonner pour*) how can I make up for forgetting your birthday?; (*se rattraper pour*) he's certainly making up for lost time now

make up to *vic* (*flatter*) don't try making up to me; they got the money by making up to the old man

map out *vtsép* **(a)** (*tracer*) have you mapped out the route yet?
  (b) (*préparer, organiser*) I've mapped out a programme

mark up *vtsép* (*augmenter le prix de*) most restaurants mark up wine by about ten per cent

marry off *vtsép* (*marier par arrangement*) she's being married off to a man who's twenty years older than her

measure up 1 *vtsép* **(a)** (*mesurer*) after measuring up the timber . . .
  (b) (*prendre la mesure de*) she measured the situation up with one glance
  2 *vi* (*être à la hauteur*) I don't think you're going to measure up to the job

meet up *vi* (*se rencontrer, se voir*) let's meet up again soon

meet with *vic* **(a)** (*rencontrer*) the proposal has met with fierce opposition; rescue attempts have so far met with failure; the suggestion met with acclaim **(b)** (*avoir rendez-vous avec, rencontrer*) the senator is meeting with his advisors next week

melt away *vi* **(a)** (*fondre et disparaître*) the ice has melted away
  (b) (*disparaître*) the onlookers melted away after the initial excitement

melt down *vtsép* (*fondre*) the gold jewellery will have been melted down by now and will be impossible to identify

mess about/around *Fam* **1** *vtsép* **(a)** (*s'amuser avec, faire tourner en bourrique*) first we're going, then we're not going – I wish you would stop messing me about! **(b)** (*changer l'ordre de, de façon gênante*) they've messed the programmes around again
  2 *vi* **(a)** (*faire l'idiot*) stop messing about! **(b)** (*traîner*) he's

been messing about in the garden all day **(c)** (*s'amuser avec*) don't mess around with something that doesn't belong to you

mess up *vtsép* **(a)** (*salir, mettre en désordre*) don't mess the kitchen up **(b)** (*gâcher, bousiller*) you've really messed your marriage up; by changing his mind at the last minute he's messed things up for all of us

miss out 1 *vtsép* (*omettre, oublier*) have I missed anyone out?
   2 *vi* (*rater quelque chose de valable*) you missed out on a great concert; (*rater son coup*) you missed out there

mix up *vtsép* **(a)** (*préparer, pour un mélange*) will you mix up some of my medicine for me? **(b)** (*embrouiller*) don't talk to me when I'm trying to count or you'll mix me up; (*confondre*) he mixes her up with her mother **(c)** (*tremper, mêler*) everyone in that family is mixed up in something dishonest

move along 1 *vtsép** (*faire partir*) policemen had to move the crowd along
   2 *vi* **(a)** (*se pousser*) move along and let the lady sit down **(b)** (*partir*) I really ought to be moving along; all the policeman said of course was "move along, there's nothing to see" **(c)** (*passer*) moving along to my next question

move in 1 *vtsép* **(a)** (*envoyer*) the government has decided to move troops in to quell the riots in the city **(b)** (*déménager*) the company can't move us in for another two weeks
   2 *vi* **(a)** (*avancer, d'une façon menaçante*) troops are now moving in on the beleaguered capital **(b)** (*emménager*) people are moving in next door

move on 1 *vtsép* (*faire partir*) the police moved us on
   2 *vi* (*passer, avancer*) can we move on to the next item on the agenda?

move out 1 *vtsép* (*enlever, faire sortir*) you'll have to move the car out of the garage; (*faire déménager*) they're being moved out of their homes to make way for a new road; (*faire partir*) the new government has promised to move its soldiers out
   2 *vi* **(a)** (*déménager*) the people next door have decided to move out **(b)** (*se retirer*) troops are already moving out

move up 1 *vtsép* **(a)** (*monter, changer de place vers le haut*) move this section up; his regiment was moved up to the front

    (b) (*promouvoir*) they've moved him up to be assistant manager
    2 *vi* (*s'avancer*) troops are moving up to the combat zone

muddle along/on *vi* (*se débrouiller tant bien que mal*) they were
    muddling along quite happily and then management brought in a
    team of consultants to look at efficiency

muddle up *vtsép* (*mélanger, confondre*) he's managed to muddle the
    dates up; (*embrouiller*) you're muddling me up

muscle in *vi Fam* (*s'imposer*) he's not keen on people muscling in on
    his territory; I'm not going to let anyone muscle in (*c.-à-d. je ne
    vais laisser personne s'immiscer dans mes affaires*)

N

narrow down 1 *vi* (*se réduire*) the question narrows down to this . . .
    2 *vtsép* (*réduire, à partir d'une grande quantité*) we've
    narrowed the candidates down to four

nod off *vi Fam* (*s'endormir*) Grandpa was sitting nodding off in front
    of the television

notch up *vtsép Fam* (*marquer*) she has notched up yet another win

O

open on to *vic* (*donner sur*) the back door opens on to a paved courtyard

open out 1 *vi* (*s'ouvrir, s'épanouir*) the roses are beginning to open out
    2 *vtsép* (*déplier*) it's difficult to open out your newspaper on a
    crowded commuter train

open up 1 *vi* **(a)** (*s'ouvrir*) another couple of warm days and the
    roses will have opened up; new markets are opening up all
    the time; there are some new shops opening up on the high
    street **(b)** (*s'ouvrir, se montrer franc*) he never opens up to
    anybody **(c)** (*ouvrir, pour un endroit fermé*) police – open up!;
    the shop-keeper was just opening up when I passed

2 *vtsép* **(a)** (*commencer à exploiter*) the rain forest is being opened up for development **(b)** (*ouvrir, pour les portes*) when did you open the shop up this morning? **(c)** (*commencer, pour une affaire*) opening up a restaurant in this part of town is a risky venture

opt out *vi* (*choisir de ne plus participer*) I'm opting out of the committee because I have too many other commitments

own up *vi* (*avouer*) I know it was you I saw so you might as well own up; he rarely owns up to his mistakes

P

pack away *vtsép* **(a)** (*ranger*) maybe we packed our winter clothes away a little too soon **(b)** *Fam* (*se goinfrer de*) I've never seen anyone who can pack it away like you

pack in 1 *vtsép* **(a)** (*coincer, dans une valise, un tiroir, etc.*) you can't possibly pack anything more in **(b)** (*attirer, en grand nombre*) her latest film is packing them in **(c)** *Fam* (*arrêter*) he's decided to pack his job in; go next door and tell them to pack that noise in **(d)** *Fam* (*plaquer, pour un(e) petit(e) ami(e), etc.*) are you going to pack him in or not?
    2 *vi* **(a)** (*rentrer, tenir*) I don't know how all those people manage to pack in to one train **(b)** *Fam* (*tomber en panne*) the lawnmower's packed in on me

pack off *vtsép* (*envoyer, se débarrasser de*) I'll call you back once I've packed the kids off to school

pack out *vtsép* (*remplir, bourrer*) the fans packed the hall out; the pub was packed out so we went somewhere else

pack up *vi* **(a)** (*faire ses bagages*) pack up – we're not staying here another night **(b)** (*se préparer à quitter le travail*) are you packing up already? **(c)** *Fam* (*tomber en panne*) the lawnmower has just packed up so I can't cut the grass

palm off *vtsép Fam* **(a)** (*refiler, donner, pour quelque chose qu'on ne veut pas*) they're palming the children off on us for the weekend; be careful he doesn't try to palm any rotten fruit off on you

(b) (*se débarrasser de, d'une façon allusive*) the last time I complained, the company palmed me off with a standard letter

pass away *vi* Euphémique (*s'éteindre, mourir*) the old lady passed away in her sleep

pass by 1 *vi* **(a)** (*passer*) luckily a taxi was passing by just at that moment **(b)** (*passer, pour le temps*) time is passing by – are you going to meet the deadline?
    2 *vic* (*passer devant*) we pass by that house every morning
    3 *vtts* (*locution*) do you ever feel that life has passed you by?
est-ce que tu ne penses jamais que la vie t'est passée sous le nez ?

pass off 1 *vi* **(a)** (*se dérouler*) the ceremony passed off without a hitch
    (b) (*dissiper*) is the nausea passing off?
    2 *vtsép* (*faire passer pour*) he passed her off as a duchess

pass on 1 *vi* **(a)** Euphémique (*s'éteindre, mourir*) when did your father pass on? **(b)** (*passer*) why don't we pass on to the next item on the agenda and come back to this later?
    2 *vtsép* (*dire, pour une information*) don't pass this on, but . . .; (*passer, donner*) I passed the file on to him yesterday

pass out 1 *vi* (*s'évanouir*) one look at the needle and she passed out; I must have passed out
    2 *vtsép* (*distribuer*) he passed copies of the memo out to the people at the meeting

pass over 1 *vtsép* (*oublier, ignorer*) they've passed me over for promotion again
    2 *vi* Euphémique (*s'éteindre, mourir*) the clairvoyant began to talk about "our loved ones who have passed over"

pass up *vtsép* (*laisser passer*) imagine passing up a job like that!; she has had to pass up the offer

patch up *vtsép* **(a)** (*réparer temporairement, bricoler*) I've managed to patch the car up so that it gets us into town at least; (*soigner rapidement*) the army doctor just patched him up and sent him back to the front **(b)** (*locution*) to patch things up *se raccommoder, se réconcilier*

pay back *vtsép* **(a)** (*rembourser*) have you paid that money back yet?
    (b) (*se venger sur*) I'll pay you back for this!

pay off *vtsép* **(a)** (*licencier*) the company is going to pay half its labour force off at the end of the month **(b)** (*finir de rembourser*) when we've paid the mortgage off, . . . **(c)** (*acheter, corrompre par l'argent*) the policeman admitted to having been paid off

pay out *vtsép* **(a)** (*dépenser*) he's had to pay out a lot on car repairs lately **(b)** (*payer*) the wages were paid out this morning **(c)** (*laisser filer, pour une corde*) pay out some more line

pay up 1 *vtsép* **(a)** (*payer, pour une dette*) has she paid up what she owes you? **(b)** (*payer complètement*) my subscription is paid up **2** *vi* (*payer*) I've asked him twice to pay up but I'm still waiting

pick off *vtsép* **(a)** (**enlever, petit à petit*) why spend all that time putting nail varnish on when you just pick it off a day later? (*ramasser) pick those papers off the floor **(b)** (**cueillir, ramasser*) the birds have picked all the cherries off **(c)** (*abattre, à la carabine*) the sniper picked them off one by one

pick on *vic* **(a)** (*choisir*) who have you picked on for your bridesmaid?; why pick on me to answer? **(b)** *Fam* (*harceler*) stop picking on the boy, he's doing his best

pick out *vtsép* **(a)** (*choisir*) I've picked out one or two patterns you might like **(b)** (*identifier*) she picked the man out from an identity parade; I picked you out immediately – you were the only one wearing a red coat **(c)** (*enlever*) pick out any badly bruised fruit **(d)** (*rehausser*) the panels on the door are picked out in a deeper shade of the colour used on the walls **(e)** (*retrouver, jouer à peu près, pour un air*) he can pick out a few tunes but that's all

pick up 1 *vtsép* **(a)** (*ramasser, prendre*) he picked up a book and started to read **(b)** (*prendre en passant*) will you pick my prescription up at the chemist's?; when did he say he would be picking us up?; the bus stopped to pick up passengers **(c)** (*dénicher, dégoter*) they picked that wonderful old table up at an auction **(d)** *Fam* (*draguer*) he goes around picking up women **(e)** (*attraper, pour une maladie*) she's constantly picking up colds **(f)** (*prendre, pour des habitudes, un accent, etc.*) that child has picked up some very bad habits; (*apprendre*) I'll never pick this game up **(g)** (*arrêter, par la police*) he's been picked up for shoplifting **(h)** (*poursuivre, continuer avec*) to pick up my story, . . . **(i)** (*découvrir*) the police have picked up a trail that

might lead them to the wanted man; (*attraper*) you can pick up a
lot of foreign stations with a short-wave radio **(j)** (*corriger*)
please pick me up if I make any mistakes

2 *vtts* (*remonter le moral à*) a tonic will pick her up; what
would really pick me up would be . . .

3 *vi* **(a)** (*s'améliorer*) the weather is picking up; (*aller mieux*)
he's been quite ill but he's picked up in the last day or two
(b) (*continuer*) let's pick up where we left off **(c)** (*s'afficher*) I
don't like that crowd you've picked up with

pile up 1 *vi* (*s'accumuler*) the work tends to pile up at this time of
year; (*s'immobiliser, pour la circulation*) one of the lanes has
had to be closed and traffic is piling up

2 *vtsép* (*faire un tas de*) pile the leaves up there; *Fam*
(*amasser*) they're piling up the money

pin down *vtsép* **(a)** (*coincer, immobiliser*) they were pinned down by
wreckage; he has his opponent pinned down on the canvas
(b) (*forcer à décider, coincer*) I've tried to pin her down to a
time **(c)** (*définir*) it's just one of those feelings that are very
difficult to pin down; (*identifier*) I was sure I had seen him
before but I couldn't pin him down

pipe down *vi Fam* **(a)** (*se taire, mettre la sourdine*) I wish you two
would pipe down while I'm trying to watch television
(b) (*se la boucler*) just pipe down about it, OK?; he finally
piped down when he realized she knew more about it than he did

play about/around *vi* (*s'amuser*) it's about time he stopped playing
about and settled down; you shouldn't play around with people's
feelings

play along 1 *vi* (*coopérer*) if that's what you've decided then I'm quite
happy to play along

2 *vtts* (*manipuler, en vue d'obtenir des avantages*) he's just
playing her along until he gets what he wants

play back *vtsép* (*repasser, pour un enregistrement*) play that last bit back

play down *vtsép* (*minimiser*) she played down the extent of her
injuries; the government is trying to play down its involvement

play off 1 *vtsép* (*monter . . . contre . . ., pour en tirer profit*) she's
playing Phil off against Tom; you take pleasure in playing people
off against each other, don't you?

2 *vi* (*jouer la belle*) the two teams will play off next week

play on 1 *vi* (*continuer à jouer*) the orchestra played on despite the bombardment
    2 *vic* (*se servir de*) he's just playing on your kindness with all those hard luck stories

play out *vtsép* **(a)** (*agir, jouer*) that was quite a scene they played out for our benefit **(b)** *habituellement au passif* (*être épuisé*) he's played out as a world class boxer; I feel quite played out **(c)** (*accompagner la sortie de . . . en musique*) the organist played the congregation out

play up 1 *vi Fam* **(a)** (*faire des siennes, causer des ennuis*) the car is playing up again **(b)** (*flatter*) he plays up to anyone who can further his career
    2 *vtts* (*embêter, faire des problèmes à*) the baby has been playing me up all day

plough back *vtsép* (*réinvestir*) all the profits are ploughed back into the company

plug in 1 *vtsép* (*brancher*) plug the iron in
    2 *vi* (*brancher*) it would help if you plugged in first!

plug up *vtsép* (*remplir, boucher*) that gap will have to be plugged up

plump for *vic Fam* (*se décider pour*) I see you plumped for a car instead of a holiday

point out *vtsép* **(a)** (*montrer*) can you point him out? **(b)** (*préciser, indiquer*) she pointed out the extra work that this would entail

point up *vtsép* (*souligner, faire resssortir*) why point up the difficulties?

poke about/around 1 *vi* **(a)** (*chercher*) poke about and see what you can find; the dog was poking about in the bushes **(b)** (*mettre son nez dans les affaires des autres*) that social worker is always poking about
    2 *vic* (*fouiner dans, fouiller*) I love poking about antique shops

poke out 1 *vi* (*dépasser, sortir*) the label on your coat is poking out
    2 *vtsép* **(a)** (*sortir*) she opened the window and poked her head out **(b)** (*enlever, avec quelque chose de pointu*) careful or you'll poke my eye out!

polish off *vtsép Fam* (*finir, achever*) you polished that plate of pasta off in record time!; the sports commentators feel that Sampras will polish this opponent off too

polish up *vtsép* **(a)** (*polir, astiquer*) the silver needs to be polished up **(b)** (*améliorer*) I'm going to evening classes to polish up my maths

pop off *vi* **(a)** *Fam* (*clamser, claquer*) guess who popped off last night? **(b)** (*partir, à l'imprévu*) they're popping off for the weekend

pore over *vic* (*plonger dans*) he spends all his time poring over old manuscripts

pour out 1 *vi* (*sortir en masse*) smoke was pouring out of the windows; (*affluer, sortir en flots*) once she had composed herself, the words just poured out
 2 *vtsép* **(a)** (*servir*) will I pour out the tea?; (*verser*) pour some sugar out into a bowl **(b)** (*se montrer bavard à propos de*) I hope you didn't mind me pouring my troubles out like that

print out *vtsép* (*imprimer*) the text is edited on screen and then printed out to be sent back to the author

prop up *vtsép* (*consolider, renforcer*) they've had to prop the castle walls up; the regime is being propped up by the military; *Plaisanterie* you can usually find him propping up the bar at his local; (*appuyer*) he propped himself up against the gate

pull away 1 *vtsép* (*enlever en tirant*) they had to pull the distraught father away from the burning car
 2 *vi* **(a)** (*démarrer*) the train slowly pulled away **(b)** (*s'écarter, prendre de la distance*) the dog pulled away when I tried to pat it; why do you keep pulling away? **(c)** (*prendre de l'avance, dans une course*) she's beginning to pull away

pull down *vtsép* **(a)** (*baisser*) pull the blind down **(b)** (*démolir*) how many more buildings are they going to pull down? **(c)** (*affaiblir*) this cold is really pulling me down **(d)** *Am Fam* (*gagner, pour de l'argent*) considering his qualifications, he doesn't pull down much of a salary

pull in 1 *vtsép* **(a)** (*attirer*) the play is pulling people in by the coach-load **(b)** (*arrêter*) the police pulled him in for questioning
 2 *vi* **(a)** (*s'arrêter, se garer*) pull in here **(b)** (*s'arrêter*) we'll pull in to the next garage we see **(c)** (*arriver, pour on train ou*

un bus) the express pulled in two hours late

pull off *vtsép* **(a)** (*enlever) when I had pulled the paper off . . .; he pulled off his clothes **(b)** (*réussir*) I never thought we would pull it off; he has pulled off a remarkable achievement

pull out 1 *vtsép* **(a)** (*sortir en tirant*) I'm stuck in this mud – you'll have to pull me out; (*arracher*) he's having a tooth pulled out tomorrow **(b)** (*retirer*) the president has promised that all troops will be pulled out by the end of the year
   2 *vi* **(a)** (*sortir, souvent pour doubler*) look in your mirror before you pull out **(b)** (*partir, en train ou en bus*) when do we pull out? **(c)** (*se retirer*) troops have begun to pull out

pull over 1 *vtsép* **(a)** (**tirer, mettre en tirant*) he pulled his sweater over his head **(b)** (*faire tomber*) be careful or you'll pull the filing cabinet over on top of you
   2 *vi* (*se mettre de côté, se rabattre et s'arrêter*) the policeman asked us to pull over; (*se rabattre*) she's pulling over to let the other runners past

pull through 1 *vtts* (*faire tenir, permettre de tenir le coup*) he says it was his faith that pulled him through
   2 *vi* (*guérir*) I think we can confidently say that she will pull through

pull together 1 *vi* (*coopérer*) we must pull together on this
   2 *vtts* (*se calmer, s'organiser*) come on, pull yourself together, there's a lot to be done

pull up 1 *vtsép* **(a)** (*amener*) he pulled up a chair and joined us; (*remonter*) pull the blind up **(b)** (*réprimander*) she pulled him up about his bad language; the police pulled him up for not having his lights on
   2 *vi* **(a)** (*s'arrêter*) why are you pulling up?; the horse pulled up lame **(b)** (*rattraper une distance*) he is beginning to pull up, but I think he's left it too late

push ahead *vi* **(a)** (*avancer*) research on this is pushing ahead in various countries **(b)** (*continuer, poursuivre, malgré les difficultés*) I think we should push ahead nonetheless

push along 1 *vtsép* (*pousser*) as she pushed the pram along . . .
   2 *vi Fam* (*partir, se sauver*) I suppose I should be pushing along soon

push around *vtsép Fam* (*marcher sur les pieds à, donner des ordres à*) I'm not going to let him push us around like this

push for *vic* (*exercer une pression pour obtenir*) the company is pushing for more government funding

push off 1 *vtsép* (**enlever, en poussant*) push the lid off
    2 *vi Fam* **(a)** (*partir, s'en aller*) everyone's pushing off at five o'clock; I wish you would push off and let me finish what I'm doing **(b)** (*partir en bateau, déborder*) we pushed off in the early hours of the morning

push on 1 *vi* (*continuer*) we decided to push on
    2 *vtsép* **(a)** (*forcer pour mettre*) I had to push it on to make it fit **(b)** (*encourager*) both runners are being pushed on by the crowd

push through 1 *vic* (*se faire un chemin à travers*) we'll have to push through the crowd
    2 *vtsép** (*imposer*) the government is pushing this bill through

push up *vtsép* **(a)** (*lever, en poussant*) you have to push up the garage door **(b)** (*faire monter*) excessive wage increases are pushing up inflation

put about *vtsép* (*répandre, faire courir*) who put that rumour about?; it's being put about that . . .

put across *vtsép* **(a)** (*faire passer, pour des idées*) he didn't put that across very well; a politician who certainly knows how to put herself across (*c.-à-d. s'imposer*) **(b)** (*locution*) to put one across somebody *duper, faire marcher quelqu'un*

put away *vtsép* **(a)** (*ranger, remettre à sa place*) put your wallet away – I'm paying for this; could someone put the car away for the night? **(b)** (*économiser, mettre de côté*) she puts something away every month for the proverbial rainy day **(c)** (*engloutir, siffler, de la nourriture ou de l'alcool*) this family puts away so much meat that I'm the butcher's favourite customer; (*picoler*) he's down at the pub every night putting it away; you're putting it away a bit, aren't you? **(d)** (*enfermer, dans une prison, etc.*) that maniac should be put away somewhere

put back *vtsép* **(a)** (*remettre*) put that back where you found it
    (b) (*repousser, à une autre date, etc.*) the meeting's been put

back till next month **(c)** (*retarder l'heure de*) isn't this the week
we put the clocks back?

put down *vtsép* **(a)** (*poser*) put that down before you drop it
(b) (*déposer*) if you put me down at the next corner, I can walk
the rest of the way **(c)** (*faire atterrir*) the pilot had to put the
plane down on the motorway **(d)** (*faire baisser*) we will put this
uprising down with the utmost firmness **(e)** *Fam* (*dire du mal
de, rabaisser*) he's always putting her down; why do you keep
putting yourself down? **(f)** (*abattre, faire piquer, pour un animal*)
the cat's in a great deal of pain – I think we should have her put
down **(g)** (*payer*) how much do you have to put down as a
deposit? **(h)** (*écrire*) have you put all the details down?
(i) (*attribuer*) she puts it down to laziness

put forward *vtsép* **(a)** (*suggérer, proposer*) somebody put forward the
rather good idea that . . .; they've put him forward for a
knighthood **(b)** (*avancer, à une autre date, etc.*) the meeting has
been put forward to noon today **(c)** (*avancer l'heure de*) did you
put your watch forward?

put in 1 *vtsép* **(a)** (**mettre, dans une valise, armoire, etc.*) have you put
everything in? **(b)** (*installer*) we're finally having a telephone
put in **(c)** (*faire, travailler*) I put in a lot of overtime last month;
don't you think you should put in a bit of piano practice?
  2 *vtts* (*présenter, inscrire*) we're putting him in for the 500 and
1000 metres
  3 *vi* (*poser sa candidature pour*) has he put in for that job we
saw advertised?

put off 1 *vtsép* **(a)** (*déposer) could you put me off at the High Street?
(b) (*faire descendre) the bus conductor put the boys off because
of their behaviour **(c)** (*repousser*) let's put lunch off to another
time **(d)** (*décommander*) you can't keep putting him off like this
– just tell him you don't want to go out with him **(e)** (*éteindre*)
put the TV off
  2 *vtts* **(a)** (*dégoûter*) their stories have put me off foreign
travel; that programme on slaughter houses put him off meat for
a week **(b)** (*déranger, gêner*) you would think that all those
people standing round watching would put her off

put on 1 *vtsép* **(a)** (**mettre, pour un vêtement, etc.*) put your coat on;
she put on her glasses **(b)** (*affecter, simuler*) the boss can put on
a show of being fierce; she puts on a posh accent sometimes;

he's just putting it on (*c.-à-d. il fait semblant*) **(c)** (*jouer, faire passer*) they're not putting Hamlet on again?; why can't they put on something decent on TV for a change? **(d)** (*ajouter*) he's put on a few inches round the waist **(e)** (*allumer*) put the radio on
2 *vtts* (*avancer l'heure de*) we had to put our watches on several times when we flew to Australia

put on to *vttsc* (*indiquer*) I can put you on to an excellent restaurant; (*mettre sur la piste de*) what put the police on to him as the culprit?

put out 1 *vtsép* **(a)** (*mettre dehors*) don't forget to put the milk bottles out **(b)** (*préparer, sortir*) have you put the side plates out as well? **(c)** (*tendre*) she put her hand out **(d)** (*faire sortir, publier*) we'll be putting out a new edition very soon **(e)** (*éteindre*) put the light out **(f)** (*faire perdre conscience, pour un malade*) the drug will put you out very quickly
2 *vtts* **(a)** (*énerver*) everyone was put out by the two hour delay **(b)** (*gêner, déranger*) would one more guest put you out?; I don't want to put anyone out **(c)** (*démettre, disloquer*) don't lift that table or you'll put your back out again

put through 1 *vtsép* **(a)** (**faire accepter*) a bill has been put through Parliament that . . . **(b)** (*passer, pour un correspondant téléphonique*) will you put me through to the book department, please?
2 *vttsc* (*causer à*) you've put your mother through a great deal of anxiety with your behaviour

put up *vtsép* **(a)** (*lever*) put up your hand if you know the answer **(b)** (*construire, ériger*) a new block of flats is being put up just behind their house **(c)** (*accrocher au mur*) I want to put up a few more pictures in this room **(d)** (*augmenter*) car manufacturers are putting their prices up again **(e)** (*héberger*) could you put us up while we're in town? **(f)** (*mettre*) a lot of people have put their houses up for sale; (*présenter*) they put up a lot of resistance; she put up a good fight but had to concede defeat in the end (*c.-à-d. elle a mené un très beau combat*)

put up with *vic* (*tolérer, supporter*) why do you put up with that kind of behaviour?; it's a lot to have to put up with

Q

quieten down 1 *vi* **(a)** (*se calmer*) if you lot don't quieten down I'm going to get very cross **(b)** (*devenir calme*) business always quietens down after Christmas

   2 *vtsép* (*calmer*) it took me ages to quieten the class down; the nurse tried to quieten the child down but he kept crying for his mother

R

rain off (*Am* = **rain out**) *vtsép habituellement au passif* (*annuler pour cause de pluie*) the match was rained off

rattle through *vic* **(a)** (*rouler dans un bruit de ferraille*) the two old cars rattled through the streets **(b)** (*faire ou dire à toute vitesse*) she tends to rattle through her work; the speaker fairly rattled through his speech

read out *vtsép* (*lire à haute voix*) he read out the names of the injured

read up on *vic* (*étudier, potasser*) the play might have meant more to you if you'd read up a bit on the events it depicted

rein in 1 *vtsép* **(a)** (*ramener au pas*) the girl reined her pony in and turned back towards the stables **(b)** (*restreindre, diminuer*) he tried very hard to rein his anger in; the council wants to rein in its spending on sports facilities

   2 *vi* **(a)** (*ralentir l'allure d'un cheval*) they reined in so they could talk **(b)** (*faire des économies*) we'll have to rein in this month

rest up *vi* (*se reposer*) the doctor has told him to rest up

ring back *vi Br* (*rappeler, au téléphone*) could you ring back in half an hour?

ring in *vi Br* (*téléphoner*) you ought to have rung in to say you were ill and couldn't come to work

ring off *vi Br* (*raccrocher*) I must ring off now, there's someone at the door

ring out *vi* (*résonner*) her voice rang out; the church bells were ringing out

ring up *vtsép Br* (*téléphoner à*) why not ring her up and ask?

rip off *vtsép* **(a)** (**arracher*) as soon as they got their hands on the presents, the children ripped the paper off **(b)** *Pop* (*arnaquer*) let's choose another restaurant – I was ripped off the last time I was at this one

rip up *vtsép* (*déchirer en petits morceaux*) just rip his letter up and forget the whole business

root for *vic* (*supporter, encourager*) which side are you rooting for?; the candidate I root for invariably loses

rough out *vtsép* (*ébaucher*) could you rough out a publicity campaign?

rough up *vtsép* **(a)** (*ébouriffer*) don't rough up my hair **(b)** (*malmener, attaquer*) he was roughed up by some soccer fans; they roughed her up a bit but she's all right

round down *vtsép* (*arrondir, à un chiffre inférieur*) the price will be rounded down

round off *vtsép* **(a)** (*arrondir*) round off the edges **(b)** (*terminer*) we rounded the meal off with coffee and liqueurs; she rounded off her presentation by saying . . .

round on *vic* (*s'en prendre à, attaquer*) rounding on his tormentors, he shouted . . .

round up *vtsép* **(a)** (*rassembler*) about this time of year the cattle are rounded up; round everyone up for the meeting, will you? **(b)** (*arrondir, au chiffre supérieur*) just round the bill up to £50

rub down *vtsép* (*sécher*) the groom will rub your horse down; he rubbed himself down with the towel

rub in *vtsép* **(a)** (*faire pénétrer, en frottant ou massant*) rub the cream in well **(b)** *Fam* (*insister sur, rappeler avec insistance*) she kept rubbing in his unpunctuality; I know I was wrong – don't keep rubbing it in!

rub off 1 *vtsép** (*effacer*) rub those dirty marks off the wall; the teacher rubbed the equations off the blackboard

2 *vi* **(a)** (*partir en frottant*) the stain won't rub off **(b)** *Fig* (*déteindre*) I hope his attitude to authority doesn't rub off on you

rub out *vtsép* **(a)** (*enlever en frottant*) try rubbing the stain out with soap and water **(b)** (*gommer*) don't rub out your calculations **(c)** *Pop* (*tuer, liquider*) the gang decided to rub the witness out before she could talk to police

run about 1 *vic* (*courir*) I refuse to run about the shops looking for presents for people I don't like
    2 *vi* (*courir çà et là*) the children were running about on the beach; (*être très occupé*) she's been running about all day preparing for her mother-in-law's visit

run across *vic* (*rencontrer par hasard, tomber sur*) if you should run across John give him my regards; I've run across a word I don't know

run away with *vic* **(a)** (*partir avec, s'enfuir avec*) I know it sounds ridiculous, but his wife has run away with the milkman! **(b)** (*se sauver avec*) the man in the butcher's has run away with the week's takings **(c)** (*monter à la tête, pour l'enthousiasme, l'imagination, etc.*) jogging five times a week is what I call letting your enthusiasm run away with you; if I'm not careful, she'll run away with the idea that I'm very easy-going (*c.-à-d. elle se mettra dans la tête que*) **(d)** (*utiliser*) repairs to the house have run away with most of our savings

run back 1 *vi* **(a)** (*rentrer en courant*) I ran back to the car **(b)** (*revenir vers son partenaire, pour un homme ou une femme*) he'll come running back once he's had his fling
    2 *vtts* (*ramener en voiture*) don't worry about the last bus – I'll run you back

run down 1 *vi* **(a)** (*descendre les escaliers*) run down and see who's at the door **(b)** (*perdre son pouvoir, s'essouffler*) the government is accused of letting the industry run down; (*s'arrêter, pour une horloge, etc.*) don't wind the clock until it has completely run down; (*se décharger*) you've let the battery run down
    2 *vtsép* **(a)** (*renverser, pour un véhicule*) she was run down by a bus **(b)** (*dire du mal de*) you shouldn't run everyone down so **(c)** (*décharger*) remember to switch off the lights or they'll run the battery down; (*baisser la production de*) the factory is being deliberately run down **(d)** (*trouver après de longues recherches,*

dénicher) the police finally ran him down in Hove

run in 1 *vi* (*entrer en courant*) she came running in to tell us
  2 *vtsép* **(a)** *Br* (*rôder*) it will be another couple of weeks before we've run the new machine in **(b)** *Fam* (*arrêter*) the police ran him in for drunk driving

run into *vic* **(a)** (*rentrer dans*) he ran into an old lady as he raced for his train **(b)** (*rencontrer par hasard*) guess who I ran into last week **(c)** (*s'élever à*) the cost will run into millions

run off 1 *vi* (*partir en courant*) he ran off when he saw me coming; (*partir*) I haven't seen next door's dog for ages – I hope he's run off
  2 *vtsép* **(a)** (*tirer*) will you run off six copies of this? **(b)** (*écrire vite, écrire au fil de la plume*) she runs these magazine articles off in her spare time **(c)** (*perdre en courant*) he's a bit overweight and wants to run off a few pounds

run out 1 *vi* (*s'achever*) your time is running out
  2 *vtsép* (*éliminer, au cricket*) he was run out for ten

run out of *vic* (*être à bout de*) I have run out of patience with you; (*manquer de, être à court de*) we're running out of butter; with two miles to go we ran out of petrol

run over 1 *vi* **(a)** (*faire un saut*) I won't be a minute – I'm just running over to the shops **(b)** (*dépasser le temps accordé*) television broadcasts of sports events often run over into the next programme **(c)** (*déborder*) the sink is running over
  2 *vic* (*examiner rapidement*) the doctor will want to run over your case history; let's run over the arrangements one last time
  3 *vtts* (*amener en voiture*) I'm running Mum over to Grandad's – do you want to come?
  4 *vtsép* (*renverser en voiture*) he ran an old lady over

run through 1 *vic* **(a)** (*utiliser*) I hate to think how many clean shirts he runs through in a week **(b)** (*revoir, répéter*) would you like me to run through your speech with you?
  2 *vtsép* (*poignarder*) the coachman ran the highwayman through

run up 1 *vi* **(a)** (*monter, en courant*) run up and fetch my purse for me **(b)** (*accourir*) people ran up to see if they could help
  2 *vtsép* **(a)** (*faire vite, pour des vêtements*) the dressmaker said she could run the suit up for me in a couple of days

(b) (*accumuler*) you've run up a lot of bills this month
(c) (*hisser, pour les drapeaux*) they run the flag up on special occasions

rush at *vi* **(a)** (*attaquer*) he rushed at the burglar **(b)** (*faire sans réfléchir*) it's not the kind of job that can be rushed at – take your time

rush through 1 *vtsép* **(a)** (*envoyer de toute urgence*) the necessary equipment has been rushed through to the rescue workers **(b)** (******exécuter d'urgence*) could you rush my order through?
2 *vttsc* (*faire passer à toute allure*) they rushed us through Customs; (*faire dépêcher pour finir*) you rushed me through lunch and now you're rushing me through dinner – what's the hurry?

rustle up *vtsép* *Fam* (*préparer à la hâte, pour un plat ou une boisson*) could you rustle up a meal for me?

S

save up 1 *vi* (*faire des économies*) if you want a new motorbike you'll have to start saving up, won't you?
2 *vtsép* **(a)** (*économiser*) you should save up part of your pocket money for Christmas presents **(b)** (*garder, mettre de côté*) one of the children's programmes on TV has asked viewers to save up silver paper

score off 1 *vtsép** (*rayer, enlever*) score his name off the guest list
2 *vic* (*marquer un point sur, dans un débat*) the speaker scored off the government when he reminded them of their campaign promises

score out *vtsép* (*rayer, barrer*) score any mistakes out neatly

scrape along *vi* (*se débrouiller, surtout financièrement*) she's scraping along until her next pay cheque

scrape by *vi* (*passer de justesse*) I don't mind scraping by, as long as I pass the exam; he's just been scraping by since he lost his job (*c.-à-d. il joint à peine les deux bouts*)

scrape together/up *vtsép* (*trouver, avec difficulté*) I'll scrape the money together for you somehow

scream out 1 *vi* (*pousser un cri*) the pain made him scream out
   2 *vtsép* (*crier*) the sergeant major screamed out his orders

screw up *vtsép* **(a)** (*froisser, chiffonner*) she screwed the letter up and threw it in the fire **(b)** (*faire des grimaces avec*) don't screw your face up like that **(c)** *Fam* (*bousiller*) this rush job has screwed up my plans for the weekend **(d)** *Fam* (*gâcher*) you screwed the whole thing up – next time let me do the talking **(e)** *Fam* (*rendre neurotique*) he claims it was his parents that screwed him up; she's all screwed up that girl

see about *vic* **(a)** (*s'occuper de*) you'll have to see about those cracks in the ceiling **(b)** (*considérer, voir*) I'll see about it; *Ironique* so they're going to win, are they? well, we'll see about that

see across *vtts* (*faire traverser*) she saw me across the road

see in 1 *vi* (*voir dedans*) they always keep the curtains drawn so people can't see in
   2 *vtsép* (*faire entrer*) always see guests in

see off *vtsép* (*dire au revoir, à la gare, à l'aéroport*) who's coming to see you off?

see out 1 *vi* (*voir dehors*) another passenger changed seats with the little boy so he could see out
   2 *vtsép* **(a)** (*raccompagner à la porte*) my husband will see you out, doctor **(b)** (*durer*) I don't think my boots will see the winter out

see over/round *vic* (*visiter*) would you like to see over our new house?

see through 1 *vic* (*ne pas se laisser duper par, voir clair à propos de*) why do you persist with these stories? – everyone can see through them
   2 *vtts* (*aider à supporter, pour une difficulté*) friends and neighbours are seeing them through this bad time; a couple of hundred gallons of oil should see us through the winter

see to *vic* (*s'occuper de*) let your husband see to the baby – you relax for a bit

see up *vtsép* (*accompagner à un étage supérieur*) do you know where his room is or do you want me to see you up?

seize up *vi* (*ne plus marcher, se coincer*) if you don't put some oil in soon the engine will seize up; (*s'ankyloser*) my knee always seizes up at the most inconvenient times

seize (up) on *vic* (*sauter sur, pour une occasion, une idée, etc.*) it seemed like an excellent idea and we seized on it immediately

sell off *vtsép* (*liquider, solder*) the shoe shop is closing down soon and has started to sell off its stock

sell out 1 *vtsép* **(a)** *habituellement au passif* (*ne plus avoir en stock*) how can a supermarket be sold out of butter? **(b)** (*vendre*) the rebel leaders were accused of selling their supporters out
   2 *vi* **(a)** (*liquider son stock*) all of the shops I tried had sold out **(b)** (*vendre une affaire*) they are selling out since they want to retire **(c)** (*trahir*) we will negotiate but we will never sell out

sell up 1 *vtsép habituellement au passif* (*forcer à vendre*) something has to be done to prevent farmers being sold up and losing their livelihood
   2 *vi* (*vendre, liquider*) since she can no longer run the business on her own, she has decided to sell up

send away *vtsép* (*envoyer, faire partir*) a boy of seven is too young to be sent away to school

send away for *vic* (*se faire envoyer, demander par correspondance*) send away for your free gift now; you should send away for an application form

send down *vtsép* **(a)** (*faire descendre*) the people upstairs sent a lovely cake down for us **(b)** (*faire baisser*) the rumours have sent share prices down **(c)** *Br Fam* (*mettre en prison, coffrer*) the judge sent her down for two years **(d)** *Br* (*expulser de l'université*) all of the students involved in the incident were sent down for a term

send for *vic* (*appeler, faire venir*) I think we should send for the doctor

send in *vtsép* (*envoyer*) a lot of viewers have sent in comments on the programme we aired last week; (*faire entrer*) send Mr Martin in as soon as he arrives please

send off *vtsép* **(a)** (*envoyer par la poste*) have you sent that letter off yet? **(b)** (**au football, renvoyer du terrain*) he was sent off for spitting at the referee

send on *vtsép* **(a)** (*faire suivre*) would you send on any letters that come for me? **(b)** (*expédier par avance*) we've decided to send our luggage on so we don't have as much to carry

send out *vtsép* **(a)** (*faire sortir, renvoyer*) the teacher sent him out of the classroom for talking **(b)** (*envoyer*) I've forgotten to buy milk but I'll send one of the kids out for it **(c)** (*émettre*) the satellite has stopped sending out signals **(d)** (*envoyer par la poste*) those invitations should have been sent out a week ago

send out for 1 *vic* (*faire apporter*) do you want to send out for a sandwich?
    2 *vttsc* (*envoyer chercher*) send the office junior out for coffee

send up *vtsép* **(a)** (*lancer dans le ciel*) the crew sent up a distress rocket **(b)** (*faire monter*) news of the takeover bid sent up the company's share prices **(c)** (*ridiculiser*) politicians are very easy to send up; don't you know when you're being sent up?
(d) *Am Fam* (*coffrer, mettre en prison*) he was sent up for armed robbery

serve out *vtsép* **(a)** (*distribuer*) the soup kitchen needs volunteers to serve food out **(b)** (*achever*) Dad had only just served out his apprenticeship when the war started

set about *vic* **(a)** (*se mettre à, pour une corvée*) she set about the washing up **(b)** (*commencr à*) be sure to take expert advice before you set about rewiring the house **(c)** (*attaquer physiquement ou oralement*) the old lady set about the boys with her stick; Mum set about me for leaving my room in such a mess

set against *vttsc* **(a)** (*monter contre*) something must have set him against the idea; it was her friends who set her against me
(b) (*utiliser, pour réduire des obligations financières*) some expenses can be set against taxes **(c)** (*étudier à la lumière de*) we must set the government's promises against its performance in the past

set apart *vtsép* (*distinguer*) what sets her apart from all the other children in my class is . . .

set aside *vtsép* **(a)** (*mettre de côté*) could you set aside what you're working on and do this instead?; I've decided to set aside some money every week; setting that particular aspect of the issue aside . . . **(b)** (*annuler*) the Supreme Court has set aside the decision

set back *vtsép* **(a)** (*mettre en retrait*) they set the frontage back a few feet; the cottage is set back quite a bit from the road **(b)** (*retarder*) the strike has set the company back at least a month in its deliveries **(c)** *Fam* (*coûter*) that new car must have set him back a bit; will it set me back more than a thousand?

set down *vtsép* **(a)** (*poser, déposer*) you can set those cases down in the hall **(b)** (*laisser descendre*) the bus stopped to set down one or two passengers **(c)** (*fixer, pour des lois*) permissible levels of pollution are set down in the regulations **(d)** (*noter*) the policeman set down the details in his notebook

set forth *vtsép* (*présenter*) would you like to set forth your suggestions to the committee?; this document sets forth a detailed description of . . .

set in *vi* (*se déclarer*) the doctors are worried that gangrene might set in; (*arriver*) winter seems to be setting in early this year

set off 1 *vtsép* **(a)** (*faire partir*) terrorists have set off yet another bomb in a crowded street **(b)** (*causer, entraîner*) what set the argument off? **(c)** (*faire rire, pleurer, etc.*) that last joke of his set us all off; if you say any more you'll only set her off again; he is so allergic to pollen that even a vase of cut flowers sets him off **(d)** (*mettre en valeur, réhausser*) those velvet curtains really set the room off **(e)** (*compenser . . . par, pour une perte, etc.*) can I set these expenses off against my tax liability?
2 *vi* (*partir en voyage*) we'll have to set off at dawn

set on 1 *vttsc* (*envoyer sur, pour une attaque*) if you don't get off my land immediately, I'll set the dogs on you
2 *vic* (*attaquer*) travellers were often set on by highwaymen

set out 1 *vtsép* **(a)** (*présenter*) the desserts were set out on a trolley in an eye-catching display **(b)** (*fixer, indiquer*) this document sets out the steps that must be taken
2 *vi* **(a)** (*partir en voyage*) they set out late last night

(b) (*commencer*) I didn't realize when I set out just how long the job was going to take me **(c)** (*locution*) to set out to do something *faire quelque chose délibérément*

set to 1 *vi* (*commencer à travailler, s'y mettre*) isn't it about time that we set to and cleaned out the garage?
  2 *vic* (*commencer*) when are the builders going to set to work?

set up 1 *vi* **(a)** (*s'établir*) they've decided to set up in business for themselves; she's setting up as a hairdresser **(b)** (*se faire passer pour*) he sets himself up as a poet
  2 *vtsép* **(a)** (*monter*) marquees will be set up on the front lawn **(b)** (*organiser, monter, pour un rendez-vous, etc.*) I'd like to set up an appointment with the doctor **(c)** (*installer*) he's set her up in a flat of her own; (*monter, constituer*) a task force will be set up to investigate the matter **(d)** (*causer, entraîner*) these pills won't set up a reaction, will they? **(e)** *Fam* (*monter un coup contre*) there's no point in claiming you were set up – no one will believe you

settle down 1 *vi* **(a)** (*s'installer*) I had just settled down with a book when the phone rang **(b)** (*se calmer*) now settle down, children **(c)** (*se concentrer sur*) he must settle down to his homework **(d)** (*s'installer, se marier, etc.*) when are you going to settle down and get married?
  2 *vtsép* **(a)** (*installer*) just let me settle the baby down for the night **(b)** (*calmer*) I couldn't settle my class down at all today

settle for *vic* (*accepter à la place*) we haven't got any brandy I'm afraid – will you settle for Scotch?; is that a fixed price for the house or would the seller settle for less?

settle in 1 *vi* (*s'installer*) how are you settling in the new house?; he'll soon settle in at the job
  2 *vtsép* (*installer*) I'm just going to settle the new secretary in and then I'm having a holiday; do you want us to come over and help settle you in?

settle on *vic* (*décider de, après réflexion*) have you settled on a date for the wedding yet?

settle up *vi* **(a)** (*régler la note*) can I leave you to settle up? **(b)** (*régler ses comptes à*) he said he would settle up with us later

shake off *vtsép* **(a)** (*enlever en secouant, secouer*) shake the snow off your coat before you come in **(b)** (*se débarrasser de, pour une* *maladie, de la mauvaise humeur, etc.*) I can't seem to shake this cold off **(c)** (*échapper à*) she shook the detective off by going into the ladies and leaving by a back door

shake up *vtsép* **(a)** (*mélanger, secouer pour mélanger*) shake it up a bit – all the solids are at the bottom; don't shake the champagne up **(b)** (*secouer, pour des coussins, etc.*) let me shake your pillows up for you **(c)** (*démonter, ébranler*) the news of the accident shook her up; I was badly shaken up by my narrow escape **(d)** (*secouer les puces à*) this committee needs shaking up a bit; this will shake their ideas up

shell out *vtsép Fam* (*payer, casquer*) I'm not going to shell out any more on that motorbike of his; how much do we each have to shell out for petrol?

shoot down *vtsép* **(a)** (*abattre, descendre, par missile, par arme*) he was shot down over France; the guerrillas claim to have shot down three planes in the last week **(b)** *Fam* (*démolir, pour un argument, etc.*) she shot his argument down; if he doesn't like your proposal he'll shoot it down

shoot out 1 *vi* (*sortir brusquement*) bulbs are shooting out all over the garden
 2 *vtsép* (*avancer vite, sortir*) she shot out her hand and grabbed him before he could fall

shoot up 1 *vi* **(a)** (*monter en flèche*) house prices have shot up in the last year; (*se lever*) hands were shooting up all over the room to ask questions **(b)** (*se shooter*) a government poster showing kids shooting up
 2 *vtsép* (*détruire par les bombardements*) the runways are so badly shot up that they are unuseable

shop around *vi* (*comparer les prix des produits*) it pays to shop around

shout down *vtsép* (*désapprouver, rejeter avec violence*) union members shouted down management's proposal; don't shout her down – listen to what she has to say

show off 1 *vi* (*crâner, frimer*) he was flexing his muscles and generally showing off
 2 *vtsép* **(a)** (*faire admirer*) I think I'll go for a drive round town and show the new car off **(b)** (*mettre en valeur*) wearing white always shows off a tan

show up 1 *vi* **(a)** (*apparaître, se voir*) the dirt really shows up on a
pale carpet **(b)** *Fam* (*se pointer*) he showed up wearing a new
suit; she's always showing up late
    2 *vtsép* **(a)** (*rendre manifeste*) the loss of export markets shows
up the company's failure to modernize **(b)** *Fam* (*embarrasser*) I
don't want you showing me up in front of people, so don't tell
any of your crude jokes **(c)** (*faire monter*) the porter will show
you up to your room

shrug off *vtsép* (*ignorer, ne pas tenir compte de*) he shrugs off all
criticism

shut away *vtsép* (*enfermer, mettre à l'écart*) he's been shut away in
prison for the last year; ever since her husband's death, she has
shut herself away

shut down *vtsép* & *vi* = **close down**

shut in *vtsép* (*enfermer*) shut the dog in

shut off 1 *vtsép* **(a)** (*éteindre*) shall I shut the television off?
(b) (*isoler*) don't they feel shut off living in the depths of the
countryside?
    2 *vi* (*s'arrêter de marcher*) I want a kettle that shuts off
automatically

shut out *vtsép* **(a)** (*enfermer dehors, fermer la porte à*) the door's
locked – they've shut us out; I've forgotten my key and now I'm
shut out; close the door and shut the noise out **(b)** *Fig* (*exclure*)
people want to help – why do you insist on shutting them out?
(c) (*cacher*) we're going to plant some trees to shut out the view
of the railway line

shut up 1 *vtsép* **(a)** (*enfermer*) shut the cat up somewhere – you know
Mrs Williams is allergic **(b)** (*fermer*) they're away shutting up
their cottage for the winter **(c)** *Fam* (*calmer*) shut those kids up
– I'm trying to concentrate
    2 *vi Fam* (*la boucler*) don't tell me to shut up!

shy away *vi* (*se reculer nerveusement*) she shied away when he tried to
put his arm around her

shy away from *vic* (*éviter par peur*) he has shied away from driving
ever since the accident

sift out *vtsép* **(a)** (*enlever, en passant au tamis*) sift out any impurities

(b) (*éliminer*) we have sifted out the most obviously unsuitable candidates

sign away *vtsép* (*signer l'abandon de*) read the small print to be sure you're not signing away any of your rights

sign for *vic* (*signer, pour un reçu*) there's a registered letter for you – will you sign for it please?

sign in 1 *vi* (*signer en entrant, signer le registre d'entrée*) it's a rule of the club that all visitors must sign in
  2 *vtsép* (*faire entrer, en signant pour*) I'm a member, so I can sign you in

sign off *vi* **(a)** (*terminer l'émission*) they usually sign off for the day at midnight; he always signs off with that catch phrase **(b)** *Fam* (*phrase utilisée en fin de lettre : je vous quitte*) I think I'll sign off now and go to bed

sign on *vi Br* (*pointer, à l'agence pour l'emploi*) how long do you have to be out of work before you can sign on?; I have to sign on every Monday

sign up 1 *vtsép* (*engager*) the committee wants to sign up more volunteers to help with the fund drive
  2 *vi* **(a)** (*s'engager dans l'armée*) my uncle tried to sign up when he was only 15 **(b)** (*s'inscrire, pour un cours*) she has signed up for a class in car maintenance

simmer down *vi* (*se calmer*) I'll tell you what he said once I've simmered down

single out *vtsép* (*sélectionner*) why single her out for praise? – we all contributed to the success of the project

sink in *vi* **(a)** (*s'imbiber, pénétrer*) pour the syrup over the cake and allow it to sink in **(b)** (*faire son effet, être compris*) his remark didn't sink in until she was halfway down the stairs

sit about/around *vi* (*attendre sans rien faire*) we had to sit about in the airport lounge for two hours

sit back *vi* **(a)** (*s'installer confortablement dans un fauteuil*) now sit back and watch the next episode of our thriller **(b)** (*rester sans rien faire*) we can't just sit back if we think something's wrong next door

sit down 1 *vi* (*s'asseoir*) you'd better sit down – I've got some bad news
2 *vtts* (*faire asseoir*) the doctor sat her down and explained the operation

sit in *vi* **(a)** (*occuper des locaux en signe de protestation*) students used to sit in regularly in the sixties **(b)** (*remplacer*) the chairwoman is ill and has asked me to sit in for her at the meeting

sit on *vic* **(a)** (*être membre de*) how many people sit on the committee?
(b) (*garder dans le secret*) reporters were asked to sit on the news until the hostages were safely out of the country
(c) (*garder sous le coude*) the company decided to sit on the consultant's recommendations **(d)** *Fam* (*fermer le bec à*) I'm sorry I had to sit on you like that but you were about to be indiscreet

sit out *vtsép* **(a)** (*ne pas danser*) I'd rather sit this one out
(b) (*supporter jusqu'à la fin*) we sat the concert out to the bitter end but it didn't get any better

sit up 1 *vi* **(a)** (*se tenir assis*) she was sitting up in bed when I arrived; sit up straight for goodness sake and don't slouch! **(b)** (*s'asseoir*) sit up – I've brought you breakfast in bed **(c)** (*rester éveillé*) we sat up until midnight waiting for them to arrive
2 *vtts* (*asseoir*) the nurse sat the old man up

size up *vtsép Fam* (*juger*) she looked round the room, sizing everyone up

skim off *vtsép** (*écrémer, souvent Fig*) he always skims off the best applicants for his department

skim over/through *vic* (*parcourir*) the lawyer skimmed over his client's statement

slap on *vtsép* Fam* **(a)** (*appliquer n'importe comment*) just slap some paint on and that will hide the marks **(b)** (*ajouter*) I bet the government slaps some more on the cost of a pint in the next budget

sleep around *vi Fam* (*coucher à droite à gauche*) Aids has stopped people sleeping around

sleep in *vi* **(a)** *Fam* (*faire la grasse matinée*) I always sleep in on Sunday **(b)** (*habiter sur le lieu de travail*) she has two maids sleeping in

sleep off *vtsép* (*dormir pour faire passer quelque chose*) he's upstairs sleeping his hangover off

sleep on 1 *vi* (*continuer à dormir*) let her sleep on for as long as she likes

    2 *vic* (*remettre au lendemain, pour une décision*) you don't have to make your mind up now – sleep on it and then call me

sleep together *vi* (*coucher ensemble, avoir des relations sexuelles*) when did you start to sleep together?

sleep with *vic* (*coucher avec, avoir des relations sexuelles avec*) she's been sleeping with him for a year

slip away *vi* (*partir, surtout sans se faire remarquer*) she slipped away from the party; the time just slips away when I'm with him

slip by 1 *vi* (*passer rapidement*) the time has slipped by

    2 *vic* (*échapper à l'attention de*) how did that mistake manage to slip by you?

slip in 1 *vi* (*entrer, surtout sans se faire remarquer*) he slipped in to the room

    2 *vtsép* (*placer*) she slipped in a remark about . . .

slip off 1 *vi* (*partir, surtout sans se faire remarquer*) we didn't see you go – when did you slip off?

    2 *vtsép* (*enlever rapidement*) she slipped off her coat

slip on *vtsép* (*enfiler, pour un vêtement*) she slipped a dress on and ran to answer the door

slip out *vi* **(a)** (*sortir, surtout sans se faire remarquer*) we slipped out halfway through the concert **(b)** (*échapper, pour des remarques*) she's very apologetic about giving the secret away – it just slipped out when she was talking to him

slip up *vi Fam* (*gaffer, faire une gaffe*) slip up one more time and you're fired

slow down/up 1 *vi* (*ralentir*) slow down – there's a speed limit here; slow down – I can't understand what you're saying

    2 *vtsép* (*ralentir, retarder*) can't you walk any faster? you're slowing everyone down

smooth down *vtsép* **(a)** (*lisser*) the duck smoothed down her ruffled feathers **(b)** (*calmer, apaiser*) he's really very upset – give me a few minutes to smooth him down

smooth out *vtsép* **(a)** (*faire disparaître, pour des plis, etc.*) she smoothed out the creases from the tablecloth **(b)** (*résoudre, pour une difficulté*) we have a little problem we hope you can help us smooth out

smooth over *vtsép* (*éteindre, calmer, rendre insignifiant*) the chairman smoothed over the dispute with a light remark

snap out *vtsép* (*dire d'un ton brusque*) the sergeant snapped out an order

snap out of *vic* (*se sortir de, pour une humeur*) you must snap out of this depression

snap up *vtsép Fam* (*sauter sur, s'arracher, pour une marchandise intéressante*) the towels are so cheap people are snapping them up

snarl up *vtsép* (*bloquer*) because of the accident, traffic is all snarled up on the motorway

snow under *vttsc Fam habituellement au passif* (*submerger*) we have been snowed under with requests for a repeat of the programme about bird migration

soldier on *vi* (*persévérer*) I know you're all very tired but if you could soldier on till the project is finished, I'd be very grateful

sort out *vtsép* **(a)** (*ranger*) I've sorted out all those tools that you had just thrown in the drawer **(b)** (*enlever*) the women on the production line sort out the flawed goods with incredible speed **(c)** (*résoudre*) maybe he needs some psychiatric help to sort out his problems **(d)** *Pop* (*régler son compte à, verbalement ou physiquement*) it's about time someone sorted him out

sound off *vi* (*rouspéter, râler*) she is always sounding off about rude shop assistants

sound out *vtsép* (*demander l'opinion de*) I want to recommend you for the job but I thought I should sound you out first and see if you'd be interested

spell out *vtsép* **(a)** (*épeler*) it's rather an unusual name so I'll spell it out for you **(b)** (*expliquer bien clairement*) the chairman spelled out what a strike would mean for the company's future; do I have to spell it out for you?

spin out *vtsép* **(a)** (*faire durer*) can you spin the housekeeping money out until the end of the month? **(b)** (*prolonger*) I'd like to spin my leave out for another couple of days

splash down *vi* (*amerrir, pour un engin spatial*) the capsule splashed down at 13.00 hours just off Haiti

splash out *vi Fam* (*dépenser beaucoup d'argent*) let's splash out for once and stay in the best hotels

split up 1 *vtsép* (*répartir*) we're going to split the money up among our children
    2 *vi* (*se séparer, pour un couple*) I hear they're splitting up

spring up *vi* (*surgir, apparaître brusquement*) weeds are springing up all over the garden after the rain; the company sprang up almost overnight

square up *vi* **(a)** (*régler un compte, des dettes*) can we square up later?; I'll square up with you when I get paid if that's all right **(b)** (*se préparer à se battre physiquement*) the two men were so angry with each other they began to square up **(c)** (*faire face*) it was wonderful the way you squared up to that bully

stamp out *vtsép* (*enrayer, juguler*) the military government has vowed to stamp out unrest

stand by 1 *vi* **(a)** (*rester sans intervenir*) people just stood by and watched the policeman being beaten up **(b)** (*attendre*) viewers were told to stand by for further developments
    2 *vic* (*honorer*) the government has promised to stand by its election promises

stand down *vi* (*prendre sa retraite*) he will stand down as chairman of the football club at the end of the year

stand for *vic* **(a)** (*se présenter pour, à une élection*) I have decided to stand for the chairmanship of the committee; she is standing for election **(b)** (*représenter*) in a recipe, "tsp" stands for teaspoonful **(c)** (*tolérer*) I won't stand for that kind of behaviour

stand in *vi* (*prendre le remplacement*) Mr Wilson has very kindly agreed to stand in at short notice for our scheduled speaker

stand out *vi* **(a)** (*se distinguer*) he is so tall that he stands out in a crowd; what makes her stand out is . . . **(b)** (*tenir bon, résister*) we are standing out against management's attempts to break our strike

stand up 1 *vi* **(a)** (*se lever*) everyone stood up when the president entered the room **(b)** (*être valable, pour un argument*) the prosecution hasn't got enough evidence for the charge to stand up
   2 *vtsép* (*poser un lapin à, faire faux bond à*) poor old Tom – that's the second time this month she's stood him up

stand up for *vic* (*défendre, se battre pour*) my parents stood up for me when I was in trouble; stand up for what you believe in

stand up to *vic* (*affronter, faire face à*) I admired the way she stood up to that aggressive drunk

start off 1 *vi* (*partir*) the runners will be starting off in the coolness of the early morning; (*commencer*) to put your audience at ease, start off with a joke or two
   2 *vtsép* **(a)** (*commencer*) start your presentation off with a brief history of the problem **(b)** (*faire commencer*) there's the baby crying again – what started her off this time?

start up 1 *vi* **(a)** (*démarrer*) she heard a car starting up next door **(b)** (*ouvrir, pour une affaire, un commerce*) there's a new dry cleaner's starting up on the corner
   2 *vtsép* **(a)** (*démarrer*) start the engines up **(b)** (*ouvrir, pour une affaire, un commerce*) they're starting up another restaurant

stay off 1 *vi* **(a)** (*ne pas aller au travail, à l'école*) he's decided to stay off and see if he can cure this cold **(b)** (*ne pas commencer, pour le mauvais temps*) do you think the rain will stay off until the washing's dry?
   2 *vic* (*ne pas aller à*) can I stay off school today?

stay out *vi* **(a)** (*ne pas rentrer chez soi*) what do you mean by staying out until this time of night? **(b)** (*poursuivre la grève*) the women have decided to stay out until their demands are met

step in *vi* (*intervenir*) the government should step in and order the strikers back to work

step up *vtsép* (*accélérer, augmenter*) research into this disease must be stepped up; the company is stepping up production of the vaccine

stick around *vi Fam* (*rester dans les parages*) stick around, we may need you

stick out 1 *vi* **(a)** (*dépasser, sortir*) the label on your dress is sticking out; his ears stick out (*c.-à-d. il a les oreilles décollées*) **(b)** (*se faire remarquer*) she sticks out because of the way she dresses
2 *vtsép* (*faire dépasser de, faire sortir de*) stick your head out the window and see if they're coming

stick to *vic* **(a)** (*coller à*) the cloth is sticking to the table **(b)** (*s'en tenir à, suivre, pour une décision, des plans, etc.*) she's sticking to her plans despite her parents' opposition; it's a very tough programme of work – do you think you'll stick to it?; (*se contenter de*) if red wine gives you a headache, stick to white

stop by *vi* (*passer, dans un magasin, chez quelqu'un*) stop by at the post office on your way home; we'll stop by and see you next week

stop off *vi* (*faire une courte halte*) they're stopping off at Bali for a couple of days on their way back

stop over *vi* (*faire une étape, pour des voyageurs, en avion, etc.*) we stopped over at Manchester on the flight to Toronto

straighten out 1 *vtsép* **(a)** (*ajuster, tirer, pour des tissus*) she straightened out the crumpled bedclothes **(b)** (*mettre au point, au clair*) we need to straighten a few things out in this relationship
2 *vi* (*devenir droit, se redresser, pour une route, etc.*) after twisting and turning for a couple of hundred yards, the path finally straightened out

straighten up 1 *vtsép* **(a)** (*mettre d'aplomb*) he cannot pass a picture on the wall without straightening it up **(b)** (*ranger*) straighten your room up a bit – it's very untidy
2 *vi* (*se dresser*) she straightened up and rubbed her back

strike back *vi* (*répondre*) the government struck back at its critics with a strong defence of its actions

strike off *vtsép** (*rayer*) your name has been struck off (the list)

strike out 1 *vtsép* (*éliminer, rayer*) strike out whichever does not apply
 2 *vi* **(a)** (*donner des coups, frapper*) he struck out at his
   opponent **(b)** (*aller dans une direction définie*) we're all tired –
   let's strike out for home **(c)** (*devenir indépendant, se lancer*) I'm
   striking out on my own

strike up 1 *vtsép* (*commencer à jouer*) the orchestra struck up a waltz;
   (*lier*) they struck up a friendship at school
 2 *vi* (*commencer à jouer, pour un orchestre, etc.*) the band
   struck up

string along *vtsép Fam* (*faire marcher*) that garage is just stringing you
   along – the car can't possibly be repaired; he just strung her
   along till he'd taken all her money and then he vanished

string up *vtsép Fam* (*pendre*) they should string child abusers up from
   the nearest lamp post

strip down *vtsép* (*démonter complètement*) the garage can't find the
   fault without stripping the engine down

strip off 1 *vtsép* (*faire tomber*) the wind stripped all the leaves off the
   trees; (*enlever*) he stripped off all his clothes and jumped into
   the water; we'll have to strip off about six layers of paint from
   this door
 2 *vi* (*se déshabiller*) strip off and let the doctor examine you

sum up 1 *vtsép* **(a)** (*résumer*) the chairman summed up the
   committee's discussions **(b)** (*apprécier d'un coup d'œil,
   rapidement*) summing up the situation, he . . .
 2 *vi* (*récapituler*) when summing up, the judge warned the jury
   against . . .

summon up *vtsép* (*rassembler, pour le courage, les forces*) I
   summoned up all my courage and asked to speak to the manager

swallow up *vtsép* (*engloutir*) I watched them walk down the road and
   they were soon swallowed up by the mist; the sea swallowed
   them up

swear in *vtsép* (*assermenter*) when the witness had been sworn in . . .;
   the new president was sworn in today

sweat out *vtsép* **(a)** (*se débarrasser de . . . en transpirant*) have a
   sauna and sweat your cold out **(b)** (*supporter, endurer*) you were

found guilty and now you're just going to have to sweat your
sentence out

switch back *vi* (*revenir à, retourner à*) we tried electricity but we've
decided to switch back to gas

switch off/on 1 *vtsép* (*allumer/éteindre un appareil électrique, un
interrupteur, etc.*) switch the radio off/on
    2 *vi* (*s'allumer, s'éteindre, pour une source électrique*) where
does the power switch off/on?

switch over *vi* (*changer de chaîne, de station, pour la télévision ou la
radio*) shall I switch over? – the news is on the other side

switch round *vtsép* (*permuter, changer de place*) someone switched
the drinks around and the Duchess got the poison by
mistake

T

tail away/off *vi* (*diminuer*) the noise of the lorry tailed away in the
distance; (*baisser peu à peu*) her voice tailed off as she realized
that no one was listening

tail back *vi* (*se trouver pare-chocs contre pare-chocs*) the traffic tailed
back all the way to the intersection

take aback *vtis* (*étonner, prendre de surprise*) he quite took me aback
with his insolence; the enemy was completely taken aback by
the speed of our attack

take after *vic* (*tenir de, pour des enfants et leurs parents*) don't blame
me – it's her father she takes after

take apart *vtsép* **(a)** (*démonter*) the radio hasn't worked since he took
it apart **(b)** *Fam* (*en sport, battre à plate couture*) who would
have expected the Wimbledon title-holder to be taken apart by a
completely unknown player?

take around *vtsép** (*faire visiter*) would you like someone to take you
around?

take away 1 *vi* (*enlever*) having to go home by public transport takes away from the pleasure of going out

    2 *vtsép* **(a)** (*soustraire*) what do you get if you take 28 away from 70? **(b)** (*emmener*) they took the man next door away in an ambulance last night **(c)** (*acheter pour emporter, pour des plats tout faits*) how about some curry to take away?

take back 1 *vtsép* **(a)** (*rendre, ramener à l'endroit d'origine*) take these library books back, will you? **(b)** (*chercher, pour quelque chose qu'on avait laissé*) when is Tony coming to take back those records you borrowed? **(c)** (*retirer, pour des commentaires*) now that I know her better, I take back all that I said about her **(d)** (*accepter le retour de*) will the shop take it back if it doesn't fit?; she's a fool to take him back

    2 *vtts* (*rappeler à, pour un souvenir, etc.*) these old songs take me back to when I was a teenager

take down *vtsép* **(a)** (*descendre, décrocher, de plus haut, etc.*) it's time we took the curtains down for a wash; take all your posters down **(b)** (*démonter, enlever*) when are the workmen going to take down the scaffolding?; the shops still haven't taken down their Christmas decorations **(c)** (*prendre en note*) the reporter took down very little of what was said at the meeting

take home *vtsép* (*gagner, en salaire net*) how much does she take home every week?

take in *vtsép* **(a)** (*amener quelque part*) take your coat in to the cleaner's tomorrow **(b)** (*donner abri à, abriter*) they take in all the stray cats in the neighbourhood; taking in lodgers is not my idea of fun **(c)** (*reprendre, pour un vêtement*) could you take this skirt in? **(d)** (*comprendre, absorber*) he reeled off so many facts and figures that I couldn't take them all in **(e)** (*inclure*) the Prime Minister's tour will take in a number of urban renewal projects **(f)** *Am* (*aller voir*) do you want to take in a movie?; let's take a few of the sights in first **(g)** (*rouler, mentir à*) he took the old lady in by telling her he had known her son; don't be taken in by appearances (*c.-à-d. ne vous laissez pas prendre par les apparences*)

take off 1 *vi* **(a)** (*décoller, pour un avion*) we took off an hour late **(b)** *Fam* (*décoller, prendre son essor*) the company's sales really took off last month **(c)** *Fam* (*partir*) they're taking off for France next week; (*quitter le travail*) he's taking off early tonight

2 *vtsép* **(a)** (**enlever, ôter*) take your hat off; (*retirer*) the policeman was taken off the murder enquiry because he knew the people involved **(b)** (*amputer*) they had to take her leg off below the knee **(c)** (*réduire*) he needs to take a few pounds off (*c.-à-d. il doit perdre du poids*); the saleswoman took a pound off because of this stain (*c.-à-d. elle a baissé le prix d'une livre*) **(d)** (*prendre comme congé*) why don't you take the rest of the day off? **(e)** (*imiter*) he takes the president off extremely well

take on 1 *vi Fam* (*s'en faire*) don't take on so, he's not badly hurt

  2 *vtsép* **(a)** (*avoir la charge, la responsabilité de*) when I married you I didn't realize I'd be taking on your whole family too; she's exhausted with all the extra work she's been taking on recently **(b)** (*recruter, embaucher*) that new electronics firm took on 200 people this week **(c)** (*s'attaquer à*) why did you agree to take him on? – he's twice your size; it was a mistake to take on the best snooker player in the club **(d)** (*prendre, pour une attitude, un sens*) his face took on a cunning look; life has taken on a whole new meaning since I met you **(e)** (*prendre à bord*) the train made an unscheduled stop to take on passengers

take out *vtsép* **(a)** (*faire sortir*) if you want to work in the garage, you'll have to take the car out; (*faire partir*) washing won't take that stain out – the dress will have to be dry cleaned **(b)** (*arracher*) I'm having two teeth taken out tomorrow **(c)** (*retirer, pour de l'argent*) how much do you think we need to take out of our account? **(d)** (*sortir, inviter*) he took her out to dinner at a very fancy restaurant **(e)** (*souscrire à*) have you taken out insurance on the new car?; (*prendre*) how about taking out a subscription to this computer magazine? **(f)** (*passer, pour de la mauvaise humeur, de la colère, etc.*) why should he take his anger out on us? **(g)** (*locution*) (*fatiguer*) kids take a lot out of you; that really took it out of me **(h)** *Fam* (*détruire*) our men took out three enemy encampments

take over 1 *vi* (*prendre le pouvoir, la direction, etc.*) the new chairman will take over next week; (*envahir*) we ought to do something about the garden – the weeds are taking over

  2 *vtsép* **(a)** (*prendre la direction/le pouvoir de*) she will be taking over the running of the hotel **(b)** (**faire visiter, montrer*) a guide will take you over (the house)

take round *vtsép* **(a)** (*amener quelque part*) take this cake round to your grandmother's for me **(b)** (**faire visiter*) the supervisor was asked to take the trade delegates round (the factory)

take to *vic* **(a)** (*se prendre d'amitié pour*) I've never really taken to the people next door **(b)** (*prendre l'habitude de*) he has taken to treating me like an enemy **(c)** (*s'enfuir dans*) the outlaws took to the hills

take up 1 *vi* (*continuer*) to take up where I left off . . .
   2 *vtsép* **(a)** (*soulever*) during their search, the policemen even took up the floorboards; she took up the newspaper and pretended to read **(b)** (*monter à l'étage*) take this tray up to your mother **(c)** (*raccourcir*) these curtains need to be taken up a couple of inches **(d)** (*occuper*) I've taken up too much of your time; the bed is so large it just about takes up the entire room **(e)** (*discuter de, parler de*) I think you should take the question of training up with the personnel manager **(f)** (*commencer, pour un emploi, un passe-temps*) he must be mad taking up jogging at his age!; when she first took up the appointment . . . **(g)** (*accepter*) I'm going to take up that offer of a weekend in the country **(h)** (*continuer, poursuivre*) her sister took up the thread of the conversation

take up on *vttsc* **(a)** (*reprendre sur, dans un débat*) the Leader of the Opposition took the Prime Minister up on that last point **(b)** (*accepter, pour une offre, etc.*) if they don't take me upon this offer it's their loss not mine; (*faire tenir à, pour une promesse*) have you taken him up on his promise of . . .?; I'll take you up on that sometime (*c.-à-d. ça sera pour une prochaine fois*)

take upon *vttsc* (*prendre la responsabilité de*) you took that task upon yourself; why did she take it upon herself to call the police?

take up with *vic* (*se lier avec, surtout pour de mauvaises fréquentations*) I'm afraid he has taken up with a bad lot

talk at *vic* (*s'adresser d'une façon pompeuse à*) he tends to talk at people rather than to them

talk away 1 *vi* (*parler à n'en plus finir*) the old lady was talking away about her youth
   2 *vtsép* (*passer . . . à discuter*) we talked half the night away

talk back *vi* (*répondre avec insolence, surtout pour des enfants*) don't talk back to your father

talk down *vtsép* (*aider à atterrir par radio-contrôle*) the fog was so thick at the airport that several planes had to be talked down

talk down to *vic* (*parler avec condescendance à, comme à un enfant*) I wish she wouldn't talk down to me – I'm not stupid

talk over *vtsép* (*discuter de*) they've decided to talk things over and see if they can reach some kind of agreement

talk round 1 *vtts* (*faire changer d'avis*) Dad won't let me go to that pop concert – could you try talking him round?
   2 *vic* (*tourner autour de*) they seemed nervous about tackling the problem directly and just talked round it

tamper with *vic* (*trafiquer, falsifier, saboter dans un but criminel*) after the car accident, he claimed that the brakes had been tampered with

tangle up *vtsép* **(a)** (*emmêler*) the kitten tangled all the wool up
   (b) *habituellement au passif* (*accrocher*) he got tangled up in the barbed wire when he tried to climb the fence
   (c) (*mêler*) I'm sure she's tangled up in something dishonest

tangle with *vic Fam* (*se disputer, se battre*) he tangled with a drunk about some stupid football game

tear apart *vtsép* **(a)** (*détruire*) the country is being torn apart by civil war **(b)** (*fouiller, mettre sens dessus dessous, pour chercher quelque chose*) the police tore the place apart looking for drugs

tear away 1 *vtsép* (*déchirer, arracher*) I tore away the wrapping paper
   2 *vtts* (*arracher*) if you can tear yourself away from that television set for a minute

tear into *vic* (*attaquer physiquement ou verbalement, s'en prendre à*) the lion tore into the flesh of the deer it had killed; the boss tore into me for being late for the meeting

tear off *vtsép* (*détacher, arracher*) she tore the label off the suitcase

tear up *vtsép* **(a)** (*déchirer en petits morceaux*) his letter made her so angry she tore it up and threw it in the fire **(b)** *Fig* (*annuler*) the football player threatened to tear up his contract if the club didn't pay him more

tell off *vtts* (*gronder, réprimander*) I told him off for his impudence

tell on *vic* **(a)** (*causer des effets négatifs à*) the strain of waiting for news is telling on her **(b)** (*dénoncer*) Mum knows about the practical joke we were planning – someone must have told on us

thaw out *vi* (*dégeler*) leave the meat to thaw out; *Fig* (*se réchauffer, se mettre à l'aise*) have a cup ot tea and thaw out; he's pretty unsociable but he does thaw out sometimes

thin out 1 *vi* (*perdre ses cheveux*) he's thinning out on top; (*devenir épars*) audiences are thinning out; his hair is thinning out **2** *vtsép* (*éclaircir*) thin the plants out in autumn

think about *vic* **(a)** (*penser à*) it's strange that you should have phoned just when I was thinking about you **(b)** (*penser, envisager de*) I'm thinking about going to the cinema tonight – do you want to come?

think back *vi* (*essayer de se souvenir, faire un effort de mémoire*) the policemen asked him to think back and try to remember what had happened; thinking back, I don't believe we did send them a Christmas card

think of *vic* **(a)** (*penser à, avoir des égards pour*) it's about time she started thinking of other people all the time **(b)** (*se souvenir de*) I can't think of his telephone number at the moment **(c)** (*imaginer*) just think of it – a holiday in the Caribbean! **(d)** (*penser de, avoir une opinion sur*) what do you think of the latest fashions?; I don't think much of their new house (*c.-à-d. je n'ai pas une grande opinion sur*) **(e)** (*considérer, envisager*) we wouldn't think of letting our daughter hitchhike across Europe on her own **(f)** (*avoir l'idée de, trouver*) who thought of coming to this restaurant?; I've thought of a solution to the problem

think out/through *vtsép* (*réfléchir à fond sur, considérer scrupuleusement*) have you thought out the effect that this proposal will have on our employees?; let's think things through

think over *vtsép* (*peser le pour et le contre de*) I told him I would think his offer over

think up *vtsép* (*trouver, pour une idée, etc.*) they've thought up a brilliant idea

throw away *vtsép* **(a)** (*jeter*) throw those old papers away **(b)** (*gâcher, gaspiller*) she threw away her chance of a place at university; you're just throwing your money away buying all those records

throw back *vtsép* **(a)** (*rejeter*) the fish was so small that the angler threw it back **(b)** (*renverser*) she threw her head back

throw in *vtsép* (*donner en prime à ce qui a été acheté*) the man in the furniture shop said that if we took the bed, he would throw in the mattress for thirty pounds

throw off *vtsép* **(a)** (*jeter, se débarrasser en hâte de*) he threw off his outer clothes and jumped into the river **(b)** (*se débarrasser de, pour une maladie, etc.*) I can't seem to throw off this virus

throw out *vtsép* **(a)** (*jeter*) don't throw those photographs out **(b)** (*rejeter, pour une proposition*) after discussion, the committee threw the proposal out **(c)** (*faire sortir, pour une personne qui se conduit mal*) the manager of the cinema threatened to throw the boys out if they didn't behave themselves

throw together *vtsép* **(a)** *Fam* (*faire à la hâte, à la va-vite*) it's not very well made, it looks a bit thrown together **(b)** (*jeter, mettre, rassembler*) he threw some clothes together in a suitcase and raced to the airport **(c)** (*rassembler, unir, pour des personnes*) fate threw the two of them together; on such a small cruise ship, everyone is thrown together, like it or not

throw up 1 *vi Fam* (*vomir*) no wonder you threw up, mixing your drinks like that
    2 *vtsép* (*laisser passer, pour une chance, une occasion*) imagine throwing up a chance to go to the United States

tick off *vtsép* **(a)** (*cocher*) will you tick people's names off as they come in to vote? **(b)** *Fam* (*gronder, réprimander*) the teacher ticked him off for being late

tick over *vi* (*marcher, fonctionner, pour une machine ou un commerce, etc.*) the restaurant is ticking over quite well

tide over *vtts* (*dépanner, pendant une courte période, avec de l'argent, etc.*) could you lend me five pounds to tide me over until the end of the week?

tie down *vtsép* (*contraindre*) children tie you down; I don't want to be tied down to any specific date

tie in *vi* (*correspondre*) how does the suspect's story tie in with his wife's?

tie up 1 *vi* (*se tenir, pour des conséquences issues d'une même cause*) his debts, the robbery, and now a new car – it all ties up
  2 *vtsép* **(a)** (*immobiliser, pour de l'argent*) his money is tied up until he is twenty-five; my capital is tied up in stocks and shares
  (b) (*être occupé, pour des raisons de travail spécialement*) she'll be tied up all this afternoon

tighten up *vtsép* **(a)** (*serrer*) he bent to tighten up his shoelaces
  (b) (*rendre plus strict, renforcer*) they're tightening up the rules on tax shelters; the company has decided that security must be tightened up

tip off *vtsép Fam* (*informer, donner un tuyau à*) someone must have tipped him off that the police were on their way; the reporter was tipped off about an interesting story

tone down *vtsép* **(a)** (*rendre plus doux, adoucir*) we toned our original colour scheme down **(b)** *Fig* (*modérer*) the reporter was told to tone his article down or the paper would be sued

top up *vtsép* (*remplir, pour un verre*) he kept topping my glass up; (*resservir, pour une boisson*) can I top you up?

touch down *vi* (*atterrir, pour un avion, un engin spatial*) Concorde touched down exactly on schedule

touch up *vtsép* **(a)** (*retoucher, remaquiller*) this bit of the window frame needs to be touched up; she's just gone to touch up her make-up **(b)** *Fam* (*peloter*) if you don't stop touching me up I'll slap your face

touch (up) on *vic* (*évoquer en passant*) his speech didn't even touch on the pollution problem

toughen up *vtsép* (*endurcir*) he's one of those parents who send their sons to boarding school to toughen them up

trail away/off *vi* (*se taire, pour une voix, s'éteindre pour un bruit*) his voice trailed away with embarrassment

trot out *vtsép Fam* (*réciter, sortir, pour des arguments, etc. que l'on a déjà entendus*) don't trot out the same old excuses; he's not going to trot that speech out again, is he?

try for *vic* (*essayer d'obtenir*) she is trying for a place at music school; he's trying for the record

try on *vtsép* (*essayer, pour des vêtements, des chaussures, etc. que l'on veut peut-être acheter*) I've been trying dresses on all morning

try out *vtsép* (*mettre à l'essai*) the football club is trying him out in goal; (*essayer*) you can have the car for a day to try it out

turn against 1 *vic* (*s'opposer à*) why have you turned against me? **2** *vttsc* (*monter contre*) she claims that her ex-husband is turning their children against her

turn back 1 *vi* (*revenir sur ses pas, faire demi-tour*) we turned back because the path had become too faint to follow **2** *vtsép* **(a)** (*refuser l'entrée de, refouler*) the refugees were turned back at the border **(b)** (*rabattre*) she reluctantly turned back the bedclothes and got up **(c)** (*retarder, pour une montre, une horloge*) we turned our watches back an hour

turn down *vtsép* **(a)** (*rabattre*) since the rain had stopped, he turned his coat collar down **(b)** (*baisser, réduire, pour la chaleur, le son, etc.*) turn the gas down a bit; please turn the radio down – it's far too loud **(c)** (*refuser*) I've been turned down for that job I applied for; (*rejeter*) she turned down his offer of a weekend in Paris

turn in 1 *vi Fam* (*aller au lit, aller se coucher*) it's late – why don't we turn in? **2** *vtsép* **(a)** (*dénoncer à la police*) his former wife turned him in **(b)** (*rendre*) at the end of the war, lots of soldiers kept their handguns as souvenirs instead of turning them in; hundreds of weapons were turned in during the amnesty

turn off 1 *vi* (*tourner, pour un véhicule*) you turn off at the second street on the left **2** *vtsép* **(a)** (*éteindre, pour la radio, un moteur, etc.*) be sure to turn the stove off; (*fermer*) who didn't turn the tap off? **(b)** *Fam* (*dégoûter*) people who pick their noses in public turn me off

turn on 1 *vtsép* **(a)** (*allumer, pour une machine, la télévision, etc.*) turn the gas on for me **(b)** *Fam* (*plaire énormément, souvent d'un point de vue sexuel*) rock music turns her on; he is turned on by her

    2 *vic* **(a)** (*attaquer physiquement ou verbalement, par surprise*) one of her dogs turned on her; he turned on me when I suggested that he retire **(b)** (*dépendre de*) the company's success turns on the skills of its employees

turn out 1 *vi* **(a)** (*être présent à, assister à*) not many people turned out for his funeral **(b)** (*se révéler, s'avérer*) it's one of those silly stories where the heroine turns out to be a lost heiress **(c)** (*donner, à la fin*) how did the cake turn out?; (*se finir*) everything will turn out fine

    2 *vtsép* **(a)** (*éteindre*) it's time you turned the light out and went to sleep **(b)** (*vider*) I turned out my handbag to look for my keys **(c)** (*produire*) we're now turning out 100 computers a day **(d)** (*mettre à la porte*) the old man was turned out of his cottage

turn over 1 *vi* (*se retourner*) he turned over in bed; (*chavirer*) the lifeboat turned over and sank in seconds

    2 *vtsép* **(a)** (*se rendre*) the suspect was turned over to the police; they have turned the running of the restaurant over to their son-in-law **(b)** *habituellement non séparé* (*gagner autour de, faire un profit de . . . environ*) he must be turning over a good thousand a week

turn round 1 *vi* **(a)** (*faire demi-tour, se retourner*) he turned round and looked at her **(b)** *Fam* (*pour indiquer qu'une action est imprévu*) he just turned round and punched the other chap; one day she'll just turn round and leave you

    2 *vic* (*tourner*) turn round the next corner

    3 *vtsép* **(a)** (*renverser la situation*) the company was headed for bankruptcy but the new management team turned it round **(b)** (*exécuter*) how quickly can you turn this order round? **(c)** (*tourner*) she turned the chair round and sat down

turn up 1 *vi* **(a)** *Fam* (*arriver, venir*) he always turns up late; she turned up at the party with her new boyfriend **(b)** (*être trouvé*) if you're sure that you lost it indoors, then it's bound to turn up one day **(c)** (*arriver, se produire*) things always have a habit of turning up when you least expect them to

2 *vtsép* **(a)** (*remonter*) he turned his collar up in the wind **(b)** (*augmenter, monter, mettre plus fort*) turn the television up will you, I can hardly hear; turn the heat up a bit

U

urge on *vtsép* (*pousser, talonner*) the marathon runner said he managed to finish the race only because the crowd urged him on; her family is urging her on to go to university

use up *vtsép* (*finir*) use up the last of the milk before it turns sour; (*épuiser*) the children used up all their energy playing

V

venture on *vic* (*entreprendre, pour quelque chose de risqué*) he refused to venture on any criticism of the book until he had read it

verge on *vic* (*être aux bords de*) I was verging on tears; the sailors were told that their behaviour verged on mutiny

vote down *vtsép* (*rejeter, par le vote*) the amendment to the law was voted down

vote in *vtsép* (*élire*) the other members of the committee voted her in as chairwoman

vote on *vic* (*mettre au vote*) union members will be asked to vote on management's latest offer; it was voted on last night

W

wade in *vi Fam* (*se mêler à*) when the fight started, everybody waded in; our discussion wasn't really anything to do with her, but she waded in anyway

wade into *vic Fam* (*attaquer, avec détermination*) he got up early and waded into the job of cleaning the windows; I'm sorry – I shouldn't have waded into you for something so minor

wait behind *vi* (*rester en arrière*) she volunteered to wait behind until the doctor came

wait in *vi* (*rester chez soi, au bureau, etc.*) I was late because I had to wait in for the telephone engineer

wait on 1 *vi* (*continuer à attendre*) he waited on in the hope that she would eventually arrive
    2 *vic* (*servir*) the waitress who was waiting on them seemed to have vanished

wait up *vi* (*ne pas se coucher, veiller*) don't wait up – I'll be very late

wake up 1 *vi* **(a)** (*se réveiller*) she woke up when the church bells started ringing **(b)** *Fig* (*ouvrir les yeux*) his mother never did wake up to the fact that he was a thief
    2 *vtsép* **(a)** (*réveiller*) don't wake me up too early tomorrow **(b)** *Fig* (*secouer, éveiller*) this country needs waking up

walk into *vic* **(a)** (*entrer, pénétrer dans*) she walked into the room; the suspect walked right into the trap the police had set for him **(b)** (*rentrer dans, en collision avec*) I almost walked into a lamp post

walk off 1 *vtsép* (*prendre l'air pour éliminer les effets de*) let's go out and walk our Christmas dinner off
    2 *vi* (*partir*) he walked off and left us standing there

walk off with *vic Fam* **(a)** (*remporter haut la main*) she walked off with all the first prizes for her flowers **(b)** (*voler*) the bank manager has walked off with a million pounds **(c)** (*prendre, pour quelque chose qui ne nous appartient pas*) who keeps walking off with the scissors?

walk out *vi* **(a)** (*partir*) she walked out of the room **(b)** (*laisser tomber,* *quitter*) you can't just walk out on your wife and children!

walk over *vic* (*faire tomber, vaincre, dans un combat*) the champion walked all over another opponent today

walk through *vic* (*réussir avec facilité*) you'll walk through the job interview

walk up *vi* **(a)** (*monter à pied*) the lift was out of order so we had to walk up **(b)** (*approcher*) a complete stranger walked up and started talking to me

warm up 1 *vi* **(a)** (*se réchauffer*) I hope it starts warming up now that spring is here **(b)** (*s'échauffer, pour des sportifs*) tennis players get a couple of minutes to warm up before the match
2 *vtsép* **(a)** (*faire chauffer*) warm up some soup for yourself **(b)** (*chauffer, pour l'ambiance, etc.*) the star of the show doesn't appear until the other acts have warmed the audience up **(c)** (*mettre de l'ambiance à*) can't we do anything to warm this dinner party up?

warn off *vtsép** (*déconseiller*) I was going to buy it but someone warned me off

wash down *vtsép* (*faire passer un repas, un médicament, etc. grâce à un liquide*) have a glass of wine to wash your meal down

wash off 1 *vi* (*disparaître, partir au lavage*) do you think these stains will wash off?
2 *vtsép** (*enlever en lavant*) just let me wash the oil off my hands

wash out *vtsép* **(a)** (*rincer*) wash your mouth out please **(b)** *habituellement au passif* (*être annulé, pour cause de pluie*) the women's tennis final has been washed out

wash over *vic* (*passer au dessus de, pour des soucis, des remarques, etc.*) his mother's death seems to have washed over him; anything I say just washes over her

wash up 1 *vi* **(a)** *Br* (*faire la vaisselle*) whose turn is it to wash up? **(b)** *Am* (*se laver*) don't serve supper until I've washed up
2 *vtsép* **(a)** *Br* (*laver, pour la vaisselle, etc.*) why I am always left with the greasy pots to wash up? **(b)** *Fam habituellement au passif* (*être fichu, pour une carrière, pour une occasion*) he's washed up as a boxer **(c)** (*ramener sur le rivage, pour la mer*) a body was found washed up on the beach

watch out *vi* (*faire attention*) watch out for bones when you're eating the fish; watch out – you nearly broke the window

water down *vtsép* (*baptiser, couper d'eau*) water this down with a drop of soda, will you?; *Fig* (*édulcorer*) the drama critic accused the editor of watering his review down

wave down *vtsép* (*arrêter, en faisant un signe*) he didn't see the policeman waving him down

wave on *vtsép* (*faire un signe à . . . de poursuivre sa course*) the border guard waved them on without looking at their passports

wear away *vtsép* (*éroder, ronger*) the sea is wearing the coastline away

wear down *vtsép* **(a)** (*user*) I've worn the heels of my shoes down **(b)** (*épuiser*) she is worn down by looking after all those children

wear off *vi* (*disparaître, s'atténuer*) the effect of the anaesthetic is wearing off

wear out 1 *vtsép* **(a)** (*user*) that's the second pair of shoes he's worn out in six months **(b)** (*épuiser*) she's wearing herself out with the preparations for her daughter's wedding
  2 *vi* (*s'user*) the carpet is wearing out

weed out *vtsép* *Fig* (*éliminer, en sélectionnant*) we have weeded out the least promising candidates

weigh down *vtsép* (*surcharger*) don't weigh me down with anything more to carry; *Fig* (*ronger*) they are both weighed down with grief

weigh in *vi* **(a)** (*se faire peser, pour un boxer, un jockey, des bagages*) the champion weighed in at just under the limit; have you weighed in yet? **(b)** (*intervenir dans une discussion*) I wish she wouldn't keep weighing in with comments that are totally irrelevant

weigh up *vtsép* (*juger, se faire une idée de*) he boasts that he can weigh people up with a single glance; weighing up the situation, she . . .

while away *vtsép* (*faire passer, passer, en attendant de faire quelque chose*) how did you while away all those hours you had to spend in the airport lounge?

whip away *vtsép Fam* (*enlever brusquement, arracher*) the waiter whipped our plates away before we'd finished eating

whip out *Fam* **1** *vtsép* (*sortir brusquement d'un sac, d'une poche, etc.*) he whipped out his wallet
    2 *vi* (*courir, faire un saut*) I'm just whipping out to the car for my briefcase

whip round *Fam vi* **(a)** (*faire un saut*) whip round to the chemist's for me **(b)** (*faire une collecte*) we whipped round to get a retirement present for him

whip up *vtsép* **(a)** (*émouvoir, faire vibrer, attiser*) such speeches are intended to whip an audience up **(b)** (*rassembler, faire venir, attirer*) what can we do to whip up support for the campaign? **(c)** (*battre*) whip up some cream; make an omelette by whipping up some eggs **(d)** *Fam* (*faire à la va-vite, pour un repas*) I whipped up a meal for them

whisk away *vtsép* **(a)** (*chasser d'un coup de la main*) whisk the wasps away from the jam **(b)** *Fam* (*ramener rapidement*) the president was whisked away by helicopter

whittle away *vtsép* (*battre en brèche, réduire progresssivement*) she is whittling away her opponent's lead; support for the government is being whittled away by its evident failure to control inflation

whittle down *vtsép* (*diminuer, avec une idée d'effort*) we've whittled the number of candidates down

win hack *vtsép* (*regagner*) he won back all the money he had lost the previous week

win out/through *vi* (*l'emporter, gagner*) he finally won out over his parents' objections; we won through in the end

win over/round *vtsép* (*convaincre*) they are trying to win me over to the idea of a holiday abroad; (*séduire*) she is charming and has quite won us over

wind down **1** *vtsép* (*réduire progressivement*) the company has decided to wind down its operations in that part of the world
    2 *vi* (*tirer à sa fin*) we went home since the party was winding down

wind up 1 *vtsép* **(a)** (*remonter, pour un réveil, une horloge*) the clock
needs to be wound up **(b)** (*finir*) we wound up our holiday with
a weekend in Paris **(c)** *Fam* (*se payer la tête de*) he really wound
her up with those remarks about her dress; don't you know when
you're being wound up?
   2 *vi* = **end up**

winkle out *vtsép Fam* (*tirer, extirper*) I finally winkled the
information out of him; it's no good trying to winkle any money
out of me

wipe off *vtsép** (*effacer*) the teacher wiped the equation off the board;
wipe that grin off your face!

wipe out *vtsép* **(a)** (*effacer, anéantir*) she has completely wiped out the
memory of the crash; the power failure wiped out three weeks'
keyboarding **(b)** (*dilapider, pour de l'argent, de l'énergie*) his
gambling debts wiped out his entire fortune; (*épuiser*) I feel
wiped out **(c)** (*détruire, tuer*) enemy fire wiped out the village;
whole families have been wiped out by the disease

work in *vtsép* (*mentionner, dans un discours, etc.*) I think we should
work something in about the help we received from other
people; (*incorporer*) work the other ingredients in

work off *vtsép* (*passer, dépenser, pour de la mauvaise humeur,
l'énergie, etc.*) she worked her anger off on the squash court

work on *vic* **(a)** (*travailler sur*) he is working on a new project
   (b) (*utiliser comme base*) we'll have to work on what we have
   (c) (*persuader*) I've tried working on him but without much
success

work out 1 *vi* **(a)** (*se monter à, s'élever à*) how much do you make that
work out to? **(b)** (*marcher, réussir*) that relationship will never
work out **(c)** (*faire de l'exercice, s'entraîner dans un gymnase*)
she's been working out all morning
   2 *vtsép* **(a)** (*résoudre*) once you've worked out the problem . . .;
they'll have to work things out between themselves – I'm not
getting involved **(b)** (*concevoir*) he's worked out a plan

work up *vtsép* **(a)** (*développer, pour des sentiments*) I can't work up
any enthusiasm for this project **(b)** (*exciter*) she was getting all
worked up at the prospect of a holiday

work up to *vic* (*se préparer à*) he's working up to proposing marriage to her; (*en venir à*) it was easy to see what she was working up to

wriggle out of *vic* (*éviter, se dégager de, pour une obligation*) why did you let them wriggle out of doing their homework?; you can't wriggle out of this one

write away for *vic* (*écrire pour commander, commander par lettre*) if you want to know more, write away for our free brochure

write in *vi* (*envoyer des lettres, écrire*) a great many viewers have written in with their comments about last week's programme

write off 1 *vtsép* **(a)** (*annuler*) his debts have been written off **(b)** (*considérer comme sans valeur, donner une critique très sévère de*) the critics wrote the play off **(c)** (*bousiller, pour les voitures, etc.*) she wrote her father's car off **2** *vi* (*commander par lettre*) I've written off for tickets

write out *vtsép* **(a)** (*rédiger, écrire au propre*) have you written out your essay? **(b)** (*écrire*) just write me out a cheque; (*faire, rédiger, préparer*) the shop assistant wrote out the receipt **(c)** (*retirer, pour un rôle dans le script d'une pièce*) her part has been written out

write up *vtsép* (*préparer*) he's writing up a report on his business trip

Z

zap up *vtsép Fam* (*peaufiner, rendre plus attirant, plus plaisant*) the prose style could do with a bit of zapping up; they've certainly zapped up the colour scheme

zero in on *vic* (*se diriger droit sur*) the missile zeroes in on its target from a range of . . .; (*mettre le doigt sur*) they immediately zeroed in on the one weak point in the argument

zip up 1 *vtsép* (*fermer avec une fermeture éclair* (R)) she zipped her skirt up; zip me up, will you? **2** *vi* (*se fermer, avec une fermeture éclair* (R)) the dress zips up at the back

Index

Les codes dans cet index de verbes renvoient aux modèles de verbes, comme cela a été expliqué pages 18 à 21. Un code P9 indique que le verbe est irrégulier (voir pages 25 à 33). Les verbes en *-ate* et en *-ize* se conjuguent toujours selon le modèle P4 et ont été omis. Pour les verbes commençant par *de-, dis-, mis-, out-, over-, re-* et *un-*, se reporter au second élément. (*Am*) indique que l'orthographe américaine est expliquée au modèle P5.

abase P4
abet P5
abhor P5
abide P4 *ou* P4P9
abide by P4
abjure P4
abolish P2
abridge P4
absolve P4
abuse P4
abut P5
accede P4
access P2
accompany P6
accomplish P2
accrue P4
accuse P4
ache P4
achieve P4
acknowledge P4
acquiesce P4
acquire P4
acquit P5
ad-lib P5
address P2
adhere P4
adjudge P4
adjure P4
admire P4
admit P5
adore P4
advance P4

adventure P4
advertise P4
advise P4
age P4
agree P3
allege P4
allot P5
allude to P4
allure P4
ally P6
amass P2
amaze P4
amble P4
ambush P2
amplify P6
amuse P4
analyse P4
angle P4
announce P4
annul P5
appal P5
appease P4
apply P6
appraise P4
apprentice P4
apprise P4
approach P2
approve P4
arch P2
argue P4
arise P4P9
arouse P4

arrange P4
arrive P4
ascribe P4
assess P2
assuage P4
assume P4
assure P4
astonish P2
atone P4
attach P2
attribute P4
attune P4
avenge P4
aver P5
average P4
awake P4 *ou* P4P9
axe P4

babble P4
baby P6
baby-sit P5P9
baffle P4
bag P5
bake P4
balance P4
bale out P4
ban P5
bandage P4
bandy P6
banish P2
bar P5

barbecue P4
bare P4
barge P4
barrel P5 (*Am*)
barricade in P4
base P4
bash P2
baste P4
bat P5
bathe P4
battle P4
beach P2
bear P1P9
beat P1P9
beatify P6
beautify P6
become P4P9
bed P5
bedazzle P4
bedevil P5 (*Am*)
beetle along P4
befall P1P9
befit P5
befog P5
befuddle P4
beg P5
beget P5P9
begin P5P9
begrudge P4
beguile P4
behave P4
behold P1P9
behove P4
belch P2
belie P7
believe P4
belittle P4
belly out P6
bend P1P9
benefit P1 *ou* P5
bereave P4 *ou* P4P9
beseech P2 *ou* P2P9
beset P5P9
besiege P4
besmirch P2
bespeak P1P9

bestir P5
bestride P4P9
bet P2P9
betake P4P9
betide P4
bevel P5 (*Am*)
bewitch P2
bias P2 *ou* P10
bid P5P9
bide P4
bind P1P9
birch P2
bite P4P9
bivouac P8
blab P5
blackleg P5
blame P4
blanch P2
blare P4
blaspheme P4
blaze P4
bleach P2
bleed P1P9
bless P2
blot P5
blotch P2
blow P1P9
blue P4
blur P5
blush P2
bob P5
bode P4
bog down P5
boggle P4
bone P4
bootleg P5
booze P4
bop P5
bore P4
boss about P2
botch P2
bottle P4
bounce P4
box P2
brace P4
brag P5

brake P4
brave P4
breach P2
break P1P9
breathalyse P4
breathe P4
breed P1P9
bribe P4
bridge P4
brim P5
bring P1P9
bristle P4
broach P2
broadcast P1P9
bronze P4
browse P4
bruise P4
brush P2
bubble P4
buckle P4
bud P5
budge P4
bug P5
build P1P9
bulge P4
bulldoze P4
bully P6
bum P5
bundle P4
bungle P4
burgle P4
burn P1 *ou* P1P9
burnish P2
burst P1P9
bury P6
bus P2 *ou* P10
bust P1P9
bustle P4
busy P6
buy P1P9
buzz P2

cable P4
caddie P7
caddy P6

cadge P4
cage P4
cajole P4
cake P4
calcify P6
calve P4
camouflage P4
can (*tin*) P5
cancel P5 (*Am*)
candy P6
cane P4
canoe P4
canvass P2
cap P5
capture P4
care P4
caress P2
caricature P4
carry P6
cascade P4
cash P2
catalogue P4
catch P2P9
cause P4
cave P4
cavil P5 (*Am*)
cease P4
cede P4
censure P4
centre P4
certify P6
chafe P4
challenge P4
chance P4
change P4
channel P5 (*Am*)
chap P5
chaperone P4
char P5
charge P4
chase P4
chat P5
cherish P2
chide P4P9
chime P4
chip P5

chisel P5 (*Am*)
chivvy P6
choke P4
choose P4P9
chop P5
chortle P4
chuckle P4
chug P5
chum up P5
cinch P2
circle P4
circumscribe P4
cite P4
clam up P5
clap P5
clarify P6
clash P2
class P2
classify P6
cleanse P4
cleave P4 *ou* P4P9
clench P2
climax P2
clinch P2
cling P1P9
clip P5
clog P5
clone P4
close P4
clot P5
clothe P4 *ou* P4P9
club P5
clue up P4
clutch P2
coach P2
coalesce P4
coax P2
cobble P4
code P4
coerce P4
cohere P4
coincide P4
collapse P4
collide P4
combine P4
come P4P9

commence P4
commit P5
commute P4
compare P4
compel P5
compere P4
compete P4
compile P4
complete P4
comply P6
compose P4
compress P2
comprise P4
compromise P4
con P5
concede P4
conceive P4
conclude P4
concur P5
concuss P2
condense P4
condole P4
condone P4
confer P5
confess P2
confide P4
confine P4
confuse P4
conjecture P4
conjure away P4
connive P4
conserve P4
console P4
conspire P4
constitute P4
consume P4
continue P4
contravene P4
contribute P4
contrive P4
control P5
convalesce P4
convene P4
converge P4
converse P4
convince P4

convulse P4
cop P5
cope P4
copy P6
core P4
corpse P4
corral P5
corrode P4
cosh P2
cost P1P9
counsel P5 (*Am*)
couple P4
course P4
cox P2
crackle P4
cradle P4
cram P5
crane P4
crap P5
crash P2
crate P4
crave P4
crease P4
create P4
creep P1P9
cringe P4
crinkle P4
cripple P4
crop P5
cross P2
crouch P2
crow P1P9
crucify P6
cruise P4
crumble P4
crumple P4
crunch P2
crush P2
cry P6
cube P4
cuddle P4
cudgel P5 (*Am*)
cue P3
cup P5
curdle P4
cure P4

curry P6
curse P4
curtsy P6
curve P4
cut P5P9
cycle P4

dab P5
dabble P4
dally P6
dam P5
damage P4
dance P4
dangle P4
dare P4 *ou* P4P9
dash P2
date P4
dawdle P4
daze P4
dazzle P4
deal P1P9
debauch P2
debug P5
deceive P4
decide P4
declare P4
decline P4
decrease P4
decree P3
decry P6
deduce P4
defer P5
define P4
defy P6
deify P6
delete P4
delude P4
delve P4
demolish P2
demote P4
demur P5
denounce P4
deny P6
deplete P4
deplore P4

depose P4
depress P2
deprive P4
deride P4
derive P4
describe P4
deserve P4
desire P4
despatch P2
despise P4
destine P4
detach P2
deter P5
determine P4
devalue P4
devise P4
devolve P4
devote P4
diagnose P4
dial P5 (*Am*)
dice P4
die P7
dig P5P9
dignify P6
digress P2
dilute P4
dim P5
diminish P2
dimple P4
dine P4
dip P5
dirty P6
disable P4
disadvantage P4
disagree P3
discipline P4
discourage P4
discourse P4
discuss P2
disentangle P4
disgruntle P4
disguise P4
dish P2
disinter P5
dismantle P4
dismiss P2

disparage P4
dispatch P2
dispel P5
dispense P4
disperse P4
dispose P4
dissolve P4
dissuade P4
distance P4
distil P5
distinguish P2
distress P2
distribute P4
ditch P2
dive P4 *ou* P4P9
diverge P4
diversify P6
divide P4
divorce P4
divulge P4
do P2P9
dodge P4
dog P5
dole out P4
don P5
doodle P4
dope P4
dose P4
doss P2
dot P5
dote on P4
double P4
doze P4
drag P5
drape P4
draw P1P9
dream P1 *ou* P1P9
dredge P4
drench P2
dress P2
dribble P4
drink P1P9
drip P5
drive P4P9
drivel P5 (*Am*)
drizzle P4

drone P4
drop P5
drowse P4
drug P5
drum P5
dry P6
duel P5 (*Am*)
dupe P4
dwell P1P9
dwindle P4
dye P4
dynamite P4

ease P4
eat P1P9
echo P2
eddy P6
edge P4
edit P1
efface P4
effervesce P4
eke out P4
elapse P4
electrify P6
electrocute P4
elope P4
elude P4
embarrass P2
embed P5
embellish P2
embezzle P4
embody P6
emboss P2
embrace P4
emerge P4
emit P5
empty P6
emulate P4
emulsify P6
enable P4
enamel P5 (*Am*)
encircle P4
enclose P4
encompass P2
encourage P4

encroach P2
endorse P4
endure P4
enforce P4
engage P4
engrave P4
engross P2
enhance P4
enlarge P4
enquire P4
enrage P4
enrapture P4
enrich P2
enrol P5
enshrine P4
ensue P4
ensure P4
enthral P5
enthuse P4
entice P4
entitle P4
entrench P2
envisage P4
envy P6
equal P5 (*Am*)
equip P5
erase P4
erode P4
escape P4
establish P2
etch P2
evade P4
evoke P4
evolve P4
examine P4
excel P5
excite P4
exclude P4
excuse P4
execute P4
exemplify P6
exercise P4
exhale P4
exile P4
expedite P4
expel P5

experience P4
expire P4
explode P4
explore P4
expose P4
express P2
extinguish P2
extol P5
extradite P4
exude P4
eye P4

face P4
facet P1 *ou* P5
fade P4
fake P4
fall P1P9
falsify P6
famish P2
fan P5
fancy P6
fare P4
fatigue P4
fax P2
faze P4
feature P4
feed P1P9
feel P1P9
fence P4
ferry P6
fetch P2
fete P4
fib P5
fiddle P4
fight P1P9
figure P4
filch P2
file P4
filigree P3
finance P4
find P1P9
fine P4
finish P2
fire P4
fish P2

fit P5 *ou* P5P9
fix P2
fizz P2
fizzle P4
flag P5
flake P4
flame P4
flannel P5 *(Am)*
flap P5
flare P4
flash P2
flee P3P9
fleece P4
flesh out P2
flex P2
flinch P2
fling P1P9
flip P5
flit P5
flog P5
flop P5
flounce P4
flourish P2
flush P2
fly P6P9
fob P5
focus P2
fog P5
fondle P4
forage P4
forbid P5P9
force P4
forecast P1P9
forego P2P9
foresee P3P9
foretell P1P9
forge P4
forget P5P9
forgive P4P9
forgo P2P9
format P5
forsake P4P9
forswear P1P9
fortify P6
fox P2
fracture P4

franchise P4
free P3
freeze P4P9
fret P5
fricassee P3
fringe P4
frolic P8
fry P6
fudge P4
fuel P5 *(Am)*
fulfil P5
fumble P4
fume P4
funnel P5 *(Am)*
fur up P5
furnish P2
fuse P4
fuss P2

gab P5
gabble P4
gad about P5
gag P5
gainsay P1P9
gamble P4
gambol P5 *(Am)*
game P4
gape P4
garage P4
garble P4
gargle P4
garnish P2
garrotte P4
gas P5
gash P2
gauge P4
gaze P4
gel P5
gen up P5
gesture P4
get P5P9
gibe P4
giggle P4
gild P1 *ou* P1P9
gird P1 *ou* P1P9

girdle P4
give P4P9
glance P4
glare P4
glass P2
glaze P4
glide P4
glimpse P4
glorify P6
glory P6
gloss over P2
glue P4
glut with P5
gnash P2
go P2P9
gobble P4
goggle P4
gore P4
gorge P4
gouge P4
grab P5
grace P4
grade P4
grapple P4
grass P2
grate P4
gratify P6
gravel P5 (Am)
graze P4
grease P4
grieve P4
grin P5
grind P1P9
grip P5
gripe P4
grit P5
grope P4
gross P2
grouch P2
grovel P5 (Am)
grow P1P9
grub P5
grudge P4
grumble P4
guarantee P3
guess P2

guide P4
gum P5
gun P5
gurgle P4
gush P2
gut P5
guzzle P4

haemorrhage P4
haggle P4
halve P4
ham P5
handicap P5
handle P4
hang P1 *ou* P1P9
harangue P4
harass P2
hare P4
harness P2
harry P6
hash P2
hassle P4
hatch P2
hate P4
have P4P9
hear P1P9
heave P4 *ou* P4P9
heckle P4
hedge P4
hem P5
hew down P1 *ou*
    P1P9
hiccup P1 *ou* P5
hide P4P9
hike P4
hinge P4
hire P4
hiss P2
hit P5P9
hitch P2
hive P4
hoax P2
hobble P4
hobnob P5
hoe P3

hog P5
hold P1P9
hole P4
home P4
hop P5
hope P4
hose P4
hot up P5
house P4
huddle P4
hug P5
hum P5
humble P4
humidify P6
hunch P2
hurry P6
hurt P1P9
hurtle P4
hush P2
hustle P4

ice P4
identify P6
idle P4
ignite P4
ignore P4
imagine P4
imbibe P4
imbue P4
immerse P4
impale P4
impeach P2
impede P4
impel P5
impinge P4
implore P4
imply P6
impose P4
impoverish P2
impress P2
improve P4
improvise P4
incense P4
inch P2
incite P4

incline P4
include P4
inconvenience P4
increase P4
incur P5
indemnify P6
index P2
induce P4
indulge P4
infer P5
inflame P4
inflate P4
influence P4
infringe P4
infuse P4
inhale P4
inhere P4
initial P5 (*Am*)
injure P4
inlay P1P9
inscribe P4
inset P5P9
inspire P4
instil P5
institute P4
insure P4
intensify P6
intercede P4
interfere P4
interleave P4
interpose P4
intersperse P4
intervene P4
intone P4
intrigue P4
introduce P4
intrude P4
inure P4
invade P4
inveigle P4
invite P4
invoice P4
invoke P4
involve P4
issue P4
itch P2

jab P5
jam P5
jangle P4
jar P5
jazz P2
jet P5
jib P5
jibe P4
jig P5
jiggle P4
jingle P4
jive P4
job P5
jog P5
joggle P4
joke P4
jostle P4
jot down P5
judge P4
jug P5
juggle P4
jumble P4
justify P6
jut P5
juxtapose P4

keep P1P9
kid P5
kidnap P5 (*Am*)
kindle P4
kip P5
kiss P2
kit out *ou* up P5
knee P3
kneel P1 *ou* P1P9
knife P4
knit P5 *ou* P5P9
knot P5
know P1P9
knuckle down P4
KO P3 (KO's, etc.)

label P5 (*Am*)
lace P4

ladle P4
lag P5
lam P5
lame P4
languish P2
lap P5
lapse P4
lash P2
lasso P3 *ou* P2
latch on P2
launch P2
lavish P2
lay P1P9
laze P4
lead P1P9
lean P1 *ou* P1P9
leap P1 *ou* P1P9
leapfrog P5
learn P1 *ou* P1P9
lease P4
leave P4P9
lecture P4
lend P1P9
let P5P9
level P5 (*Am*)
levy P6
liaise P4
libel P5 (*Am*)
license P4
lie P7P9
light P1 *ou* P1P9
like P4
line P4
liquefy P6
live P4
loathe P4
lob P5
lobby P6
lodge P4
log P5
loose P4
lop P5
lope P4
lose P4P9
lounge P4
louse P4

love P4
lug P5
lunch P2
lunge P4
lurch P2
lure P4
lynch P2

machine P4
magnify P6
make P4P9
man P5
manage P4
mangle P4
manicure P4
manoeuvre P4
manufacture P4
map P5
mar P5
march P2
marry P6
marshal P5 (*Am*)
marvel P5 (*Am*)
mash P2
masquerade P4
mass P2
massacre P4
massage P4
mat P5
match P2
mate P4
mature P4
mean P1P9
measure P4
meddle P4
meet P1P9
melt P1 *ou* P1P9
menace P4
merge P4
mesh P2
mess P2
mime P4
mimic P8
mince P4
mine P4

mingle P4
mislay P1P9
mislead P1P9
misread P1P9
miss P2
mistake P4P9
mix P2
mob P5
model P5 (*Am*)
modify P6
mop P5
mope about *ou* around
    P4
mortgage P4
mortify P6
motivate P4
move P4
mow down P1 *ou*
    P1P9
muddle P4
muddy P6
muffle P4
mug P5
multiply P6
mumble P4
munch P2
muscle in P4
muse P4
muss P2
mute P4
mutiny P6
muzzle P4
mystify P6

nab P5
nag P5
name P4
nap P5
needle P4
nerve P4
nestle P4
net P5
nibble P4
nip P5
nobble P4

nod P5
nonplus P10
nose P4
nosh P2
notch P2
note P4
notice P4
notify P6
nourish P2
nudge P4
nullify P6
nurse P4
nurture P4
nuzzle P4

oblige P4
obscure P4
observe P4
obsess P2
occupy P6
occur P5
offset P5P9
ogle P4
omit P5
ooze P4
oppose P4
oppress P2
ossify P6
outwit P5
overawe P4
overlay P6
owe P4

pace P4
pacify P6
package P4
pad P5
paddle P4
page P4
pal up P5
pan P5
panel P5 (*Am*)
panic P8
parachute P4

parade P4
paralyze P4
paraphrase P4
parcel out P5 (*Am*)
parch P2
pare P4
parody P6
parole P4
pass P2
paste P4
pat P5
patch P2
patrol P5
pause P4
pave P4
pay P1P9
pedal P5 (*Am*)
peddle P4
pee P3
peeve P4
peg P5
pen P5
pencil P5 (*Am*)
pep up P5
perceive P4
perch P2
perfume P4
perish P2
perjure P4
permit P5
perplex P2
persecute P4
persevere P4
personify P6
perspire P4
persuade P4
peruse P4
pervade P4
pet P5
petrify P6
phase P4
phone P4
photocopy P6
phrase P4
pickle P4
picnic P8

picture P4
piddle P4
piece together P4
pierce P4
pig P5
pile P4
pillory P6
pin P5
pinch P2
pine P4
pip P5
pipe P4
pique P4
pirouette P4
piss P2
pit P5
pitch P2
pity P6
place P4
plague P4
plan P5
plane P4
plate P4
plead P1 *ou* P1P9
please P4
pledge P4
plod P5
plop P5
plot P5
plug P5
plunge P4
ply P6
poach P2
poke P4
police P4
polish P2
pollute P4
pop P5
pore over P4
pose P4
possess P2
postpone P4
pot P5
pounce P4
practise P4
praise P4

prance P4
preach P2
precede P4
preclude P4
predispose P4
prefer P5
prefix P2
prejudice P4
prepare P4
presage P4
prescribe P4
preserve P4
preset P5P9
preside P4
press P2
pressure P4
presume P4
prettify P6
price P4
prickle P4
pride P4
prime P4
prise P4
privilege P4
prize P4
probe P4
process P2
procure P4
prod P5
produce P4
profane P4
profess P2
profile P4
program P5
programme P4
progress P2
promenade P4
promise P4
promote P4
pronounce P4
prop P5
propel P5
prophesy P6
propose P4
proscribe P4
prosecute P4

prostitute P4
protrude P4
prove P4
provide P4
provoke P4
prune P4
pry P6
psychoanalyse P4
publish P2
puke P4
pulse P4
pummel P5 (*Am*)
pun P5
punch P2
puncture P4
punish P2
purchase P4
purée P3
purge P4
purify P6
purse P4
pursue P4
push P2
put P5P9
putrefy P6
puzzle P4

quadruple P4
quake P4
qualify P6
quantify P6
quarantine P4
quarrel P5 (*Am*)
quarry P6
quash P2
quench P2
query P6
queue P4
quibble P4
quit P5P9
quiz P5
quote P4

race P4
rag P5
rage P4
raise P4
rake P4
rally P6
ram P5
ramble P4
ramify P6
rampage P4
ranch P2
range P4
rankle P4
rap P5
rape P4
rat P5
rate P4
ratify P6
rattle P4
ravage P4
rave P4
ravish P2
raze P4
razz P2
reach P2
read P1P9
reappraise P4
rebel P5
rebuke P4
rebut P5
recap P5
recede P4
receive P4
recess P2
recite P4
recline P4
recompense P4
reconcile P4
reconnoitre P4
rectify P6
recur P5
recycle P4
redo P2P9
redress P2
reduce P4
refer P5

referee P3
refine P4
refit P5 *ou* P5P9
refresh P2
refurbish P2
refuse P4
refute P4
regale P4
regress P2
regret P5
rehash P2
rehearse P4
reimburse P4
reinforce P4
rejoice P4
relapse P4
relate P4
relax P2
re-lay (*carpet*) P1P9
relay (*information*) P1
release P4
relieve P4
relinquish P2
relish P2
relive P4
rely P6
remedy P6
reminisce P4
remit P5
remove P4
rend P1P9
renege P4
renounce P4
repel P5
reply P6
repose P4
repress P2
reprieve P4
reproach P2
reprove P4
repulse P4
repute P4
require P4
requite P4
rescue P4
research P2

resemble P4
reserve P4
reside P4
resolve P4
respire P4
restore P4
resume P4
retch P2
retire P4
retread (*tyre*) P1
retrench P2
retrieve P4
retrogress P2
rev P5
revel P5 (*Am*)
revenge P4
revere P4
reverse P4
revile P4
revise P4
revive P4
revivify P6
revoke P4
revolve P4
rhyme P4
rib P5
ricochet P1 *ou* P5
rid P5P9
riddle P4
ride P4P9
ridge P4
ridicule P4
rifle P4
rig P5
rile P4
ring P1P9
rinse P4
rip P5
ripple P4
rise P4P9
rival P5 (*Am*)
rivet P5
rob P5
robe P4
romance P4
rope P4

rot P5
route P4
rove P4
rub P5
rue P4
ruffle P4
rule P4
rumble P4
rummage P4
rumple P4
run P5P9
rupture P4
rush P2
rustle P4
rut P5

sabotage P4
sacrifice P4
saddle P4
sag P5
sally P6
salute P4
salvage P4
salve P4
sample P4
sanctify P6
sandwich P2
sap P5
satisfy P6
savage P4
save P4
saw P1P9
say P1P9
scab P5
scale P4
scan P5
scar P5
scare P4
scavenge P4
schedule P4
scheme P4
scorch P2
score P4
scrabble P4
scrag P5

scram P5
scramble P4
scrap P5
scrape P4
scratch P2
screech P2
scribble P4
scrounge P4
scrub P5
scrunch P2
scruple P4
scud P5
scuffle P4
sculpture P4
scurry P6
scuttle P4
scythe P4
search P2
secede P4
seclude P4
secrete P4
secure P4
seduce P4
see P1P9
seek P1P9
seethe P4
seize P4
sell P1P9
send P1P9
sense P4
sentence P4
serenade P4
serve P4
service P4
set P5P9
settle P4
sew P1P9
sex P2
shackle P4
shade P4
shag P5
shake P4P9
sham P5
shamble P4
shame P4
shape P4

share P4
shave P4
shear P1P9
sheathe P4
shed P5P9
shellac P8
shelve P4
shin P5
shine P4P9
shingle P4
ship P5
shit P5 *ou* P5P9
shoe P4P9
shoot P1P9
shop P5
shore P4
shove P4
shovel P5 *(Am)*
show P1 *ou* P1P9
shred P5
shrink P1P9
shrivel P5 *(Am)*
shrug P5
shuffle P4
shun P5
shush P2
shut P5P9
shy P6
side P4
sidle P4
signal P5 *(Am)*
signify P6
silence P4
silhouette P4
simplify P6
sin P5
sing P1P9
singe P4
single out P4
sink P1P9
sip P5
sire P4
sit P5P9
site P4
size up P4

sizzle P4
skate P4
skedaddle P4
sketch P2
skid P5
skim P5
skin P5
skip P5
skive P4
slake P4
slam P5
slap P5
slash P2
slate P4
slave P4
sleep P1P9
slice P4
slide P4P9
slim P5
sling P1P9
slink P1P9
slip P5
slit P5P9
slog P5
slop P5
slope P4
slosh P2
slot P5
slouch P2
slug P5
sluice P4
slum P5
slur P5
smash P2
smell P1 *ou* P1P9
smile P4
smite P4P9
smoke P4
smooch P2
smudge P4
smuggle P4
snaffle P4
snafu P2
snag P5
snake P4
snap P5

snare P4
snatch P2
sneak P1 *ou* P1P9
sneeze P4
sniffle P4
snip P5
snipe P4
snitch P2
snivel P5 *(Am)*
snog P5
snooze P4
snore P4
snub P5
snuffle P4
snuggle P4
sob P5
solace P4
sole P4
solidify P6
solve P4
soothe P4
sow P1P9
space P4
span P5
spangle P4
spar P5
spare P4
sparkle P4
speak P1P9
specify P6
speckle P4
speechify P6
speed P1P9 *ou* P1
spell P1P9 *ou* P1
spend P1P9
spice P4
spike P4
spill P1P9 *ou* P1
spin P5P9
spiral P5 *(Am)*
spit P5P9
spite P4
splash P2
splice P4
split P5P9
splurge P4

spoil P1 *ou* P1P9
sponge P4
spot P5
spread P1P9
spread-eagle P4
spring P1P9
sprinkle P4
spruce up P4
spur P5
spy P6
squabble P4
square P4
squash P2
squat P5
squeeze P4
squelch P2
squiggle P4
squire P4
stab P5
stable P4
stage P4
stake P4
stalemate P4
stampede P4
stand P1P9
staple P4
star P5
starch P2
starc P4
startle P4
starve P4
stash P2
state P4
staunch P2
steady P6
steal P1P9
stem P5
stencil P5 *(Am)*
step P5
stereotype P4
stet P5
stick P1P9
stifle P4
sting P1P9
stink P1P9
stir P5

stitch P2
stoke P4
stone P4
stop P5
store P4
straddle P4
strafe P4
straggle P4
strangle P4
strap P5
streamline P4
stress P2
stretch P2
strew P1 *ou* P1P9
stride P4
strike P4
string along P1P9
strip P5
stroke P4
strop P5
structure P4
struggle P4
strum P5
strut P5
stub P5
stucco P1 *ou* P2
stud P5
study P6
stultify P6
stumble P4
stun P5
stupefy P6
style P4
subdue P4
sublease P4
submerge P4
submit P5
subscribe P4
subside P4
substitute P4
subsume P4
subtitle P4
suckle P4
sue P4
suffice P4
suffuse P4

sully P6
sum up P5
sun P5
sunbathe P4
sup P5
supersede P4
supervise P4
supply P6
suppose P4
suppress P2
surface P4
surge P4
surmise P4
surpass P2
surprise P4
survive P4
suss P2
swab P5
swaddle P4
swan around P5
swap P5
swash P2
swat P5
swathe P4
swear P1P9
sweat P1 *ou* P1P9
sweep P1P9
swell P1 *ou* P1P9
swerve P4
swig P5
swim P5P9
swindle P4
swing P1P9
swipe P4
swish P2
switch P2
swivel P5 *(Am)*
swoosh P2
swot P5
syringe P4

table P4
tackle P4
tag P5
take P4P9

talc P8 *ou* P1
tally P6
tame P4
tan P5
tangle P4
tap P5
tape P4
tar P5
tarnish P2
tarry P6
taste P4
tat P5
tattle P4
tax P2
taxi P2
teach P2P9
tear P1P9
tease P4
tee P3
teethe P4
telecast P1P9
telephone P4
telescope P4
televise P4
telex P2
tell P1P9
tense P4
terrace P4
terrify P6
testify P6
thatch P2
thieve P4
thin P5
think P1P9
thrash P2
thresh P2
thrive P4 *ou* P4P9
throb P5
throttle P4
throw P1P9
thrum P5
thrust P1P9
thud P5
tickle P4
tide over P4
tidy P6

tie P7
tile P4
time P4
tin P5
tinge P4
tingle P4
tinkle P4
tip P5
tipple P4
tire P4
toady P6
toddle P4
toe P3
tog up P5
tone P4
tongue P4
top P5
topple P4
torture P4
toss P2
tot up P5
total P5 (*Am*)
tote P4
touch P2
tousle P4
towel P5 (*Am*)
trace P4
trade P4
traduce P4
traffic P8
traipse P4
trample P4
transcribe P4
transfer P5
transfigure P4
transfix P2
transfuse P4
transgress P2
transmit P5
transmogrify P6
transpire P4
transpose P4
trap P5
travel P5 (*Am*)
traverse P4
tread P1P9

treadle P4
treasure P4
treble P4
tree P3
trek P5
trellis P2
tremble P4
trench P2
trespass P2
trickle P4
trifle P4
trim P5
trip P5
triple P4
trot P5
trouble P4
trounce P4
trudge P4
true up P4
trundle P4
truss P2
try P6
tug P5
tumble P4
tune P4
tunnel P5 (*Am*)
tussle P4
tut P5
twiddle P4
twig P5
twin P5
twine P4
twinkle P4
twit P5
twitch P2
type P4
typify P6

umpire P4
understand P1P9
undertake P4P9
unify P6
unite P4
unravel P5 (*Am*)
up P5

urge P4
use P4

vanish P2
vanquish P2
varnish P2
vary P6
venture P4
verge on P4
verify P6
vet P5
vex P2
videotape P4
vie P7
vilify P6
vitrify P6
voice P4
vote P4
vouch P2
vouchsafe P4
voyage P4

wad P5
waddle P4
wade P4
waffle P4
wag P5
wage P4
waggle P4
waive P4
wake P4 *ou* P4P9

wangle P4
war P5
warble P4
wash P2
waste P4
watch P2
wave P4
wax P2
wear P1P9
weave P4P9
wed P5
wedge P4
weep P1P9
welcome P4
welsh P2
wench P2
wet P5 *ou* P5P9
wham P5
wheedle P4
wheeze P4
while away P4
whine P4
whip P5
whistle P4
whittle P4
whizz P2
wholesale P4
whoosh P2
whop P5
whore P4
wiggle P4
win P5P9
wince P4

winch P2
wind P1P9
wine P4
winkle P4
wipe P4
wire P4
wise up P4
wish P2
witness P2
wobble P4
worry P6
wrangle P4
wrap P5
wreathe P4
wrench P2
wrestle P4
wriggle P4
wring P1P9
wrinkle P4
write P4P9
writhe P4

yap P5
yodel P5 *(Am)*
yoke P4

zap P5
· zero in P2
zigzag P5
zip P5